Pro iOS Continuous Integration

Romain Pouclet

Apress·

Pro iOS Continuous Integration

ISBN-13 (pbk): 978-1-4842-0125-1

ISBN-13 (electronic): 978-1-4842-0124-4

Publisher: Heinz Weinheimer
Lead Editor: Michelle Lowman
Development Editor: Douglas Pundick
Technical Reviewers: Scott Gardner, Felipe Guitierrez, Abigal Goodwill
Editorial Board: Steve Anglin, Mark Beckner, Ewan Buckingham, Gary Cornell, Louise Corrigan,
    Jim DeWolf, Jonathan Gennick, Jonathan Hassell, Robert Hutchinson, Michelle Lowman,
    James Markham, Matthew Moodie, Jeff Olson, Jeffrey Pepper, Douglas Pundick,
    Ben Renow-Clarke, Dominic Shakeshaft, Gwenan Spearing, Matt Wade, Steve Weiss
Coordinating Editor: Kevin Walter
Copy Editor: Lori Cavanaugh
Compositor: SPi Global
Indexer: SPi Global
Artist: SPi Global
Cover Designer: Anna Ishchenko

Distributed to the book trade worldwide by Springer Science+Business Media New York, 233 Spring Street, 6th Floor, New York, NY 10013. Phone 1-800-SPRINGER, fax (201) 348-4505, e-mail orders-ny@springer-sbm.com, or visit www.springeronline.com. Apress Media, LLC is a California LLC and the sole member (owner) is Springer Science + Business Media Finance Inc (SSBM Finance Inc). SSBM Finance Inc is a Delaware corporation.

For information on translations, please e-mail rights@apress.com, or visit www.apress.com.

Apress and friends of ED books may be purchased in bulk for academic, corporate, or promotional use. eBook versions and licenses are also available for most titles. For more information, reference our Special Bulk Sales–eBook Licensing web page at www.apress.com/bulk-sales.

Any source code or other supplementary material referenced by the author in this text is available to readers at www.apress.com/9781430264392. For detailed information about how to locate your book's source code, go to www.apress.com/source-code/.

I'd like to dedicate this book to Camille, the woman I'm lucky enough to awake near to every morning. I couldn't have done this without you. I'd also like to thank my two cats, Crumble and Hermione, without who I would have probably finished this book sooner.

Contents at a Glance

Contents

About the Author

Romain Pouclet is a developer living in Montreal with his girlfriend and two cats. He previously lived in France where he studied computer science and mobile development. He has worked on various kinds of projects, from websites to rich interface and mobile applications. He currently works as an iOS developer for a Canadian company while learning how to walk a Slackline.

About the Technical Reviewers

Scott Gardner is an enterprise iOS app architect, developer, and consultant. He resides in the Midwest with his wife and daughter

Abigail Goodwill is a student at the University of Colorado Colorado Springs. She is studying English with a concentration in Literature, as well as Computer Science. She is an aspiring novelist who spends a great deal of her time writing stories and training Mixed Martial Arts. She one day hopes to publish a *New York Times* bestseller.

Felipe Gutierrez is a software architect, with a bachelors and master degree in computer science from Instituto Tecnologico y de Estudios Superiores de Monterrey Campus Ciudad de Mexico. With over 20 years of IT experience, during which time he developed programs for companies in multiple vertical industries, such as government, retail, healthcare, education, and banking. Right now, he is currently working as a senior consultant for EMC/Pivotal, specializing in the Spring Framework, Groovy, and RabbitMQ, among other technologies. He works as a consultant for big companies like Nokia, Apple, Redbox, and Qualcomm, among others. He is also author of the book: Introducing Spring Framework, from Apress.

Acknowledgments

When Apress gave me the opportunity to write a book about continuous integration in iOS, I was both excited and scared at the same time. Excited because writing a book has been in the back of my mind since I started working as a technical reviewer in 2008. Scared because when I started gathering all the things I wanted to talk about in this book, I realized I had underestimated the amount of work that it would require. But then again I had the chance to work with awesome people.

I'd like to thank all the people at Apress that were here to help me write this book. Now that I think about it, using "we" when I speak to you in this book is not simply an educational thing: I really wasn't alone writing this book. First, a big thanks to Louise Corrigan who was my very first contact with Apress, she really was the one that bootstrapped the whole thing, starting with making my proposal pretty. Thanks a lot to Michelle Lowman who then stepped in and took this project to the next level and always stayed on alert while the WWDC was approaching at the same time than my deadline for the first chapter about the Xcode bots.

I couldn't have done this without my day-to-day contacts who kept the whole thing organized: Douglas Pundick, who caught a huge number of unclear sentences and other misuses of style and Kevin Walter, who I discovered, rooted for the enemy as the frenzy of hockey you can only find in Canada started to rub off on me. Thank you both for providing the tools, help, and encouragement when needed.

The technical editors that were picked to work on this project, Scott Gardner, Abby Goodwill, and Felipe Gutierrez should be proud of the quality and the usefulness of the feedback they provided me with. Thanks you all for being here, you were my safety net.

I also would like to thank my company, TechSolCom, who gave me the opportunity to play with a lot of great toys, as they trusted me with the continuous integration of all our iOS projects.

I want to thank Marc Weistroff who was here when all this started and, as I was one more time complaining about Jenkins, made me understand that there is a lot more than meets the eyes. He also provided great support when I wondered if I really was up to this challenge.

Further thanks go to Benjamin Hubert, my friend of many years who supported me for the past three months, as I kept him posted of my progress in the middle of all those GIFs posted on IM. Thanks a lot for the support and looking forward to be your best man!

Last but not least, I want to thank my girlfriend Camille for her patience during those past months while I was here but not really here, writing on my laptop 3 meters from her. She kept me working at this continuously and I couldn't thank her enough for getting me back on track when needed. Here's to many more years by your side, and then some.

Introduction

There are as many definitions of Continuous integration as there is programming language out there, probably more. All of these opinionated definitions have been discussed all over the Internet: what it is, how it can help, which tools to use… Only a few of them are complete, exhaustive guides about where to start and where to go, let alone in the iOS ecosystem. In all fairness, the iOS platform is still relatively new.

Because you have to learn how to walk before you can run, this book will give you a tour of the iOS ecosystem from a developer point of view. If you're interested in reading this book, you probably already have spent a few hours in front of Xcode, but do you know that it will make your life a lot easier with automated testing and versioning? Did you know that you could easily use multiple versions of Xcode? Even more importantly, do you know how it works under the hood? That's the kind of thing this book will teach you.

Continuous integration is a matter of deciding of the best workflow and choosing the right tools. We didn't want to sound as if you should take our opinion as a work of gospel, so we chose to give you all the knowledge you need before covering two different continuous integration platforms, Jenkins and Bamboo. We'll show you how to get started as quickly as possible and how to take a sample application, build it, test it, and finally release it to your testers. Once we'll have covered how these third party tools, we'll cover the OS X Server and the Xcode, which are official tools provided by Apple. Far from being perfect, they provide enough neat advantages to give all those non-official alternatives a scare.

For all those solutions, we'll show you how to integrate tools to run your automated tests and analyze your code, making sure you're spending all this time to automate the workflow of an application that is well coded and works has expected.

In the end, it will be up to you to decide which tool suits you and your company best.

Chapter 1

Introduction to Continuous Integration

In the world of software engineering, the more time that passes the bigger your software usually becomes. It may be because your application is a huge, full-featured tool that does a lot of things or it may be simply because your code has become more and more complex. At this point, you have to start making decisions and choosing the tools you will use and the principles you will follow to make your life easier. The sole purpose of continuous integration is exactly that - making your life easier.

You may be reading this book because you're an independent software engineer or leading a team of iOS developers. We will help you find the tools you need and teach you how to make them fit in your day-to-day workflow.

What is Continuous Integration?

Continuous integration is a software engineering principle with a very self-explanatory name. During the life cycle of a project, you will be continuously integrating small pieces of software into your project. Then, as the project grows, you'll need to make sure these pieces actually fit the way they are supposed to. It may sound like a very metaphoric way of saying you will merge branches using your favorite version control system, but that's actually what happens - no matter which tool you will be using or how often you will be integrating code.

The principle of continuous integration is never far from the concept of "automated testing" and "Software Quality Assurance" (SQA). Indeed, integrating pieces of software is one thing, but making sure they fit - meaning they don't break your software, respect your coding conventions, or hurt the final product in any way - is a whole other thing.

Apple History 101

At the time of writing this book, Apple has just released the final version of Xcode 5.1. This 5.0 version was a pretty big release for Apple. It arrived at the same time that iOS 7 did, which was a whole new operating system with a completely new paradigm. What is even more interesting for us is that Apple finally stepped up in the world of continuous integration by starting to promote new tools. We will try to cover as many of these tools as we can in the following chapters.

Of course, the community of iOS developers didn't wait for Apple to finally make a move, and the principle of continuous integration had been advocated for way before the first public release of the iOS SDK. In the case of Cruise Control, Jenkins, Apache Continuum, etc., it was mostly a matter of adapting existing tools to new technologies.

The first version of Xcode was released in 2003. More than ten years later, Apple has finally started giving us officially supported tools such as the Xcode Bots. Needless to say, we have come a long way!

Pros & Cons

The advantages of continuous integration are numerous. The most important is the immediate feedback you get when working on a part of your application. It may be because you broke your test suite or you did not follow your team's coding conventions. It may even be simply because one of the generated reports told you that you were writing code that was too complex. In the end, that feedback results in considerable time saved and not spent - or even wasted - debugging.

Equally important is the peace of mind you and your team will get from being able to diagnose broken code, bugs, or poor quality code early.

Finally, integrating a new, significant, portion of code usually means deploying a new version of your application that a member of your QA team will need to test. When working as part of a team, there is always someone coming to your desk, asking you to install the latest version of the application you are working on on his device; don't be that guy! Be the smart one who automated everything. Building, automated testing, code coverage… all these concepts are simply a shell command execution away; why not let them work for you? As Douglas McIlroy, a well-known UNIX contributor said, "What you do today can be automated tomorrow." That could not be more true in the world of iOS development.

Making a build of your application available for the member of your team, your clients, or your boss to download, is complicated. For mobile, it's actually a multi-step process requiring building, code-signing, and finally deploying.

While we will show in the next chapters that it is totally achievable to do this by yourself, some services were born with the purpose of easing that process. Testflight, Hockey, or even Cloudbees, to name a few are some of the numerous services out there filling the gap. Some are free, some come with a price, some are in the cloud, and some are self-hosted, but all of them share the same common goal.

This book does not aim at comparing these services and telling you which one is the best. It will not give you an exhaustive list, and it will certainly not turn you into an expert in the utilization of the one we chose to talk about.

"There is no single development, in either technology or management technique, which by itself promises even one order of magnitude [tenfold] improvement within a decade in productivity, in reliability, in simplicity."

"No Silver Bullet — Essence and Accidents of Software Engineering" - Fred Brooks (1986)

Of course, all of this is not magic. Being able to receive immediate feedback, while a neat advantage, comes at a cost. Setting up a continuous integration system takes time. This time is not lost - don't get us wrong - but that's something you have to take into account. You may not need a full-featured, continuous integration platform that builds your app every five minutes when you are working alone on a two-screen application. Sometimes, you have to be pragmatic.

Plus, your tools are only as good as the way you use them. You may not be able to take the feedback from your CI platform for granted if you set it up incorrectly.

The Road Ahead

Each chapter will try to cover a very specific part of the principle of continuous integration for iOS. Reading this book is kind of like taking a journey. You will start by learning how to build an iOS application and release it to your team using the simplest approach, and end with a fully set up continuous integration installation. Here is an overview of the chapters we will cover together.

Chapter 2 - Continuous Integration Tools and Features in iOS and Xcode - We will create a simple iOS application that we will use as an example for our continuous integration process, and use it as an example for the rest of the book. In this chapter, we'll see what tools Xcode provides to help you in your day-to-day workflow.

Chapter 3 - Using Xcode to Release an Application Outside the App Store - With the application created in Chapter 2, we will see how we can create a build that you will be able to send to your testers. This will be the simplest approach of all, but you have to start somewhere, right?

Chapter 4 - Invoking the Power of the Command Line - Pressing a bunch of buttons is one thing, but knowing what they mean is another. In this chapter, you will learn how to leverage the power of the command line and what Xcode actually means by "build," among other things.

Chapter 5 - Automating Builds with Jenkins - Jenkins is probably the de-facto solution for continuous integration. You will learn how to get it started and how it can build your iOS applications.

Chapter 6 - Automating Builds with Bamboo - Atlassian is an Australian enterprise software company that develops products for software developers and project managers. One of their products is a commercial alternative to Jenkins. You will learn how to get it started and how you can use it to build your iOS applications.

Chapter 7 - Over The Air (OTA) Distribution - Continuous shipping is a bit different than continuous integration and usually the final step of a successful build process. You will learn how you can make your life and the life of your testers easier by sending them new builds of your application as soon as they are available.

Chapter 8 - Day-to-Day Use of Xcode Server and Xcode Bots - As we have said, Apple finally released its own continuous integration tools. We will teach you how to use them and how you can fit them into your day-to-day workflow.

Chapter 9 - Adding Unit Testing to the mix - Whether you've decided to go for the free solution that is Jenkins, the enterprise one that is Bamboo, or a totally different solution we haven't included, you will learn how to automate the execution of your unit and functional testing as part of your build process.

Chapter 10 - Quality Assurance - As the cherry on top, we will show you which tool can be used to maintain high-quality code.

During this journey, don't hesitate to jump directly to a chapter. You may after all want to learn how to use Jenkins, but don't care about how Bamboo works, and that would be totally fine with us!

Sample Application: Github Jobs

This book's goal is not to teach you how to create iPhone or iPad applications using Objective-C and Xcode. To get the most out of this book, make sure you're comfortable with Objective-C and Xcode first.

As an example, we will create an iOS application communicating with Github jobs' API. This application will be a very simple master/detail application. Coding the application won't take long, but be prepared to spend a lot of time configuring your project.

Prerequisites

Make sure you have Xcode 5.1 installed, as all screenshots in this book will use this version specifically. You wouldn't want to get lost because of an outdated Xcode, would you?

Without any further ado, let's dive in!

Summary

Continuous integration is a vast notion that can't be explained in a single chapter. It is a complex topic that impacts the technology you choose and the methodology you work with. This chapter merely introduced that notion of complexity. Now that you know more about the approach we took, let's start this journey by taking a tour of the tools and features available, while we work on the sample application.

Chapter 2

Continuous integration features in iOS and Xcode

Continuous integration is a matter of choosing the right tools, and the iOS community didn't wait for Apple before setting up their environments. How could they have? It has been known that Apple works in secret and releases all their new tools once a year, usually at WWDC. First, let's have a look at the things that have always been around, in Xcode specifically or in the community abroad.

If Xcode 5 came with a couple of shiny new tools for continuous integration, like the Xcode bots we will talk about later in this book, the previous versions already came with useful integrations to help you get some work done. Even if alternatives are getting more and more popular nowadays (for example, AppCode), and even if there are still people using their favorite text editor and a terminal to build the app, Xcode remains the de-facto IDE.

Of course it has its flaws, like the famous website "Text from Xcode," available at textfromxcode.com, has funnily shown in the past few years. No software is perfect, and we as developers tend to take everything for granted, but Xcode actually handles a lot for you. Let's see what it can do and how it will help us in setting up our continuous integration environment.

In this book we will be spending a lot of time in Xcode. As it wouldn't make sense to give you random screenshots to adapt to your existing application yourself, we will create a very simple application using the GitHub Jobs API.

We will start by creating the sample application and taking a tour of what the default project template gives us: what the application's info file is, where the unit tests are, and which framework do they rely on. Then, we'll move on to some more advanced stuff like versioning the project using Git and managing our dependencies using CocoaPods, a well-known dependency-manager for Xcode projects. Finally we will set up everything we need to be ready to release the application first to our beta testers and finally to the rest of the world. That will give us a great opportunity to cover in depth how Xcode will help us to manage multiple environments.

Sample application: Github jobs

GitHub is a hosting service, available at github.com, for software development projects that uses the Git revision control system. It comes with free, paying, and enterprise plans and is very well known in the community. Among other services, it comes with a dedicated job offers section for both job hunters and companies. If you want to know more about this service, visit https://jobs.github.com.

As we said earlier, this book does not does aim at teaching you how to code in Objective-C. Chances are you know enough of it if you're reading this book. That's why we are keeping the application very simple: it will call the GitHub API, retrieve a bunch of job offers, and display them in a list using a UITableView. Nothing fancy.

Creating the Application

Start by setting up a new iOS project using Apple's template. Open Xcode and hit the "Create a new Xcode project" button or, with Xcode open, choose "New ⌘ Project…" from the "File" menu. Make sure the iOS application templates are selected from the sidebar and choose "Single view application," as seen in Figure 2-1.

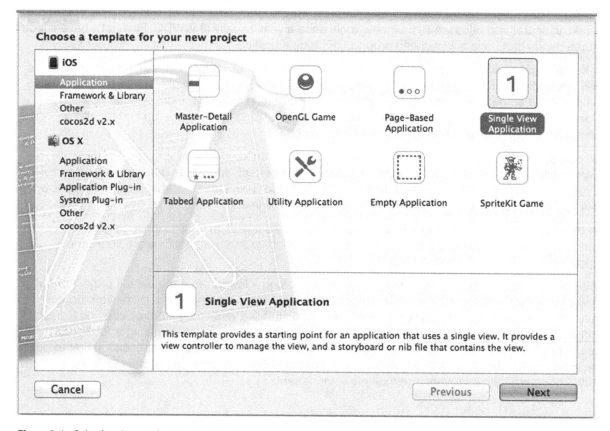

Figure 2-1. Selecting the template we want to start working on the application

Using "Github Jobs" as the product name, "com.perfectly-cooked" as the company identifier and "PCS" as the class prefix. It's the one we'll use and it will make it easier for you to understand the screenshots. The other options don't matter much, just make sure to check the "Create Git repository on…" and select "My Mac" for now. Xcode allows you to use OS X server to host your code, among other things, but we will talk about that later.

What Xcode Gives Us

We are using a standard template given by Xcode. It comes with a simple Storyboard file, an application delegate, and a UIViewController subclass. Let's take a look at the things we can use in our day-to-day workflow and how they'll fit in our continuous integration process.

Application's Info file

Every application comes with an Info file written in the property list format, you will find it under the name "MyApplicationInfo.plist" or in our case, "Github Jobs-Info.plist." When you open that file, you will basically find all the public information about the application, among other things: The name of the application and the product identifier you set earlier when you created the project.

> **Note**   **About property list format:** Property list files are files that store serialized objects using the filename extension ".plist," and thus are often referred to as Plist files. Because there are all the APIs you need in the iOS and OSX SDKs, property list files usually are the de-facto file format to store information about an application and other various settings and data.

First, open the file from your favorite text editor either by going manually to the directory where you created the application and navigating to the "Github Jobs" directory that corresponds to your application's main target (the other one is the testing target, more on that later) or by right-clicking on the file in Xcode file explorer and selecting "Open with external editor." The first lines should look like something similar to the following:

```
<?xml version="1.0" encoding="UTF-8"?>
<!DOCTYPE plist PUBLIC "-//Apple//DTD PLIST 1.0//EN"
"http://www.apple.com/DTDs/PropertyList-1.0.dtd">
<plist version="1.0">
<dict>
        <key>CFBundleDevelopmentRegion</key>
        <string>en</string>
        <key>CFBundleDisplayName</key>
        <string>${PRODUCT_NAME}</string>
        <key>CFBundleExecutable</key>
        <string>${EXECUTABLE_NAME}</string>
        <key>CFBundleIdentifier</key>
        <string>com.perfectly-cooked.${PRODUCT_NAME:rfc1034identifier}</string>
        ...
```

This is not really human friendly, to say the least. Don't worry though: Xcode doesn't expect you to edit this file manually. In fact, Xcode comes with a property list editor that will make it easier to view this file. It also turns the keys into comprehensible sentences. This way, "LSRequiresIPhoneOS" turns into "Application requires the iPhone environment."

Note that you can still view the name of the keys underneath. This can be helpful for debugging or simply because tutorials on the Internet often refers to these raw keys. From the editor, right-click on and select "Show Raw Keys/Values."

What interests us most are the two versions properties, by default, their values should be 1.0. The first one, the "Bundle versions string, short" a.k.a. CFBundleShortVersionString is the main version of the application. If you have already shipped an application on the app store, you've probably already changed its value. The second one, "Bundle version" a.k.a. CFBundleVersion, is the full version number and doesn't have to be human-readable. Most people tend to keep both in sync, but that would be a waste of configuration in our case, as the long version will be proven useful in the future.

Later in the book we will start talking about automated builds. These builds always come with an incrementing number and this is when the CFBundleVersion key comes in handy. According to Apple documentation, the CFBundleVersion specifies a version of the application, released or not, which fits perfectly. Every time our application is built, we will use the build's number to change the CFBundleVersion. To keep things clear, it is important to have coherence between those two versions.

This Info property list file contains information about the application that is made available from the NSBundle class. Its content is not limited to the keys available now, there are in fact a lot of other keys that will be added if, for example, you want your application to be opened when a certain URL scheme is called from a webpage. Xcode manages most of these keys for you, so you don't need to know them all.

Tests

An Xcode project comes with a testing target, a test class, and your very first test case. This last one is a failing one, as it basically just calls XCTFail, a C macro used to force-fail a case. Still, that's something.

Everything has been configured so you can get to work right away and start writing tests at the beginning of your project. That's something you'll be very happy about when your project becomes big and complex.

When we started writing the book, we talked a bit about how Apple took its time before actually giving you tools for continuous integration. That's not entirely true. Since Xcode 2.1, Xcode came with a version of the testing tools SenTestingKit and OCUnit, which wasn't an official Apple-labelled tool back then, but a framework created by a company called "Sen:te" (http://sente.ch).

Open the sample application and select "Github Jobs," the first element in the file explorer. Select your testing target, named "Github JobsTests" and select the "Build Settings" tab. You should see all the settings of this target. Filter these settings using the search field at the top right and look for "xctest." As the Figure 2-2 shows, you should see that a framework called XCTest is automatically linked with your application. XCTest is a brand new testing framework heavily based on the old one but way better and way more deeply integrated in the IDE and much more powerful.

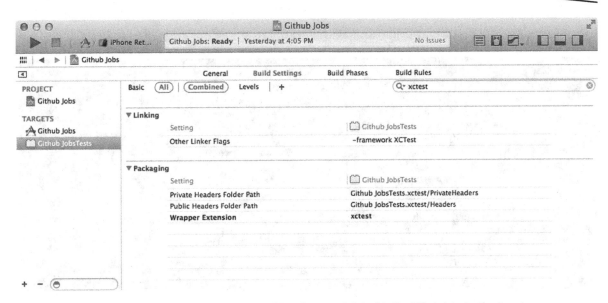

Figure 2-2. *The filtered list of build settings shows the XCTest framework linked to the Github Jobs testing target*

In the 5.1.1 release, OCUnit and the SenTestingKit framework were marked as deprecated and will be removed from a future release of Xcode. In fact, source code using OCUnit now generates warnings at compilation time.

For starters, Xcode 5 comes with a test navigator available in your sidebar or by pressing "⌘ + 5." This navigator allows you to see the recently run test cases and to re-run them by pressing a single button, making every refactoring a breeze. That's not all there is. Xcode 5 comes with new assistant editors that will help you unit-test your code. The assistants, called "Test Callers" and "Test Classes," provide access to unit tests related to the current source code in the primary editor. In our example shown in Figure 2-3, we have created a fake PCSGithubJob class (on the left) with a method whose purpose is to analyze a job offer and tell you if it will make you happy. The "Test Callers" editor (on the right) automatically jumped to the related testing method.

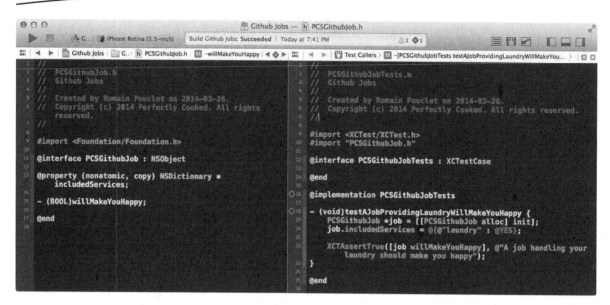

Figure 2-3. Xcode with the primary and the assistant editors opened showing the unit-testing code related to our class

Last but not least, the xcodebuild command line tool now supports the `test` action for iOS projects. Before this release it was not possible directly to run your unit-tests from the command line. We will cover more about the command line equivalent of these tools in Chapter 3.

Back in Xcode 4, when you created an iOS or OSX application, you had to check an option to add a testing target to your project and now this is the default behavior. This is a nice touch from Apple since the community of the iOS developers has always had this image of one that mostly focuses on the design and the user experience. It shows a clear will of helping the iOS developers to become more professional and start using the proper tools.

Finally, the new testing framework was actually announced at the same time as the "Xcode Bots." They are meant to help you embrace the concept of continuous integration and they fit perfectly with XCTest. Make sure to read Chapter 8 to learn more about them!

A good test suite is key in a continuous integration environment. We talked earlier about how a good environment will provide you with maximum feedback. Automated testing is one of the tools for this purpose. Whether you are an independent iOS developer working alone or a developer wondering if you should integrate the feature your coworker has been working on, making sure all the tests are green first sure will help you in making a decision.

Git Integration

Integrating pieces of codes in your project as we said in the introduction usually means merging branches using your favorite version control system. A successfully continuous integration usually means a well-established workflow. When you are working on an application, there are a couple of things that will happen. Once the first version has been released, you will start working on new features, some of them will take time, and that's why you will be working on separate branches of your repository. During this process, your users will probably send you bug reports and feedback about various glitches in the application. These will have to be fixed as soon as possible and be shipped as new minor versions of your application. Once again, because you don't want to mess with the application, you will work on separate branches just as you work on new features.

The main thing to keep in mind is that at any and every time you work you will want feedback about the tasks you are working on. You will want to know if you are currently breaking something while implementing your new feature, or if the bug that has been reported to you is being fixed. Plus, your QA team, your boss, or even your client may want that feedback as well, and probably a fresh build of your application. Because, "I'm sorry, I broke the app for now, please call me back in an hour or two" is not an acceptable answer, you will have to keep everything separated.

The good news is that branches are cheap in Git. You can create as much as you want without any trouble for you or your coworkers. The great news is Xcode comes with Git support right out of the box, as you may have noticed when you created the Github Jobs project or by looking at the big "Source Control" menu in Xcode.

Back in the old days, Xcode only supported Subversion and CVS. While the first one still exists, even if it's grown a bit out of date due to the arrival of Decentralized Version Control System (DVCS), such as Git and Mercurial, the second one was clearly a legacy from the sad old days of versioning control.

Git is a really popular Version Control Systems that works in a decentralized way. Meaning the opposite way of how SVN works, every single working copy of a project can be used as a remote and even better, can work independently.

To show you how useful it is to have Git deeply integrated in your Xcode project, let's break it. That's right, let's create a very simple conflict and see what happens. In the world of Version Control Systems, conflicts are what happen when merging two versions of a file is not possible. If you changed the same part of the same file differently in the two branches you're merging together, it won't be able to merge them and a manual intervention will be required.

In Xcode, from the Source Control menu, select "Github Jobs – master" and then, select "New Branch…". In the field that appears, fill the branch name field with "saying-hi" and press "Create." At the end of this process, you will be working on a dedicated branch for your "Saying Hi" feature. This means that your application will evolve while a stable version, the master branch, is still available somewhere.

Now, open the "AppDelegate.m" file and add a simple NSLog instruction that greets the user when the application finishes launching:

```
#import "PCSAppDelegate.h"

@implementation PCSAppDelegate

- (BOOL)application:(UIApplication *)application didFinishLaunchingWithOptions:(NSDictionary *)
launchOptions
{
    NSLog(@"Hi, I'm a sample application for a book.");

    return YES;
}

@end
```

With this greeting implemented, open the Source control menu and select "Commit…". In the form that appears, enter a simple commit message such as "Saying hi when the application starts" and press the "Commit 1 File" button. You've now made your very first commit in this feature branch.

To create a conflict, a file must have been modified at a similar place in the file in a different branch, so we need to go back to the master branch and create a commit similar to the one we've just made.

From the Source Control menu, select "Github Jobs – saying-hi" and then "Switch to Branch…". In the list that appears, select the master branch and press "Switch." We are now back to the master branch, and the NSLog instruction we've added is no longer here.

Let's repeat the process with a slightly different greeting message while still on the master branch. We chose to go with "Hi, I'm a book created for a sample application," which indeed doesn't make much sense. Commit your modification like we did before. We now have 2 branches, both with a slightly different greeting instruction at the same position in the same file.

Finally, from the Source Control menu, select "Github Jobs – master" and then "Merge from Branch…". In the list that appears, select "saying-hi" and press "Merge": a window similar to the one shown in Figure 2-4 will appear. Select the third button in the menu at the bottom of the screen to integrate the modifications on the right and press the "Merge."

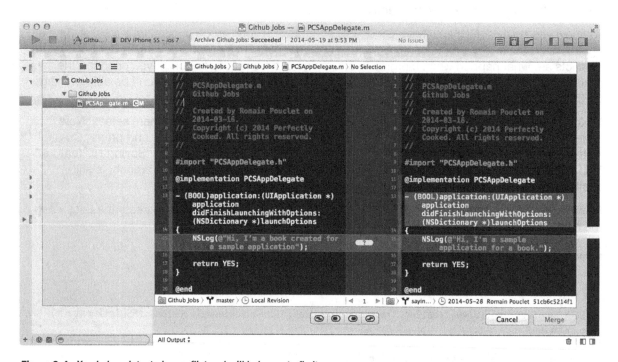

Figure 2-4. Xcode has detected a conflict and will help you to fix it

That's basically how conflicts work and that's how Xcode will assist you to fix them and keep your project clean. However, sometimes conflict will happen outside of Xcode, because you decided to merge a branch using the command line or because you started using a dedicated Git client.

That's the kind of thing Xcode will understand. When that happens and some of your files become disfigured with weird characters all over the place, building your application could simply throw you some random syntax error and let you find out why your build is failing. Xcode is much more clever than that. Indeed, you won't even be able to build your application unless the conflict is marked as resolved manually using your shell or your favorite Git client, or directly in Xcode, as shown in Figure 2-5.

Figure 2-5. Xcode has detected a conflicted file and marked it as such in the sidebar and the primary editor

To fix this conflict and mark it as resolved, edit the "AppDelegate.m" file until it looks good to you. In our case, that would be keeping only one "application:didFinishLaunchingWithOptions:" method and choosing the second message. You must remove all the conflict markers, which are the lines with the multiple chevrons and equal signs, for your application to build again. After all, in this context, they are nothing more than syntax errors. Once this is done, simply right-click on the conflicted file and select "Mark Selected File as Resolved" in the "Source Control" menu item.

Versioning control in Xcode is not all sparkles and rainbows. There are edge cases that come with Apple using file formats such as the one for the "xcodeproj" file or even "xib" and "storyboards." In Xcode 5, Apple came with a much simpler file format for those Interface Builder files, making merge operations and conflict resolutions a lot easier. From NIB to bloated XIB, to almost-readable, ten-times shorter XIB, Apple is indeed working at easing this process. Once again, we've come a long way, even if we are still waiting for a simpler file format for those "xcodeproj," which still uses an old-style brace based format to delimit the configuration hierarchy.

If there is one tip this book can give you, it's to close Xcode during merge operations involving an Xcode project or an Xcode workspace file. Usually, this happens when someone on your team is changing a setting in the "provisioning profiles" and/or "code signing" sections. As this format is hardly human-readable at all, the results from a merge can get ugly and Xcode can get a little bit "crashy."

There are still a couple of downsides to this integration directly in the IDE. For starters, it is pretty limited. You'll only be able to do the basic Git operations and will probably end up using your shell or a dedicated Git client. Also, Xcode ships its own version of Git. At the time of writing this book, the current stable version of Git is the 2.0.1, as shown in a shell after running `git --version`:

```
$ git --version
git version 1.9.1
```

This version can be easily installed using a package manager such as Homebrew or even compiled and installed manually, if you have some spare time on your hands. However, if you open a terminal and run a simple command, you should see that the version of Git used by Xcode is Apple's own version, based on 1.8.5.2:

```
bash-3.2$ $(xcode-select -print-path)/usr/bin/git --version
git version 1.8.5.2 (Apple Git-48)
```

In most cases, it won't cause any trouble, but incompatibilities between Xcode's Git version and the one you're using may arise. This was the case when Xcode 4 was the current version and the latest Git was a couple of versions ahead of the one that was shipped with it.

> **Note**   **About xcode-select:** xcode-select is one of those very useful tools shipped with a bunch of others provided by Apple's official command line tools and is very helpful if you are playing with multiple installations of Xcode, during betas for example. We'll talk about this more in Chapter 4.

CocoaPods

Someone once said, "with great projects come huge dependencies" and managing dependencies with external libraries in an iOS project has pretty much always been a pain. This is a pain you don't need in your iOS project, but Apple doesn't seem to be willing to provide an official tool besides workspaces, subprojects, and *manually* managing the search paths of your dependencies. This was before CocoaPods.

CocoaPods is a dependency manager written in Ruby, unsurprisingly inspired from RubyGems (https://rubygems.org/). If you don't know about it but have been writing Ruby in the past, its syntax used in the PodFile, in which you'll declare all your dependencies, is really easy to understand and should not give you too much of a hard time.

The use of CocoaPods really is up for debate in the iOS and Mac community. Whether you hate it or love it, in this book we definitely stand with the people who love it. In the process of continuously integrating pieces of code, letting a well-designed tool handling the management of your dependencies makes something less to worry about and gives you more time to focus on other things.

As a bonus, you can actually use CocoaPods for a specific application's dependencies, meaning you can use it to split your big application in multiple modules and let CocoaPods handle the merge.

Once again, there is no silver bullet. As it is written on the website, "CocoaPods is not ready for prime-time yet." At the time of writing this book, 0.33.1 is the latest version. It's far from being perfect but it's a lot better than no tools at all. We will be using CocoaPods in the sample application.

Speaking of which, let's code.

Coding the Sample Application

Open the "Github Jobs" project we created earlier in Xcode, select the only view controller header class present in the file explorer, and make it an **UITableViewController** instead of a simple **UIViewController**. Go to the associated implementation file, declare a "jobs" property of type NSArray, and implement the required methods from UITableViewDataSource: "tableView:numberOfRowsInSection:" and "tableView:cellForRowAtIndexPath:." At the end of this process, your implementation file should look like this:

```
#import "PCSViewController.h"

@interface PCSViewController ()

@property (nonatomic, strong) NSArray *jobs;

@end

@implementation PCSViewController

#pragma mark - Table View
- (NSInteger)numberOfSectionsInTableView:(UITableView *)tableView
{
    return 1;
}

- (NSInteger)tableView:(UITableView *)tableView numberOfRowsInSection:(NSInteger)section
{
    return self.jobs.count;
}

- (UITableViewCell *)tableView:(UITableView *)tableView
cellForRowAtIndexPath:(NSIndexPath *)indexPath
{
    UITableViewCell *cell = [tableView dequeueReusableCellWithIdentifier:@"Cell"
forIndexPath:indexPath];

    return cell;
}

@end
```

Then, open the storyboard file and remove the view controller already created by Xcode. Instead, drop a new navigation controller. It should automatically come with a table view controller. Select it and use "PCSViewController" as its class. Select the navigation item and change the title to "iOS jobs." In the TableViewController, select the first prototype cell and give it the "Cell" reuse identifier to avoid getting an exception on run later on. That's pretty much all there will be in this application. We are trying to keep it very simple.

The Github Jobs API is very simple, all you need is calling a specific URL to retrieve a JSON-encoded list of iOS job offers in New-York. Using the iOS 7.0 new NSURLSession API, go back to the implementation file of your view controller and fetch content from that famous URL in the viewWillAppear: method as follows:

```objc
- (void)viewWillAppear:(BOOL)animated {
    NSURL *url = [NSURL URLWithString:
    @"https://jobs.github.com/positions.json?description=ios&location=NY"];
    NSURLSessionDataTask *jobTask = [[NSURLSession sharedSession] dataTaskWithURL:
    url completionHandler:^(NSData *data, NSURLResponse *response, NSError *error) {
        dispatch_async(dispatch_get_main_queue(), ^{

            if (error) {
                UIAlertView *alert = [[UIAlertView alloc] initWithTitle: @"An error occured"
                                                                message: error.localizedDescription
                                                               delegate: nil
                                                      cancelButtonTitle: @"Dismiss"
                                                      otherButtonTitles: nil];
                [alert show];
                return;
            });

            NSError *jsonError = nil;
            self.jobs = [NSJSONSerialization JSONObjectWithData: data options: 0 error: &jsonError];
            [self.tableView reloadData];
        });
    }];

    [jobTask resume];
}
```

Note that we wrapped the whole content of the completion block using a function from Grand Central Dispatch (GCD) so all the UI job is performed on the main thread. Don't forget to update the tableView:cellForRowAtIndexPath: method to display the "title" property of a job.

```objc
- (UITableViewCell *)tableView:(UITableView *)tableView
cellForRowAtIndexPath:(NSIndexPath *)indexPath {
    UITableViewCell *cell = [tableView dequeueReusableCellWithIdentifier:@"Cell"
    forIndexPath:indexPath];
    cell.textLabel.text = self.jobs[indexPath.row][@"title"];

    return cell;
}
```

The application could have been a master-detail application, and selecting a row could have opened a detailed page showing the application logo, detailed information about the offer, and a direct button helping the user postulate. Instead, because a complete application is not the goal of this book, selecting a cell with simply… will open Safari mobile. To do that, implement the delegate method that will be called when the user taps on a cell in the "PCSViewController.m," as follows:

```
- (void)tableView:(UITableView *)tableView didSelectRowAtIndexPath:(NSIndexPath *)indexPath {
    NSURL *jobUrl = [NSURL URLWithString: self.jobs[indexPath.row][@"url"]];
    [[UIApplication sharedApplication] openURL: jobUrl];
}
```

The only missing part of this application is a way to show the user that work is being done and content is not available yet. We will use a very simple library called SVProgressHUD for this very purpose and we will install it using – that's right, CocoaPods.

Close your Xcode project and open a terminal. Navigate to the location of your iOS project and install CocoaPods if you haven't already, using RubyGems (see instructions below). Run the pod init command to create an empty-ish Podfile and open it. Add SVProgressHUD as a dependency, as shown in Figure 2-6:

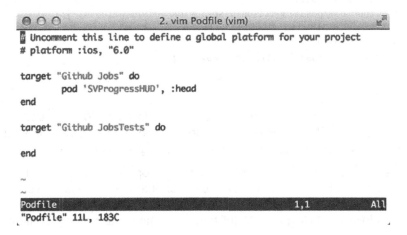

Figure 2-6. *Using vim, we are adding the SVProgressHUD library as a dependency*

Finally, run pod install and open the generated `Github Jobs.xcworkspace` instead of the previous `Github Jobs.xcodeproj`. This is why we asked to close Xcode.

Here is the whole process:

```
$ (sudo) gem install cocoapods
$ cd path/to/Github\ Jobs
$ pod init
$ vim Podfile
// edit Podfile...
$ pod install
$ open Github\ Jobs.xcworkspace
```

Installing CocoaPods   The installation of CocoaPods may, of course, vary in case you are using a Ruby version management system such as rbenv (`http://rbenv.org`) or RVM (`https://rvm.io`).

SVProgressHUD provides really easy methods to use to display messages. Let's go back to the view controller and use these methods, before and after fetching the content from the Github Jobs API. Before calling the resume method of the NSURLSessionDataTask object that we created, import the SVProgressHUD .h file and call the following class method:

```
#import <SVProgressHUD/SVProgressHUD.h>

// ...

- (void)viewWillAppear:(BOOL)animated {
    NSURL *url = [NSURL URLWithString:
    @"https://jobs.github.com/positions.json?description=ios&location=NY"];

    NSURLSessionDataTask *jobTask = ...
    [SVProgressHUD showWithStatus: @"Fetching jobs..."];
    [jobTask resume];
}
```

The SVProgressHUD library comes with two different methods, "showWithStatus:" and "showWithStatus:maskType." We are using the second one so we can have a dark background. Otherwise we wouldn't be able to properly see the HUD being animated.

Once the jobs have been fetched and the JSON has been properly decoded and turned into a list of jobs to display, we want to give the user a small indication that the process is over. To do that, add the following snippet at the end of the NSURLSession's "dataTaskWithURL: completionHandler:" completion block, as follows. Calling showWithStatus: will show a temporary confirmation message, there is no need to dismiss it manually.

```
NSURLSessionDataTask *jobTask = [[NSURLSession sharedSession] dataTaskWithURL: url
completionHandler:^(NSData *data, NSURLResponse *response, NSError *error) {
        // ...

        [SVProgressHUD showSuccessWithStatus: [NSString stringWithFormat: @"%lu jobs fetched",
        (unsigned long)[self.jobs count]]];
}];
```

When you run your application, you should see the HUD in both situations, similar to Figure 2-7.

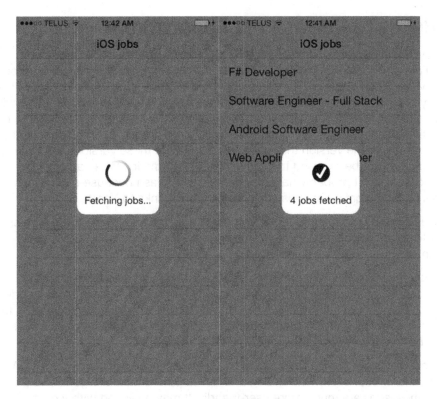

Figure 2-7. Fetching the jobs shows a spinning animation and getting the results shows a confirmation message

Installing dependencies using CocoaPods creates two things in addition to the generated PodFile: a **Podfile.lock** managing the state of the dependencies in the project and a Pods folder containing the actual dependencies. It's really a hot debate in the community, but automation has been created for a reason and we strongly suggest you ignore this folder by adding "Pods" to your ".gitignore" file: create a .gitignore file at the root of the directory where you created your project, and add "Pods." This folder will be ignored and Git will not try to commit it when your dependencies change, for example because you've switched to a more recent version.

> **About ".gitignore" files**   A gitignore file specifies a pattern of files that Git should ignore. If you don't have one already, which is totally possible considering Xcode doesn't generate one automatically, grab the one available on GitHub: `https://github.com/github/gitignore/blob/master/Global/Xcode.gitignore`.

Why Have We Done All This?

We now have an application up and running. It's not pretty and probably not very useful, but we will be able to use it in the remaining chapters of this book as an example. If you are interested in the complete application, it is available at the following URL: `https://github.com/palleas/github-jobs`.

Getting Ready to Release the Application

During the lifecycle of a project, there will be multiple versions of the application. First, there will be the one you are developing on your computer that will run in your iOS simulator or on one of your testing devices. Then, there will be one that will be used by your QA team that will review the latest features you've implemented and the bug you've fixed. Once this is done, there will be a version of your application that you will send to your client. This is the final step before pushing the application on the official App Store. Finally, there will be the production-ready application, once the client is satisfied with the version that you have sent. All of these versions will have specificities. For example, you may not be showing the same level of information when an error occurs in the application. Also, you won't probably have your application crash because of a failing assertion in your code. This multiple-configuration is easily achievable thanks to Xcode.

Of course, this is not the way it has to work; you may be an independent iOS developer and/or may not have a QA team at your disposal. We will make it easier for everybody and only have three levels of configuration:

- Debug: the level of configuration you will use when you are working on the application. It may crash from time to time when you are misusing some code and display a lot of information when errors occur. Debugging tools such as the awesome Reveal (http://revealapp.com) or libraries relaying on private APIs may be linked with your application in this configuration.

- Adhoc: this is the configuration used by the version you will send to your QA team and/or your client. The debug and development tools are gone and the error messages are much more user-friendly. It may be linked with a crash log reporter to ease the back and forth with your client, for example.

- Release: this will be the configuration used by your application when it goes live on the store.

Go back to your Xcode project, select the top-level element in the file explorer, and make sure the "Github Jobs" item in the Project section is selected. If you take a look at what's on the screen, you will see that Xcode already provides you two different configuration levels, as shown in Figure 2-8.

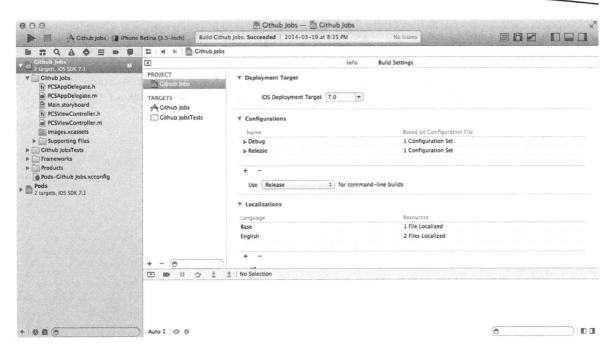

Figure 2-8. By default, an Xcode project comes with two levels of configuration: Debug and Release

Because we want a third one called "AdHoc," click on the plus sign right beneath the configuration list and select "Duplicate Debug configuration" as it's much easier to remove the things we don't want from the Debug configuration than putting back in one we need to the Release configuration. In the first cell of the row that just appeared, fill in "AdHoc." We now have three levels of configuration.

You may wonder why we chose "AdHoc" as a configuration name. "Ad Hoc" comes from Latin and means "for this." It is a popular convention given by Apple. In fact, when you go in the iOS developer center to create a distribution certificate, you can choose to create an "Ad Hoc" provisioning profile so you can deploy your application without using the App Store. We will talk a lot more about Ad Hoc provisioning profiles and over the air distribution in Chapter 7.

We now have our three configuration levels. Let's see how it will help us in our continuous integration process. Go to the build settings tab in your project configuration. You will see a lot of settings you don't want to play with, mostly because some of them look like gibberish and honestly, Apple did a good job setting up these proper default values. Let's take a look at a couple of them. You can easily jump to a specific setting by using the search field at the top of the interface and compare the different settings depending on the configuration, for example the "Build Active Architecture Only" one.

When you work on your application, you want the build to be as fast as possible. That's why you don't want to build for all the valid architectures. With the current active devices out there, from iPad 3 to iPhone 5S, you end up having to build for three different architectures: armv7, armv7s, and arm64, which makes the build slower.

If you take a look at the "Build active architecture only" you will see that this option is set to YES for the Debug configuration and set to NO for the Adhoc and Release builds. It is very important to keep the build as fast as possible, that's why there are other settings, such as "Validate Product" that are disabled for debug build. On the other hand, when your application is built by an automated build tool every once in a while, you don't care if the build is slower and actually want the extra feedback provided by these settings.

For the AdHoc configuration, select NO for this build setting, as shown in Figure 2-9. We want the extra feedback provided by the Debug configuration but we actually need the three architectures since we don't know which devices the application will be installed on. We will talk a little bit more about these architectures in chapter 4.

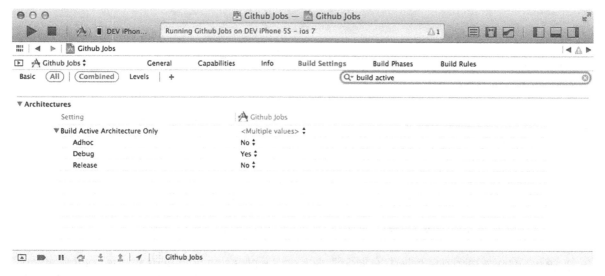

Figure 2-9. *A project comes with multiple levels of configuration for settings that can be inherited or overridden*

Look for the "static analyzer" section on the build settings. As shown in the Figure 2-10, the static analyzer is disabled during the build process.

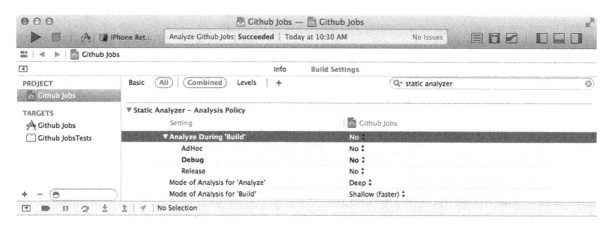

Figure 2-10. *Static code analysis is disabled for build process*

It is this way for a very simple reason: static analysis of code is slow. It is even slower when you want to have a more in depth analysis instead of a shallower one. Let's activate it for the AdHoc configuration as shown in Figure 2-11.

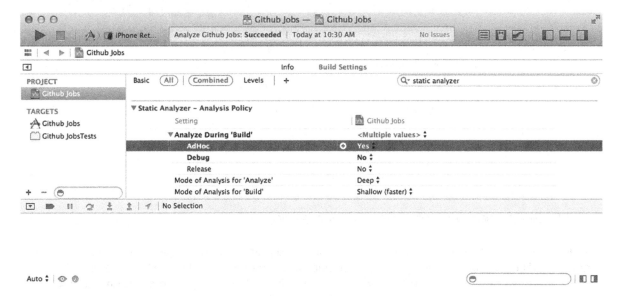

Figure 2-11. *Static code analysis is now enabled for build using the Adhoc configuration*

Of course, we are not telling you to avoid quality assurance at all in your projects. In fact, Chapter 10 will be dedicated to that subject.

Custom Build Settings

Having multiple configurations for your application does not only allow you to play with the build settings that came with the project. In a real application you may want to interact with different web services, such as YouTube, Twitter, or even a custom backend. Of course, you don't want to pollute the live application and with the example of Twitter, post a lot of testing tweets on a real account. In your different configurations, you will want different endpoints for your web services and different security tokens.

In our case, we will assume we have the source of the application and run multiple instances: a local one on our computer, a staging one for testing and review purposes, and a live one, located at http://jobs.github.com.

There is a very simple way of switching between developing tokens and web services endpoints. One of the settings provided by the compiler and easily editable from Xcode are preprocessor macros, which are evaluated at compile time, once and for all. This setting is named "GCC_PREPROCESSOR_DEFINITIONS" and can be found in Xcode under the "Preprocessor Macros" section. As you will see in Figure 2-12, Xcode already declared a DEBUG macro, only available in the Debug environment (and the Adhoc one, which is based on Debug).

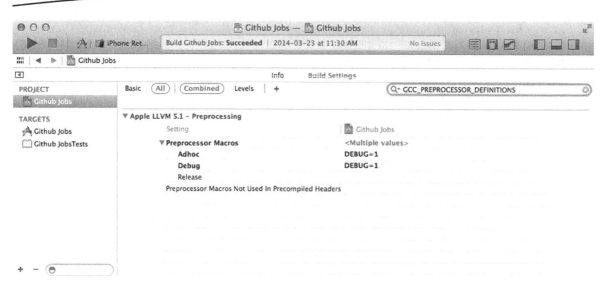

Figure 2-12. *The debug macro is available for Debug and Adhoc configurations*

In your code, it's pretty easy to use this information using preprocessor conditionals. These conditions will be evaluated during compilation and portions of code will actually be compiled and some of them will be ignored. You can use this simple trick to handle a debug environment and a production one. For example, in our code:

```
- (void)viewWillAppear:(BOOL)animated {
#if DEBUG
    NSURL *url = [NSURL URLWithString:
    @"https://127.0.0.1:9000/positions.json?description=ios&location=NY"];
#else
    NSURL *url = [NSURL URLWithString:
    @"https://jobs.github.com/positions.json?description=ios&location=NY"];
#endif
}
```

While this solution works despite the fact it will only handle two configurations, it has a couple of cons. The most important downside to this solution is the code getting more complicated. A few lines back we talked about three configurations, so we will need to add a new conditional block using #elseif.

Keeping your code clean has to be your main objective and with this approach, the code will get a lot less clear while you keep using this solution for tokens, endpoints, and images. What we really need is a way to link a URL endpoint to a configuration, and that is easily achievable with Xcode using custom build settings.

Open the "Editor" menu, then from "Add Build Setting," select "Add User-Defined Setting." In the cell that will appear, fill in "GITHUB_JOBS_ENDPOINT" and press enter. We now have a new build setting, able to contain different values depending on the configuration, as shown in Figure 2-13.

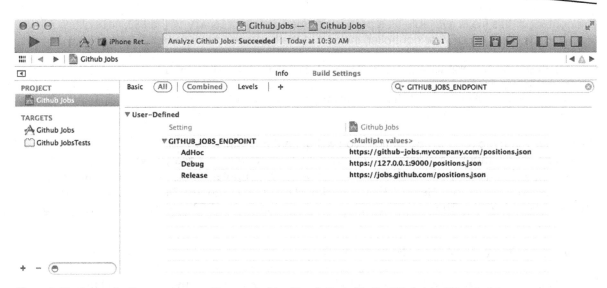

Figure 2-13. *Our application now comes with a new build setting dedicated to the Github Jobs API endpoint*

Now that this setting is available to us, there are a couple of ways to access it within our code. The easiest one is to make it available in your application Info property list file and fetch it from there during runtime.

Open the `Github Jobs-Info.plist` and click on the plus sign that appears when you hover the "Information Property List" cell. In the row that appears, enter "GithubJobsEndpoint" as the new property's key, as shown in Figure 2-14. Make sure "string" is selected in the type column and use "$(GITHUB_JOBS_ENDPOINT)" as the value: the value of this property will be automatically replaced by the content of the GITHUB_JOBS_ENDPOINT build setting, which may vary across our different configurations.

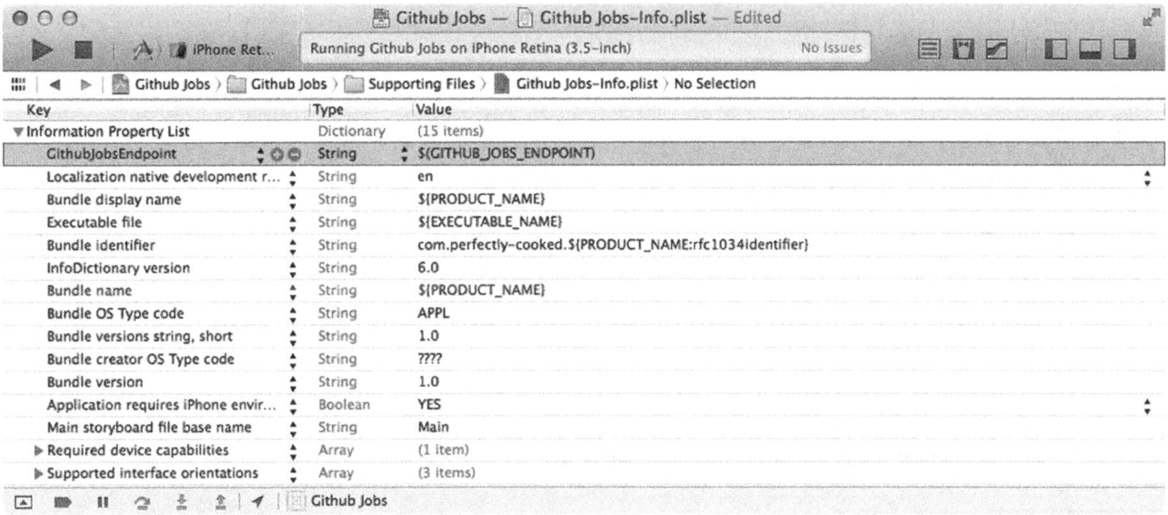

Figure 2-14. *The application manifest now contains the URL base on the value of the current configuration's endpoint setting*

The content of this file is available as a property named infoDictionary of the NSBundle class. All we need to do is use it in our view controller, instead of the hardcoded endpoint.

```
NSString *endpoint = [[NSBundle bundleForClass: [self class]] infoDictionary]
[@"GithubJobsEndpoint"];
    NSURL *url = [NSURL URLWithString: [endpoint stringByAppendingString:
    @"?description=ios&location=NY"]];
```

Note that if you try to run the application, you will get an error since you don't really have a server running on your computer and listening for requests on port 9000. In case you wanted to give it a try anyway, you can easily create an HTTP server on your computer, using ruby. To do that, create a folder called "Github Jobs Server." Fetch the JSON response from the GitHub Jobs API and store into a positions.json file. Then from the command line, start your HTTP server using the following command:

```
$ ruby -run -e httpd -- --bind-address 0.0.0.0 --port 9000.
```

It's okay to feel lost if you are not very comfortable with the command line; you haven't read Chapter 4 yet! We are only talking about this local HTTP server for the most advanced of you.

Build Phases

There is one more feature that will help you called "build phases." As the name would suggest, the build process is split into multiple subtasks. Select the Github Job top item at the top of Xcode's file navigator, select the "Github Jobs" target and navigate to the Build Phases tab. As you can see in Figure 2-15, our project comes with several build phases already.

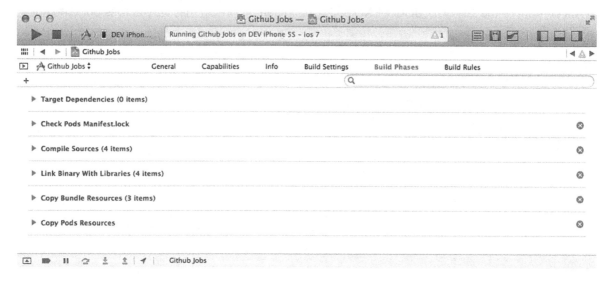

Figure 2-15. an empty project comes with a few required build steps

First, you will find "Compile source" (we are deliberately ignoring the Target Dependencies build phase), which turns all your implementation files into machine code. This is the most important part of the build process. Then, the frameworks and libraries you are using are linked into the generated binary, in the Link Binary With Libraries build phase. Finally, the "Copy Bundle resources" build phase copies your resources (images, sounds, etc.), into the final bundle.

These are the default phases when you create a project, but if you look at the build phases in the Github Jobs application, you will notice two other phases we haven't talked about. These two phases were added to your project when you ran pod init and started using CocoaPods. Their goal is to make sure your project is up to date with its dependencies, meaning you did not forgot to run a pod install after you or your coworker added a dependency. The final one copies all CocoaPods-related assets into your project. That comes in handy when you use dependencies that come with images, sounds, or even if you decided to split your application into multiple modules, as CocoaPods can also handle XIB and Storyboard files.

More important than that, this shows you that it is possible to implement custom build phases with multiple purposes. To add a new build phase, select Editor ➤ Add Build Phase ➤ Add Run Script Build Phase. A new phase will appear at the bottom with a first text field so your can select your favorite shell – most of the time, sh or bash - and a text area to enter your script. This could do anything - from incrementing the build number, to the application main icon being printed with the name of the Git branch you are on. This will bring several advantages when we talk about quality assurance in Chapter 10.

Summary

We've shown you that Xcode comes will all the tools you need to set up a more than decent continuous integration environment, from versioning system integration to testing tools. We are now ready to answer the question that comes after the build process: What should I do with my build?

The next chapter will show you how to simply distribute the application to your team.

Chapter 3

Using Xcode to Release an Application Outside the App Store

The question we need to ask ourselves now is, "What should I do with my application now?" In the previous chapter, we created a simple application that displayed a few iOS job offers around New York. This application is simple enough to be entirely explained and developed in one chapter, along with all the tools we have at our disposal, directly integrated into Xcode or not.

This sample application is far from being ready to be sent to the public. To be honest, one quick look to the application from the Apple review team would probably make them laugh before clicking the big red "reject" button. Assuming there is such a button and that it is red. That is why, at this point in the process, you will start needing feedback from your team. Let's see how we can use Xcode to get that feedback.

What We Need

For our team to test the application and send us feedback, what we need is a build of the application installed on a testing device. If you are reading this book, you may have already released an application on the App Store and you are now trying to take your process to the next level. This means that you have probably already created more than a build to send to the App Store. The next pages will probably feel like déjà-vu for you. If you are not in the mood for a "back-to-basics" session, feel free to jump directly to the next chapter, where we will be toying with the command line tools.

In chapter 2, we explained why you should always create multiple environments for your application. In our case, we have a simple application with Debug, Adhoc, and Release configurations. As we are releasing a first version of the application without using the App Store, we will be using the AdHoc configuration.

Getting Ready to Release the Application

The template we used came with default values about the application, like the version number, set to 1.0. The definition of 1.0 and what it means from a developer point of view could raise an interesting debate. For example, in the SCRUM methodology the definition of "complete" must be defined early on before actually starting to work on the project. In this context, it usually means defining a clear and concise list of requirements that a feature must adhere to for all the members of your team to call it "complete." As a convention, the 1.0 version usually means the "good enough" version, the one that can be shared with the public. Let's be honest here: we are far from the 1.0 version. We are actually closer to the "0.1" version, the one we are not ready to show to anyone.

Even if we are only aiming at the 1.0 version, an iOS application comes with two version numbers: the short version called the "marketing" one and the long version called the "build" one. In the Info. plist file, the two versions are called "Bundle versions" and the "Bundle version string, short". Let's set the short version number and the long version number to "0.1". When we will create new internal builds, we will only bump the build version number. To change the versions of the application, open the "Github JobsInfo.plist" file and change the values, as shown in Figure 3-1.

Key	Type	Value
▼ Information Property List	Dictionary	(15 items)
Localization native development r...	String	en
Bundle display name	String	${PRODUCT_NAME}
Executable file	String	${EXECUTABLE_NAME}
Bundle identifier	String	com.perfectly-cooked.${PRODUCT_NAME:rfc1034identifier}
InfoDictionary version	String	6.0
Bundle name	String	${PRODUCT_NAME}
Bundle OS Type code	String	APPL
Bundle versions string, short	String	0.1
Bundle creator OS Type code	String	????
Bundle version	String	0.1
GithubJobsEndpoint	String	$(GITHUB_JOBS_ENDPOINT)
Application requires iPhone envir...	Boolean	YES
Main storyboard file base name	String	Main
▶ Required device capabilities	Array	(1 item)
▶ Supported interface orientations	Array	(3 items)

Figure 3-1. The Github Jobs configuration file, with version numbers set to 0.1

> **About version numbers**   Xcode, and more specifically the iOS application archives, are well designed
> enough to allow you to keep version numbers meaningful. If you are not sure what version number you should
> use, reading the semantic versioning specification available on semver.org might be a good start. It's not as
> boring as it sounds!

We now have the 0.1 version of our application. It's not pretty and it doesn't do many things beside
loading a simple JSON file and displaying the results in a table view. We mentioned earlier that
reading this book would be like taking a journey. Well, we have the earliest version possible of our
application and it's a good time to start setting up the continuous integration of our project. Being
able to build the application many times a day and sending a build to a selected bunch of users is
all about collecting feedback. Let's start with an important one that will help us understand why our
application crashed, a.k.a. crash logs.

Collecting Feedback from Crash logs

There are multiple kinds of feedback you hope you will get once your build is out to your QA team, to
your beta testers or to your client. There is the obvious one about glitches in the user experience and
graphical decisions, and there is the other one about how your application crashed. Once collected
and converted in a human readable format, a crash log or crash report, looks like this (it's actually
much longer than that but we're only showing the interesting parts):

```
Incident Identifier: 9A230C6E-370E-413E-801C-D1182081BFDA
Hardware Model:      iPhone3,1
Process:             Github Jobs [2001]
Path:                /var/mobile/Applications/D4B64242-327D-486C-A2A6-ABBDB76F7B92/ Github Jobs.app/
                     Github Jobs
Identifier:          com.perfectly-cooked.Github-Jobs
Version:             1.0 (1.0.1)
Code Type:           ARM (Native)
Parent Process:      launchd [1]

Date/Time:           2013-12-15 13:12:32.342 -0500
OS Version:          iOS 7.0.4 (11B554a)
Report Version:      104

Exception Type:  EXC_BAD_ACCESS (SIGSEGV)
Exception Subtype: KERN_INVALID_ADDRESS at 0x0000000f
Triggered by Thread:  2

Thread 0:
0   CoreData                    0x30906a1c -[NSSQLCore _externalDataLinksDirectory] + 0
1   CoreData                    0x308f3d8a -[NSPersistentStoreCoordinator dealloc] + 702
2   libobjc.A.dylib             0x3ae93b06 objc_object::sidetable_release(bool) + 170
3   Traffic                     0x000d1446 0x73000 + 386118
4   libobjc.A.dylib             0x3ae93b06
...
```

This is an actual crash log coming from a different app, we've only replaced the name of the application with ours so we can describe it a bit without confusing anyone. The report shows a lot of information about the application itself (build and marketing versions, identifier...) with information about the device that runs the application. This makes it easy to determine if the application only crashes on a specific device, for example the not-so-new-anymore iPhone 5S that came with support for arm64 processors. It also shows, and that's the more interesting part, which part of the code crashed. Here we are talking about a "EXC_BAD_ACCESS" in a piece of code that perform tasks with Core Data. This can mean many things but it is usually caused by calling a method on a pointer that is no longer valid.

Apple already provides the ability to collect crash logs from applications that are distributed throught the App Store but for applications that are not ready to be sent to the store, there are tools out there that will help you to achieve the same goal, such as "PLCrashReporter", available at http://plcrashreporter.org.

To make sure you will be able to use these reports and fix the crashes, there is one setting you need to check before building the application. Go back to the "Github Jobs" Xcode project, open the build settings of the main target and look for the "Debug Information Format" setting. Apple uses a standard debugging data format called **DWARF**, a medieval fantasy reference standing for "Debugging With Attributed Record Formats." In this setting, make sure the "DWARF with dSYM File" is selected, it will generate a dSYM foder in the same folder that your application, as shown in Figure 3-2. This file is mandatory to understand potential crash logs.

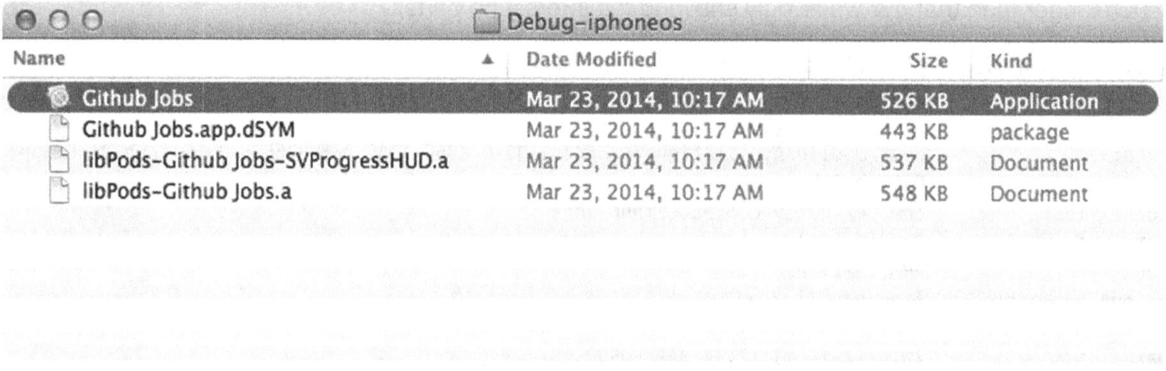

Name	Date Modified	Size	Kind
Github Jobs	Mar 23, 2014, 10:17 AM	526 KB	Application
Github Jobs.app.dSYM	Mar 23, 2014, 10:17 AM	443 KB	package
libPods-Github Jobs-SVProgressHUD.a	Mar 23, 2014, 10:17 AM	537 KB	Document
libPods-Github Jobs.a	Mar 23, 2014, 10:17 AM	548 KB	Document

Figure 3-2. The build folder contains the application and the dSYM file, among other things

To see an example, navigate to your ~/Library/Developer/Xcode/DerivedData/ folder where your temporary .app files are stored every time you build your application. Using your shell or right-clicking on the "Github Jobs.app" file in the Products groups of your Xcode project, select the "Reveal In Finder" option. You should see a dSYM file.

Generating the dSYM file takes time and is not really needed while you'll be working on the app. Chances are you will be able to detect and reproduce a crash during a debug session. Because of that, in debug configuration, the "Debug Information Format" setting is usually set on "DWARF" to speed up the build. Before building the application, make sure the setting is on "Dwarf with dSYM" for the adhoc configuration, as shown in Figure 3-3. We will not go back to this session until we actually start releasing the application using a method called "Over The Air distribution" in Chapter 7.

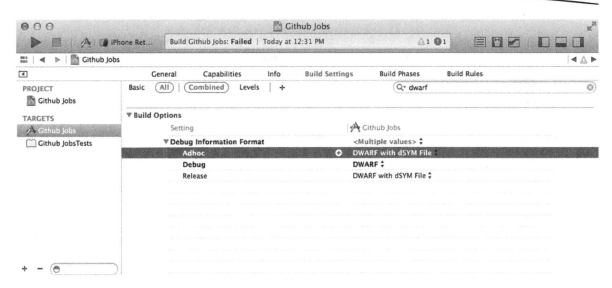

Figure 3-3. The dSYM file generation is only disabled for the Debug configuration to speed up the build

Creating the IPA file

We are now officially ready to build the very first version of our application and send it to our beta testers. To do that, all we need is to create an IPA file.

1. Unplug your devices and make sure you've selected "iOS device" in the menu that lets you select where to run the application.

2. In the Product menu, instead of pressing "Archive" directly, hold the ALT key. The "Archive" menu will turn into "Archive..." and this will open a window allowing you to select the configuration to use for the build, like the one shown in the Figure 3-4.

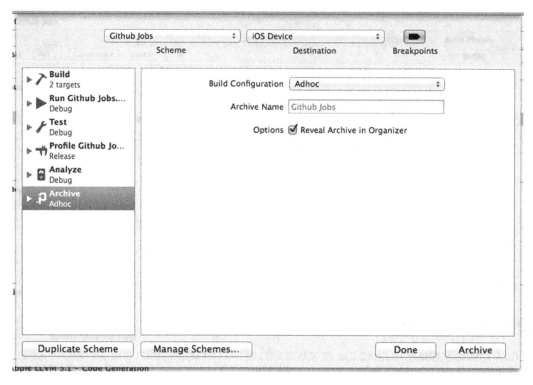

Figure 3-4. The archive panel ready to archive the application for the Adhoc configuration

3. Change the build configuration to "AdHoc" instead of release and press "Archive". If you've checked the "Reveal Archive in Organizer" option, the organizer should appear with your archive selected.

4. The next steps are just as easy, and you probably already went through them when you released an application to the App Store. Press the "Distribute..." button, select "Save for Enterprise or Ad Hoc Deployment" and select the location where to save the IPA file. Congratulations, you are now ready to distribute the very first build of your application!

Let's step back for a second and see what we have done. In Chapter 2 we created a very simple application that we are now getting ready to release. In this chapter, you've been through a boring process composed of many, many clicks only to end up with an IPA file on your desktop, probably. Well, stay with us for a couple more pages, because we are about to use the least convenient process ever invented to distribute an iOS application: iTunes!

Most people have some kind of a love/hate relationship with iTunes. From playing music and videos, to connecting to the app store and buying apps and albums as well as subscribing to podcasts, iTunes is this bloated OSX application that's been around since the beginning of this millennium, which is starting to mean something. When the iPhone came out, while Apple could have come up with a dedicated iPhone synchronization application, it instead chose to integrate this process into its historic application.

iTunes actually allows you to install applications on a device right from your desktop. Let's see how.

Installing the Application on the Tester's Device

Open iTunes and click on the "update later" button (there's always an update of iTunes waiting for you). Then, open a finder window and navigate to the directory where you exported the IPA file: in our case, the desktop directory. Double click on the "Github jobs.ipa" file and wait for the magic to happen. iTunes should activate and display your application in the "Apps" section, as shown in Figure 3-5.

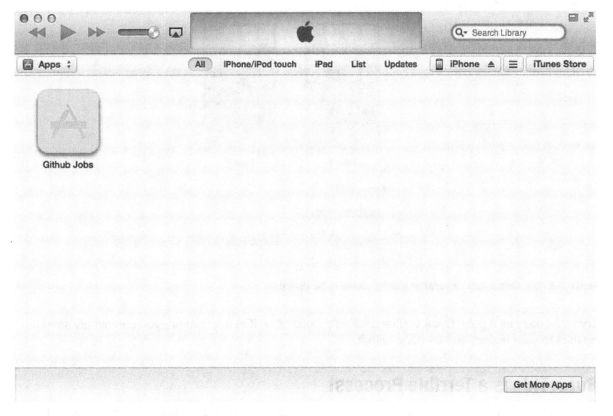

Figure 3-5. iTunes has added the Github Jobs app to your library

With this very simple operation, iTunes took the IPA file and copied it in its media folder. If you haven't changed this folder, you should be able to retrieve your application in "~/Music/iTunes/iTunes Media/Mobile Applications", one folder away from your music. Don't delete the original IPA file: we will need it later.

Now that iTunes has its own copy of our application, plug your iPhone in and click on the "iPhone" button that will appear at the top left of the window. This screen should feel like home, you've probably already been there to install a beta version of iOS or simply manage the synchronization settings of your device. Select the "apps" tab where all your applications should be listed on the left, including "Github Jobs". Press the "Install" button right next to "Github Jobs" and then hit the "Apply" button. During the synchronization process, Github Jobs will be installed on your device, as shown in Figure 3-6.

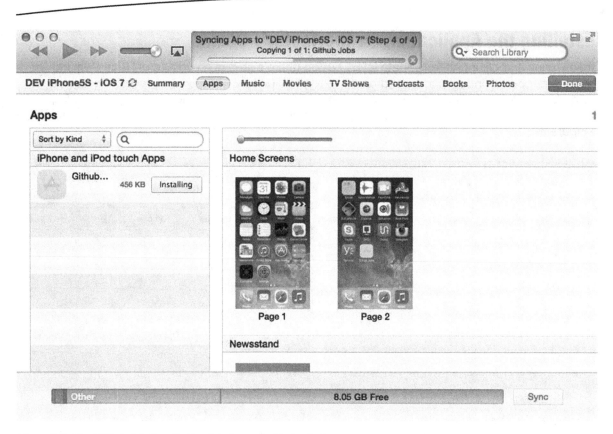

Figure 3-6. The "Github Jobs" application is being copied to the device

That's as easy as it gets. Once you've created a build of an iOS application, you can simply send it by mail to your testers and be done with it.

But... This is a Terrible Process!

You may be thinking this is a terrible process right now and it would be hard to argue with you. To be fair, we did warn you earlier.

This is exactly what we needed: more clicks! After a boring process only resulting in an IPA file generated on our desktop, we've added more steps involving another software and many clicks.

There is one more downside to this approach that comes with the complex code signing and provisioning profile process Xcode requires in order to build and ship applications. You can send the IPA to anyone but it has to be explicitly authorized in the application's provisioning profile as we will show in Chapter 7 where we'll talk about how provisioning profiles work. If you try to install an application for which you're not authorized, iTunes will fail silently and you will end up with a disabled application on your home screen.

Installing the Application on the Tester's Device

It is actually possible to understand what is going on using the iPhone Configuration Utility application available at http://support.apple.com/downloads/#iphone. This nifty little tool is exactly the kind of tool that Apple could have made, dedicated to managing iOS devices. If you are not familiar with this tool already, you really should become familiar. Go grab it and let's try again.

Open the iPhone Configuration Utility and a new Finder window. Navigate back to where you stored the original IPA file – remember when we asked you not to delete it? This is why – select it and drop it to the Utility window. Just as it was in iTunes, the "Github Jobs" application is now available for you to be installed via the desktop.

With your iPhone still plugged in, select it in the left menu and navigate to the applications tab. You should see the "Githubs Jobs" API with an "Install" button. Press it and the application will be installed automatically to your phone.

This is a little better than using iTunes to install intermediate builds of your application. Indeed, where iTunes fails miserably when you try to install an unauthorized application, the iPhone configuration utility was created for a different audience: the power users and developer. If you click on your phone in the left sidebar and open the console app you will be able to get a much more detailed feedback of what's happening in your phone. Digging into these provided logs information should get you to lines such as:

```
Mar 31 19:26:43 DEV-iPhone5S-iOS-7 lsd[75] <Warning>: LaunchServices: installation failed for app
com.perfectly-cooked.Github-Jobs
```

This is the kind of information you will need when testers won't be able to install the build you will be sending them. This tool will also help you manage your provisioning profiles, configuration profiles, and applications. It will show you detailed information about a plugged device and, last but not least, it will also help you with sending your applications by e-mail, as shown in Figure 3-7!

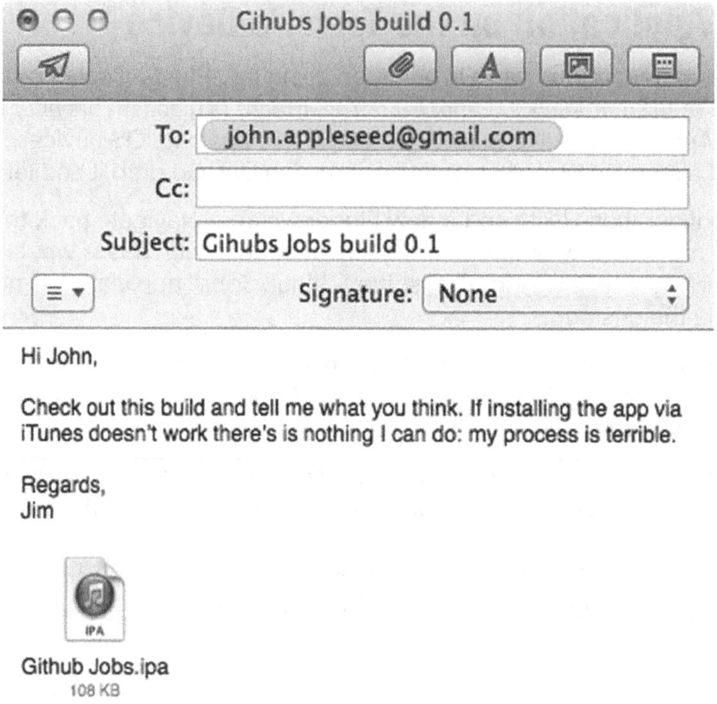

Figure 3-7. The iPhone Configuration Utility will help you distribute builds by mail

Even if this tool is slightly better than iTunes, distributing builds through e-mail is not very convenient and would only work with power users. But that's good news! Now that we have described the worst solution to distribute builds, from now on we can only get better. The next chapters will focus on how to build the application in a "smarter" way, for lack of a better term (but it's really in Chapter 7 that the magic will happen). In Chapter 7, we will show you how to automate the process we've been covering in the past 10 pages.

Installing Multiple Versions of the Application

In case the installation worked, there is still a very important thing to take care of. When you create an iOS application using Xcode, the project creation wizard asks you for a bundle identifier. Unlike the Java world where you need a complex reverse-DNS based namespace to be one of the cool guys, the bundle identifier of an iOS app is important: it is a unique identifier that helps differentiate your application from other ones and you can't have multiple applications sharing the same bundle ID.

In practice this is not a big deal, all the application does is use a reverse-DNS based bundle identifier, like in this case perfectly-cooked.com turning into "com.perfectly-cooked.GithubJobs". On the other hand, when you start distributing and asking people to install beta versions of your application, it prevents people from having the stable application and the beta one at the same time.

Fortunately for you, we showed you in chapter 2 how to manage multiple environments for your application using configurations. The bundle identifier is just one more setting that you can customize, depending on the configuration.

Go back to Xcode and select the main property list file, "Github JobsInfo.plist" and look for the "Bundle identifier" key. If your own Xcode is configured to display the raw names of these keys, look for the "CFBundleIdentifier" key.

The current bundle identifier contains "com.perfectly-cooked.${PRODUCT_NAME:rfc1034identifier}" which, once the application is compiled, is evaluated and transformed to com.perfectly-cooked. githubs-jobs. This RFC parameter describes DNS and its use for host address support. In our case, the ":rfc1034identifier" right after the wrapping brackets we've seen in Chapter 2 is a filter that turns the Product Name of the application into a RFC1034-compliant identifier (no more spaces...) and because of that, we can easily change it only for the AdHoc configuration. We want the version we'll send to our beta users to be codenamed "Github Jobs (beta)". This way, people will be able to see that they are using the beta version. They will also be able to keep the stable version of the application because thanks to the ":rfc1034identifier", the bundle identifier will be different.

Open the build settings application and look for the "Product Name" setting. Its default value should be "$(TARGET_NAME)" where TARGET_NAME is one of the many environment variables available. To change the bundle identifier, all we need to do is to change the product name of the Ad Hoc configuration, as shown in Figure 3-8.

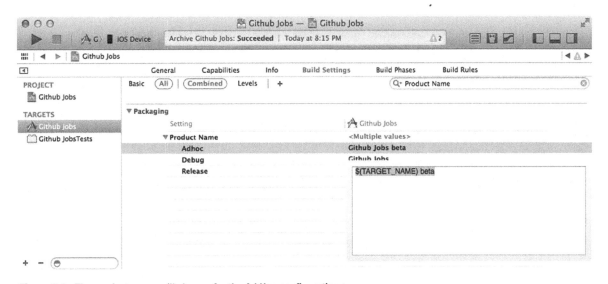

Figure 3-8. The product name will change for the Ad Hoc configuration

It is very important that we keep a human readable format for the product name setting, as this is the name of the application that will be displayed on your home screen. Note that this can cause issues with the code signing process when provisioning profiles and entitlements are locked to a very specific bundle identifier: use this technique with caution!

Updating the PRODUCT_NAME build setting will change the bundle identifier depending on the configuration. Your testers will then be able to have multiple versions of your application installed on their devices.

Summary

In this chapter, we have shown you the tools available to distribute beta versions of your application. Whether they use iTunes or the iPhone Configuration Utility, this is actually a terribly constraining workflow, far from giving you any flexibility whatsoever. It requires a lot of clicks, multiple softs, and doesn't handle potential errors very well.

In our first chapter, we've actually mentioned a guy that would install beta versions of the application when testers would ask for it with a little tap on the shoulder. This guy would plug the tester device in, build a version of the application, and give the device back. The good news is you now have all the tools and knowledge you need to be that guy. But don't be - instead, keep reading and the next chapters will show you how to automate this process and how to provide a better user experience to your testers.

Chapter 4

Invoking the Power of the Command Line

Multiple user interfaces, even well-designed and obvious ones such as the ones provided by Xcode are not enough. Indeed, the previous chapter showed you what a tedious process it was to release an application outside of the app store using Xcode and iTunes or the iPhone Configuration Utility. A good interface doesn't make everything right. In this chapter, we will go deeper and cover the tools on which most of these interfaces are based by calling them directly using the command line.

Command Line Interface?

The command line interface (often referred to as CLI) is a way for the user to interact with the computer at a lower level using text-based commands in syntax understandable by the computer. This syntax is a good compromise for both parts in terms of readability. A lot of developers are scared of it and some of them will spend their entire career without using a shell (the provided interface to execute commands) once. Why would they? Using Photoshop to design the application, Xcode to code it, while using a graphical client for the version control (if any) and the application loader to send a build to the app store, it's completely doable to develop an application without opening the shell once. The thing is using the command line gives you access to power user features and will actually come in very handy when we set up our continuous integration environment.

In this chapter, we will try to show you that the command line, in the context of iOS development, is not as scary as you may think, especially on OSX. Since you bought this book, we don't need to convince you what a great operating system OS X is for developers. You should thank its UNIX origins for that. OS X comes with a pretty decent shell for you to play in called "Terminal.app" and is available with a bunch of other tools in "/Applications/Utilities". If you take a close look at Figure 4-1, this is actually where the iPhone Configuration Utility we talked about in the previous chapter was installed.

Name	▲	Date Modified	Size	Kind
Activity Monitor		Mar 9, 2014, 5:47 PM	11.4 MB	Application
▶ Adobe Application Manager		Jul 2, 2013, 7:13 PM	--	Folder
Adobe Flash Player Install Manager		Mar 27, 2014, 5:48 PM	594 KB	Application
▶ Adobe Installers		Mar 12, 2014, 7:56 PM	--	Folder
AirPort Utility		May 21, 2013, 4:05 PM	50.5 MB	Application
AppleScript Editor		Mar 9, 2014, 5:47 PM	10.9 MB	Application
Audio MIDI Setup		Aug 25, 2013, 1:11 AM	10.9 MB	Application
Bluetooth File Exchange		Mar 9, 2014, 5:47 PM	2.6 MB	Application
Boot Camp Assistant		Mar 9, 2014, 5:47 PM	5.2 MB	Application
ColorSync Utility		Aug 25, 2013, 1:57 AM	16.1 MB	Application
Console		Mar 8, 2013, 9:40 PM	10.2 MB	Application
DigitalColor Meter		Aug 25, 2013, 1:01 AM	1 MB	Application
Disk Utility		Mar 9, 2014, 5:47 PM	22 MB	Application
Grab		Apr 16, 2013, 3:03 PM	1.7 MB	Application
Grapher		Mar 7, 2013, 5:31 PM	35.6 MB	Application
iPhone Configuration Utility		Mar 31, 2014, 8:14 PM	21.6 MB	Application
Keychain Access		Mar 9, 2014, 5:47 PM	14.3 MB	Application
Migration Assistant		Aug 25, 2013, 1:05 AM	1.7 MB	Application
System Information		Mar 9, 2014, 5:47 PM	6.5 MB	Application
Terminal		Aug 25, 2013, 1:08 AM	8.9 MB	Application
VoiceOver Utility		Mar 9, 2014, 5:47 PM	27.6 MB	Application
XQuartz		Feb 1, 2014, 5:44 PM	6.7 MB	Application

Figure 4-1. A list of utilities, mostly provided by OSX

One of the reasons developers are scared or simply not inclined to dig into their shell, is probably because of the way it looks the first time you open it on OSX. You get a black on white interface with no indication whatsoever of what you should do. We are not going to lie - the command line interface is puzzling and is mostly designed for the power user. The good news is it's actually pretty easy to become comfortable with the command line. The hard part is to know which command to run, with which parameters and when, but that will only come with experience and time.

Let's see how we can achieve what we did in the past chapter with creating a release build and using the command line.

Introducing Shenzhen

The iOS and OSX developers' community is full of remarkable people who keep writing blog posts, and releasing libraries and tools that we'll use in our project. Matt Thompson is one of these people. In addition to the NSHipster (available at `http://nshipster.com`) website where he writes about hidden gems and tips about the "overlooked bits in Objective-C and Cocoa", he created Shenzhen, a command line tool for building IPA files. Shenzhen also handles distributing apps to third-party services such as Testflight and HockeyApp, but we won't be talking about over the air (OTA) distribution until Chapter 7.

Shenzhen is written in Ruby, so the easiest way to install it is to use Rubygems. Before we start, make sure you have a recent version of Ruby installed. At the time of writing this book, the current stable release of Ruby is 2.1.1.

```
$ ruby -v
ruby 2.1.1p76 (2014-02-24 revision 45161) [x86_64-darwin13.0]
```

Once again, if you're still using the installation of Ruby shipped with OS X, you should consider upgrading to a more recent one using rbenv (http://rbenv.org/) or RVM (https://rvm.io/).

To install Shenzhen, simply run the following command:

```
$ gem install shenzhen
```

Once it's installed, a new executable named ipa will be available in your terminal. Running it without any arguments should give you the following output:

```
$ ipa
  ipa

  Build and distribute iOS apps (.ipa files)

  Commands:
    build                  Create a new .ipa file for your app
    distribute:ftp         Distribute an .ipa file over FTP
    distribute:hockeyapp   Distribute an .ipa file over HockeyApp
    distribute:s3          Distribute an .ipa file over Amazon S3
    distribute:testflight  Distribute an .ipa file over testflight
    help                   Display global or [command] help documentation.
    info                   Show mobile provisioning information about an .ipa file

  Aliases:
    distribute             distribute:testflight
    distribute:sftp        distribute:ftp --protocol sftp

  Global Options:
    --verbose
    -h, --help             Display help documentation
    -v, --version          Display version information
    -t, --trace            Display backtrace when an error occurs

  Author:
    Mattt Thompson <m@mattt.me>

  Website:
    http://mattt.me
```

As you can see, this tool does a lot of things, but we only care about the `build` command. Using the terminal, simply navigate to the root directory of the Github Jobs Xcode project and run the `build` command:

```
$ cd ~/Projects/Apress/Github\ Jobs
$ ipa build -c AdHoc -d ~/Desktop
    xcodebuild  Github Jobs.xcworkspace
        xcrun  PackageApplication
          zip  /Users/Palleas/Projects/Apress/Github Jobs/Github Jobs.app.dSYM
~/Desktop/Github Jobs.ipa successfully built
```

So what just happened here? Only a couple of things: Shenzhen built the application for the AdHoc configuration (the -c argument), archived it and created the IPA file on your Desktop (the -d argument). We also used "cd", a built-in command to change the current directory we're in, just like if we were using a Finder window. Congratulations! You've done in ten seconds and with one very understandable command what we've covered in a whole chapter!

To be fair, with Xcode and its release process, we cheated a bit. After all, Shenzhen is a full-featured tool written in almost a few hundred lines of Ruby. This is the power of command line though. Let's have a look to the tools provided by Xcode.

Juggling with Multiple Installations of Xcode

Let's start with an easy one, called xcode-select. If you remember correctly what we've covered in Chapter 2, we used this command when we wanted to know which was the version of git embedded with Xcode. xcode-select is a command line tool used to manage the active developer directory for Xcode and the tools that come with it, such as git, but also svn, clang, and make. Running the following commands in your shell will print you the current directory, which is useful if you need some of the tools provided by Xcode and don't want to hardcode the path. Once again, go back to Chapter 2 to see how to use the result of this command in a script.

```
$ xcode-select -print-path
/Applications/Xcode.app/Contents/Developer
```

If you've been using OSX long enough, it would be surprising if you haven't heard of Xcode's command line tools. Installing the command line tools is a requirement to be able to use the Homebrew package manager, for example. While it is possible to use the Xcode preferences panel to install these command line tools, xcode-select is the command-line equivalent to open the installation window shown in Figure 4-2.

```
$ xcode-select -install
xcode-select: note: install requested for command line developer tools
```

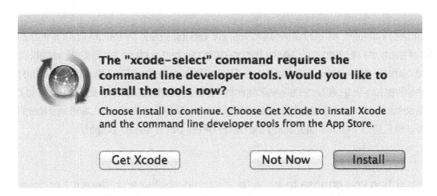

Figure 4-2. The xcode-select tool can start the installation of the Xcode command line tools

If you're an Apple registered developer, you have access to the private beta releases of Xcode and this is where xcode-select comes in handy. xcode-select allows you to switch between different versions of Xcode. Because it manages the path to the developer directory at a global level, this command has to be run as a "super user" using sudo.

```
$ sudo xcode-select --switch /Applications/XCode6-beta.app
```

This way, you will be able to use the command line tools provided by Xcode6-beta, which is helpful if you want to make sure your application still builds with new versions of Xcode or if you've found a bug with a previous version of Xcode and want to check if it has been fixed. The point is, switching between versions of Xcode is super easy thanks to this little tool. As a bonus, xcode-select will make sure the developer directory you are trying to use is valid:

```
sudo xcode-select -s /Applications/Dashboard.app
xcode-select: error: invalid developer directory '/Applications/Dashboard.app'
```

The developer directory we usually use is /Applications/Xcode.app however for historical reasons, the actual developer directory is a sub directory contained in the application package. That is why our first use of the xcode-select -p command didn't print "/Applications/Xcode.app" but "/Applications/Xcode.app/Contents/Developer". When you use xcode-select to switch to a different version of Xcode, you can use both values. If you enter the shorter one, it will automatically be expended to the full Developer directory path.

Of course, switching to a beta version of Xcode globally can be a little bit extreme and, most importantly, dangerous. Imagine an Apple computer – let's say a Mac Mini for the sake of this example – dedicated to building your applications automatically. You don't want to take the chance of switching to a beta version of Xcode and jeopardizing your whole environment. That's exactly why there is a little less aggressive way of switching to a different version of Xcode: a DEVELOPER_DIR environment variable.

> **Note**   Environment variables, as the name indicates, are variables used by the environment that a command
> runs in. A few of them are set automatically by the operating system such as the $HOME variable that contains
> the path to the current user's Home directory (e.g., /Users/Palleas) or the $PWD that contains the path to the
> current working directory (e.g., /Users/Palleas/Projects/Apress/Github Jobs). It is also possible to define some
> for the current session with a very simple syntax: MY_ENV_VARIABLE="My Value", and use them later with
> $MY_ENV_VARIABLE. With that in mind, using the DEVELOPER_DIR is just as simple.

No matter which solution you choose to go with, switching between different Xcode environments is pretty easy. For example if you feel nostalgic for an old version of Xcode or because an old project of yours won't build with the newest version, you could simply go to the "Downloads for Apple developers" page (available at `https://developer.apple.com/downloads/index.action`), download an older version of Xcode and use it.

Please note that contrary to the xcode-select approach, using an environment variable doesn't check that the directory you want to use is valid until it actually tries to use it, as in the following example, in which we are trying to use the Dashboard.app – a well-known OSX application – as a developer dir.

```
DEVELOPER_DIR=/Applications/Dashboard.app xcodebuild -v
xcrun: error: invalid DEVELOPER_DIR path (/Applications/Dashboard.app), missing xcrun at:
/Applications/Dashboard.app/usr/bin/xcrun
```

You may have noticed the use of the xcodebuild command. It is time we get our hands dirty and see how we can actually build the application using the command line. After all, that is why we are here.

Building the Application

Now that we have a general idea of where the command line tools are provided by our installation of Xcode, let's see how we can build the application right from our terminal. You've had a glimpse at the xcodebuild command in the previous section, and this is the command we are actually going to use.

Building the Application Using xcodebuild

If you run the xcodebuild command in your terminal with the help option, you might get scared.

```
$ xcodebuild -h
Usage: xcodebuild [-project <projectname>] [[-target <targetname>]...|-alltargets]
[-configuration <configurationname>] [-arch <architecture>]... [-sdk [<sdkname>|<sdkpath>]]
[-showBuildSettings] [<buildsetting>=<value>]... [<buildaction>]...
        xcodebuild [-project <projectname>] -scheme <schemeName> [-destination <destinationspecifier>]...
[-configuration <configurationname>] [-arch <architecture>]... [-sdk [<sdkname>|<sdkpath>]]
[-showBuildSettings] [<buildsetting>=<value>]... [<buildaction>]...
```

```
      xcodebuild -workspace <workspacename> -scheme <schemeName> [-destination <destinationspecifier>]...
[-configuration <configurationname>] [-arch <architecture>]... [-sdk [<sdkname>|<sdkpath>]]
[-showBuildSettings] [<buildsetting>=<value>]... [<buildaction>]...
      xcodebuild -version [-sdk [<sdkfullpath>|<sdkname>] [<infoitem>] ]
      xcodebuild -list [[-project <projectname>]|[-workspace <workspacename>]]
      xcodebuild -showsdks
      xcodebuild -exportArchive -exportFormat <format> -archivePath <xcarchivepath> -exportPath
<destinationpath> [-exportProvisioningProfile <profilename>] [-exportSigningIdentity <identityname>]
[-exportInstallerIdentity <identityname>]
```

xcodebuild is one of those tools that will do a lot for you if you learn how to use it. If you start using the command line, you will use this command often: xcodebuild is the command used to build Xcode project and workspaces, and is actually the command that Xcode uses when you hit ⌘ + B. Xcode relies on xcodebuild to perform most of the actions available in the "Product" menu, in fact here are the things that xcodebuild will do for you, available as a xcodebuild "build action": "build", "analyze", "archive", "test", "install" & "installsrc" and "clean".

Let's go back to the terminal and navigate to the directory where the Github Jobs Xcode project is stored and let's go straight to the point and build the application, using the xcodebuild command without any option or parameter. In this case, building the application is the default behavior.

```
$ xcodebuild
```

The following build commands failed:

```
Ld build/Github\ Jobs.build/Release-iphoneos/Github\ Jobs.build/Objects-normal/armv7s/Github\
Jobs normal armv7s
Ld build/Github\ Jobs.build/Release-iphoneos/Github\ Jobs.build/Objects-normal/arm64/Github\
Jobs normal arm64
Ld build/Github\ Jobs.build/Release-iphoneos/Github\ Jobs.build/Objects-normal/armv7/Github\
Jobs normal armv7
(3 failures)
```

Trying to build the application without any argument will fail and encounter exactly three errors, as you can see in the output above. There is actually one error by architecture: armv7, armv7s, and arm64 that are types of processors embedded in your iOS device. Each ARM version comes with improvements while being retro-compatible with the version that came before it. When the code is compiled, the compiler handling the process will only generate instructions for the architecture it is targeting. There are currently a lot of iPhone devices out there but Apple's policy suggests that you should support only the last few models. With different models come different processors. That is why the application is built multiple times for all the architectures out there that needs to be supported. The iPhone 3GS, 4, and 4S come with ARMV7 processors. While it is safe to assume that there aren't a lot of iPhone 3GS alive and well out there, a lot of iPhone 4S are still being used everyday. The iPhone 5 came with a ARMV7s processor and the iPhone 5S came with the ARM64 architecture. That gives you three valid architectures that need to be supported and that is why the xcodebuild instruction gives you three errors: the application cannot be built for any of the architectures. That's actually a lot to remember, that is why there is a very helpful website that presents these things in a very understandable way: http://iossupportmatrix.com/.

The first thing to notice, as we didn't specify the configuration to use, xcodebuild chose the default one: Release. However, that's not what we want. In the previous chapter we built the application using the AdHoc configuration and as we are trying to do the same thing here, we will use the –configuration option to tell xcodebuild to use the **AdHoc** configuration we created earlier in Chapter 2.

```
$ xcodebuild –configuration AdHoc
```

The following build commands failed:

```
Ld build/Github\ Jobs.build/AdHoc-iphoneos/Github\ Jobs.build/Objects-normal/armv7/Github\
Jobs normal armv7
Ld build/Github\ Jobs.build/AdHoc-iphoneos/Github\ Jobs.build/Objects-normal/armv7s/Github\
Jobs normal armv7s
Ld build/Github\ Jobs.build/AdHoc-iphoneos/Github\ Jobs.build/Objects-normal/arm64/Github\
Jobs normal arm64
(3 failures)
```

That is better, but the command still fails during the build and it doesn't seem capable of using the linker command ld. Its goal is to combine several object files and libraries, to resolve references, and to produce an output file. As it always produces a single-architecture file, it has to be used three times because of the three valid architectures of our project we mentioned earlier.

ld is one of the commands you don't really need to know about because you will never have to use it directly. The compiler will usually take care of it.

Let's try to see what the actual error is by analyzing the output of the xcodebuild command. The good news is our application is small enough so that the compilation process doesn't have to do many things such as compiling a bunch of implementation ".m" files, turning a very simple storyboard file into a Nib that will be loaded when the application starts. This means that it will be pretty easy to understand what is going on. If you navigate to the bottom of the output, where the first ld command is ran, you should find something like this:

```
ld build/Github\ Jobs.build/AdHoc-iphoneos/Github\ Jobs.build/Objects-normal/armv7/Github\
Jobs\ beta normal armv7
cd "/Users/Palleas/Projects/Apress/Github Jobs"
export IPHONEOS_DEPLOYMENT_TARGET=7.1
export PATH="/Applications/Xcode.app/Contents/Developer/Platforms/iPhoneOS.platform/Developer/usr/
bin:/Applications/Xcode.app/Contents/Developer/usr/bin"
/Applications/Xcode.app/Contents/Developer/Toolchains/XcodeDefault.xctoolchain/usr/bin/clang -arch
armv7 -isysroot /Applications/Xcode.app/Contents/Developer/Platforms/iPhoneOS.platform/Developer/
SDKs/iPhoneOS7.1.sdk -L/Users/Palleas/Projects/Apress/Github\ Jobs/build/AdHoc-iphoneos -F/Users/
Palleas/Projects/Apress/Github\ Jobs/build/AdHoc-iphoneos -filelist /Users/Palleas/Projects/Apress/
Github\ Jobs/build/Github\ Jobs.build/AdHoc-iphoneos/Github\ Jobs.build/Objects-normal/armv7/
Github\ Jobs\ beta.LinkFileList -dead_strip -ObjC -framework QuartzCore -fobjc-arc -fobjc-link-
runtime -miphoneos-version-min=7.1 -framework CoreGraphics -framework UIKit -framework Foundation
-lPods-Github\ Jobs -Xlinker -dependency_info -Xlinker /Users/Palleas/Projects/Apress/Github\
Jobs/build/Github\ Jobs.build/AdHoc-iphoneos/Github\ Jobs.build/Objects-normal/armv7/Github\
Jobs\ beta_dependency_info.dat -o /Users/Palleas/Projects/Apress/Github\ Jobs/build/Github\
Jobs.build/AdHoc-iphoneos/Github\ Jobs.build/Objects-normal/armv7/Github\ Jobs\ beta
ld: library not found for -lPods-Github Jobs
clang: error: linker command failed with exit code 1 (use -v to see invocation)
```

This blob of text is the command run during the xcodebuild process that actually invokes clang under the hood. clang is the compiler used by Xcode to compile C, C++, and Objective-C, it also provides tools such as a static code analyzer and a code-style checking tool. While discussing this in depth is not the goal of this chapter, we will cover them more in Chapter 10 when we talk about quality assurance. What is important in this paragraph is that clang is invoked with a lot of arguments. Xcode manages these arguments when you configure the build settings of your application but you can explicitly set some in the "Other linker flags" section, as shown in Figure 4-3.

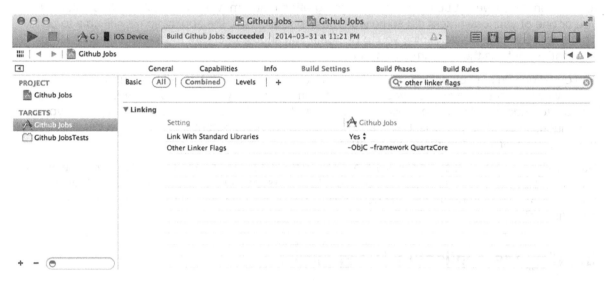

Figure 4-3. The Other linker flags setting can be used to add framework (QuartzCore) and tell the linker to treat source input files as Objective-C inputs

The issue we are having here comes with the -lPods-Github\ Jobs argument passed in the invocation of clang, which doesn't know about this library that we are asking to link the compiled application with - that is because of Cocoapods.

When you use Cocoapods to declare dependencies in the PodFile, Cocoapods actually tweak your project and ask you to use a generated Workspace file. In this workspace, you will find your original Xcode project, Github Jobs, and a new one called "Pods." It contains your dependencies that have been downloaded during the execution of the pod install which we've talked about in Chapter 2. When you build the Github Jobs application, the Pods project is actually compiled first into a static library that will be linked then with the main application. While it is 100% possible to not use a workspace and to use subprojects instead to avoid the issue we have been having, this is the default behavior and the way Apple recommends you manage your dependencies.

xcodebuild doesn't detect automatically when you are using a workspace instead of a simple project file, you have to explicitly pass it to xcodebuild using the –workspace option. When you use the –workspace option, you also have to use the -scheme one or else xcodebuild is going to yell at you:

```
$ xcodebuild -workspace Github\ Jobs.xcworkspace -scheme Github\ Jobs
```

Once this command has executed, you should see a lot more instructions on your screen and a final "Build succeeded" message. Congratulations, you have built your iOS application using the command line. At this point, the application is not actually usable. As we've said earlier, we've simply recreated what happens when you hit ⌘ + B in Xcode, not ⌘ + R (Run) and certainly not ⌘ + B (Archive). There are a few steps missing before being able to send a build of our application, the final step of our process.

Still, we are now able to build the application and that's a first indicator of the current state of the application. Once we set up our continuous integration platform, we will be able to detect if, after you or one of your coworkers did some work on the application, the application is still able to build. That's not much feedback helping you to decide if you should integrate this piece of code in the application, but it is the most important one.

The question you may be asking yourself right now is why have we done all that and written so much when we could have given you the right command directly? The answer is that you need to be able to understand how the xcodebuild command works if you expect to use it as part of your continuous integration process. Being able to dig into the huge output of xcodebuild will allow you to understand why an application won't build.

Still, xcodebuild's output still looks like gibberish to the most experienced iOS and OSX developers out there. Having to dig into a huge blob of text to understand why an application won't build is annoying and, most importantly, time consuming. This is why we started to see alternative building tools like xctool.

Building the Application Using Xctool

Don't worry; we will go straight to the point this time. xctool is a replacement for Apple's xcodebuild that makes it easier to build and test iOS and OSX applications from the command line. Created and maintained by Facebook, its goal is to provide a more human readable output when building an application and comes with nice features that make it especially helpful for continuous integration. For a while, xctool was also the only solution available to run the unit tests of an iOS application from the command line. 5.1 fixed that and it is now possible to use the xcodebuild "test" build action with iOS projects.

To install xctool, simply clone it somewhere in your computer. For the example, we have created a Tools folder in our $HOME directory and cloned it there.

```
$ mkdir ~/Tools
$ cd ~/Tools
$ git clone git@github.com:facebook/xctool.git
$ cd xctool
```

The xctool repository contains a lot of files but it's the "xctool.sh" file that interests us the most: all the commands will be run using this shell script. Cloning the repository is not enough to be able to use xctool in our project: you still have to build it. Don't be afraid though, you won't be using some complex build process you sometimes see in the documentation of open source projects. In the case of xctool, it goes straight to the point: xctool will build itself the first time you call it. The irony here is that xctool is built using... xcodebuild.

Let's start by asking the current version of xctool.

```
$ ./xctool.sh -version
=== BUILDING XCTOOL ===

  /Users/Palleas/Tools/xctool/scripts/build.sh

      ✓ Built xctool (98000 ms)

0.1.15
```

Now that we have a valid installation of xctool, let's go back to the directory were the Github Jobs project is stored and build the application from there. Note that there are other ways of installing xctool, the easier way is probably to use Homebrew, a package manager for OSX written in Ruby that will make your life a lot easier. If you haven't already, you should go grab it at http://brew.sh/. Homebrew requires the Xcode command line tools to work properly, so go back a few pages if you don't remember how to easily install them!

We have installed xctool in the ~/Tools/xctool directory. That is why we should be calling the xctool.sh script using a relative path, like this:

```
$ ~/Tools/xctool/xctool.sh -v
0.1.15
```

That's definitely not ideal though. That is why we will be using another environment variable called $PATH. This variable contains a list of all the directories accessible to the user containing an executable tool, separated by a colon. Let's add our xctool installation folder to this list.

```
$ export PATH=$HOME/Tools/xctool:$PATH
```

Please note that there is no way to simply push a value to this path variable, that's why we are simply concatenating the ~/Tools/xctool directory to the beginning of the existing variable and that is why you have to be extra careful when you modify this environment variable.

xctool is similar to xcodebuild in many ways: most of the options and arguments are the same. The tool itself is a bit stricter though, you won't be able to call it without at least specifying a -scheme argument. In our case we also want to build a workspace and not a simple Xcode project (the default behavior) and we want to use the AdHoc configuration. That's why we use the -workspace and the -configure arguments:

```
$ xctool.sh -workspace Github\ Jobs.xcworkspace -scheme Github\ Jobs
[Info] Loading settings for scheme 'Github Jobs' ... (1142 ms)

=== BUILD ===

  xcodebuild build Github Jobs
    Pods / Pods-Github Jobs-SVProgressHUD (AdHoc)
      √ Check dependencies (111 ms)
      √ Write auxiliary files (7 ms)
      ...
```

The first thing to note is that the output of xctool is much more clear. No longer a huge, hard to understand pile of text, you now have a grouped output of all the major steps of the build process. If you've run the command on your computer too, you should have noticed that the output also comes with colors.

The advantages of xctool are numerous. It is one thing to be all shiny and pretty, it is a whole other thing to provide actually helpful features. xctool provides different reporters in addition to the pretty (default) one, making it easier to integrate with continuous integration tools such as Jenkins, which we will cover in the next chapter. It also supports a JSON-based configuration file format so calling xctool stops being a pain. To use it, simply create a ".xctool-args" file with the following content:

```
[
        "-workspace", "Github Jobs.xcworkspace",
        "-scheme", "Github Jobs",
        "-configuration", "AdHoc"
]
```

Thanks to this file, it is now possible to invoke xctool without option or argument and have it build the application using the proper workspace and scheme.

Even if xctool is a really great tool, you have to remember once again that this is no silver bullet. As mentioned earlier, xctool is an alternative building solution for iOS and OSX projects to the Apple's xcodebuild, maintained by Facebook. For example, this means the tool could break with new releases of the Apple developer tools. In fact, for a long time, Xctool was not able to build Xcode 5.1 projects.

That is why you should also consider other solutions such as xcpretty. Its creator, Marin Usalj chose a different approach. Instead of creating a new build tool to fix the output readability problem, he chose to format it and make it pretty.

Formatting **xcodebuild** output using xcpretty

The easiest way to install xcpretty is, just like any other Ruby tool, to use Rubygem.

```
$ gem install xcpretty
```

Using xcpretty is then really straightforward. All you have to do is leverage a shell functionality called pipes.

```
$ xcodebuild -workspace Github\ Jobs.xcworkspace -scheme Github\ Jobs -configuration AdHoc build |
xcpretty -c
▸ Building Pods/Pods-Github Jobs-SVProgressHUD [AdHoc]
▸ Precompiling Jobs-SVProgressHUD-prefix.pch
▸ Precompiling Jobs-SVProgressHUD-prefix.pch
▸ Precompiling Jobs-SVProgressHUD-prefix.pch
▸ Precompiling Jobs-SVProgressHUD-prefix.pch
▸ Precompiling Jobs-SVProgressHUD-prefix.pch
▸ Precompiling Jobs-SVProgressHUD-prefix.pch
▸ Compiling Pods-Github\ Jobs-SVProgressHUD-dummy.o Pods-Github\ Jobs-SVProgressHUD-dummy.m
▸ Compiling Pods-Github\ Jobs-SVProgressHUD-dummy.o Pods-Github\ Jobs-SVProgressHUD-dummy.m
```

▸ Compiling SVProgressHUD.m
▸ Compiling SVProgressHUD.m
▸ Compiling Pods-Github\ Jobs-SVProgressHUD-dummy.o Pods-Github\ Jobs-SVProgressHUD-dummy.m
  Compiling SVProgressHUD.m
...

The output, once formatted, is pretty similar to the one generated by xctool: grouped into the main steps of the build and the –c option adds some color to the output. Just like xctool, it also provides multiple formatters, such as junit to easily integrate – like xctool – with Jenkins but also html, tap, or rspec.

The goal of this chapter is not to tell you that xcpretty does a better job than xctool, it's only about giving you the alternatives. Both of these solutions are about providing a better output, especially the junit one that will come in handy when we set up our unit tests in Jenkins and Bamboo in the following chapters.

Anatomy of an Xcode Project File and Scheme Sharing

Now that you've discovered how to build an iOS application from the command line using two different tools, you may have noticed a common behavior from both: they all need a valid Xcode project file or workspace (which is basically a glorified folder of Xcode projects) and more importantly, they both need a valid scheme.

You've already worked with Xcode targets, knowingly or not. A target specifies the product to build and how to build it using build phases such as compiling sources, copying headers and resources, and linking frameworks and build settings. In our "Github Jobs" Xcode project, we already have two targets - one for the main application and one that runs the unit tests. You can have as many targets as you see fit, and some targets can depend on others. A scheme is basically a collection of targets, among other things and can be stored at different levels: project level and workspace level. You can see a list of all the available schemes from the command line by using the -list argument of the xcodebuild command.

```
$ xcodebuild -list
Information about project "Github Jobs":
    Targets:
        Github Jobs
        Github JobsTests

    Build Configurations:
        Debug
        AdHoc
        Release

    If no build configuration is specified and -scheme is not passed then "Release" is used.

    Schemes:
        Github Jobs
```

If you run the same command within the workspace file, you should only see the schemes that were automatically generated by Cocoapods when it created the workspace the first time you ran the pod `install` command.

```
xcodebuild -list -workspace Github\ Jobs.xcworkspace
Information about workspace "Github Jobs":
    Schemes:
        Pods-Github Jobs
        Pods-Github Jobs-SVProgressHUD
```

In our case, we only care about the "Github Jobs" scheme. That is the one we've been using so far. By the way, don't let the message about the "Release" configuration fool you; you actually need to pass a valid scheme argument to the `xcodebuild` command when your project uses a workspace. In fact, if you don't, you will get the following error:

```
$ xcodebuild -workspace Github\ Jobs.xcworkspace build xcodebuild: error: If you specify a workspace
then you must also specify a scheme.  Use -list to see the schemes in this workspace.
```

Let's say it is time for a second developer to join the team and start working with you on the application. He will start by fetching the latest version of the source from your company's git repository, run the `pod install` command (remember we suggested you ignore the Pods folder) and want to make sure everything went well. With a terminal window already open, he will try to build the application from the command line:

```
$ xcodebuild -workspace Github\ Jobs.xcworkspace –scheme Github\ Jobs build
xcodebuild: error: The workspace 'Github Jobs' does not contain a scheme named 'Github Jobs'.
```

Remember when we mentioned that schemes could be stored at different levels? Now picture yourself in the next chapter, where this new developer is actually an automated build platform such as Jenkins or Bamboo and you got yourself a failed build for a dumb reason.

It's pretty easy to visualize all the information about a scheme from the command line or simply from the finder.

1.   Open a finder window and navigate to the folder where the Github Jobs project is stored.

2.   Right-click on the "Github Jobs.xcodeproj" and select "Show package content".

3.   Select the "xcuserdata" folder, then the "YourUser.xcuserdatad" and finally the "xcschemes" one. You should find your Github Job scheme there, as shown in Figure 4-4.

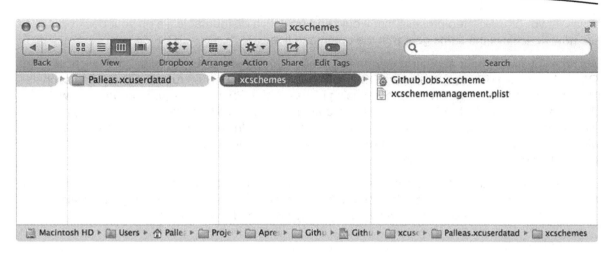

Figure 4-4. The Github Jobs scheme is a file stored somewhere in the Xcodeproj package

To be fair with Xcode and this new developer, the first time he would have opened the project in Xcode, the "Github Jobs" scheme would have been automatically created and could have been found in a new "xcuserdatad" package stored at the same level than the Palleas.xcuserdatad one. An automated build platform wouldn't open the project with Xcode though. Even if that is technically doable considering the build platform would run on an OSX computer capable of starting Xcode, that is definitely not the purpose of such a tool.

The solution lies within a UI element available in Xcode's scheme managing panel. Go back to Xcode and select the "Github Jobs" dropdown at the top left of the window, near the "Build & Run" button. Select the "Manage Schemes…" menu item. You should see a list of all the schemes available in your project. Check the first checkbox in the "Shared" column and press OK.

Two things happened. First, if you go back exploring the content of the Xcodeproj package, you should no longer see the "Github Jobs.xcscheme" file that was stored in "YourUser.xcuserdatad". Then, an "xcshareddata" folder has been created, containing the missing "Github Jobs.xcscheme" file in a similar "xcschemes" folder.

This seems a bit complicated but there are numerous reasons why we talked about this architecture. The obvious one is, as we mentioned earlier, that this could prevent you from getting a failing build from an automated build platform. More accurately, it will help you understand why your first build is failing when you will setup your continuous integration platform. No matter the number of years of experience in iOS development, every once in a while a developer will forget to check that checkbox. What is important is that sharing your schemes with your coworkers and your automated build platform allows you to work within the exact same environment. After all, a scheme is nothing but a bunch of configuration settings and it is very important to share them across your team and avoid the false positive and the "but it build successfully on my computer" messages from your coworkers.

Creating the IPA File From the Command Line

We have spent enough time building the application without being able to actually run it, let alone sending a testing version to your client or the members of your QA team. If you recall from Chapter 2 or simply from experience, creating the IPA file was an action available from the organizer window.

It was a two- or three-step process that would end up with a distributable file on your desktop. Let's see how to achieve the same goal with the command line.

It is time you learn about another tool from the Xcode ecosystem: xcrun; but first, let's talk about the IPA file format. An IPA file contains an iOS application. They can only be run on iOS devices such as iPhone and iPad and can only be opened using iTunes or the iPhone Configuration Utility as we've shown in Chapter 3. An IPA file is basically a glorified encrypted ZIP archive containing a .app file like the one we've been creating for the past ten pages or so. In fact, you could create IPA files without using any dedicated tool. That would be a waste of time considering xcrun will do that for you (and more) but technically doable.

Let's have a look at the IPA file we've created in the previous chapter. Start with renaming it to "Github Jobs.zip" and simply double click on the file from the finder. A command line equivalent of this process using the unzip command would go way faster and look like this:

```
$ unzip Github\ Jobs.ipa
Archive:  Github Jobs.ipa
   creating: Payload/
   creating: Payload/Github Jobs.app/
   creating: Payload/Github Jobs.app/_CodeSignature/
  inflating: Payload/Github Jobs.app/_CodeSignature/CodeResources
  inflating: Payload/Github Jobs.app/Assets.car
   creating: Payload/Github Jobs.app/Base.lproj/
   creating: Payload/Github Jobs.app/Base.lproj/Main.storyboardc/
  inflating: Payload/Github Jobs.app/Base.lproj/Main.storyboardc/72K-nL-OMz-view-WoX-oB-R4e.nib
  inflating: Payload/Github Jobs.app/Base.lproj/Main.storyboardc/Info.plist
  inflating: Payload/Github Jobs.app/Base.lproj/Main.storyboardc/UIViewController-1Id-ia-L1b.nib
  inflating: Payload/Github Jobs.app/embedded.mobileprovision
   creating: Payload/Github Jobs.app/en.lproj/
  inflating: Payload/Github Jobs.app/en.lproj/InfoPlist.strings
  inflating: Payload/Github Jobs.app/Github Jobs
  inflating: Payload/Github Jobs.app/Info.plist
  inflating: Payload/Github Jobs.app/LaunchImage-700-568h@2x.png
 extracting: Payload/Github Jobs.app/PkgInfo
  inflating: Payload/Github Jobs.app/ResourceRules.plist
   creating: Payload/Github Jobs.app/SVProgressHUD.bundle/
  inflating: Payload/Github Jobs.app/SVProgressHUD.bundle/angle-mask@2x.png
 extracting: Payload/Github Jobs.app/SVProgressHUD.bundle/error@2x.png
 extracting: Payload/Github Jobs.app/SVProgressHUD.bundle/success@2x.png
```

As you can see, all there is, is a Payload folder containing the application.

The xcrun executable is a command line tool that comes with Xcode just like xcodebuild and just like it, it is impacted by the location of the developer directory and the $DEVELOPER_DIR environment variable. It has two main purposes: finding development tools and executing them.

We mentioned earlier the linking executable named ld is part of the Xcode developing toolchain and can be located using xcrun, just like clang, git, or any other tool that comes with Xcode:

```
$ xcrun --find ld
/Applications/Xcode.app/Contents/Developer/Toolchains/XcodeDefault.xctoolchain/usr/bin/ld
```

```
$ xcrun --find git
/Applications/Xcode.app/Contents/Developer/usr/bin/git

$ xcrun --find clang
/Applications/Xcode.app/Contents/Developer/Toolchains/XcodeDefault.xctoolchain/usr/bin/clang
```

xcrun is also capable of running developer tools for you right after it has located them. To execute a command using xcrun, simply call it with xcrun first. Be careful though, xcrun can bypass the traditional $PATH environment variable to locate executable files. That is why you shouldn't expect it to simply use the freshly installed version of git on your computer if you ask him to do the following:

```
$ git -version
git version 1.9.1

$ xcrun git --version
git version 1.8.5.2 (Apple Git-48)
```

What is the point of this command then? Of course, it is not only to make things look more complicated just for the sake of it. Let's see how to package the application then, using the PackageApplication executable. With what we've just covered – finding executables using xcrun – you may think yourself capable of finding the PackageApplication executable but it is in fact not that simple.

```
$ xcrun PackageApplication
xcrun: error: unable to find utility "PackageApplication", not a developer tool or in PATH
```

xcrun cannot find the executable for two reasons. The first one is that it is simply not in your PATH. The second one is that PackageApplication is an executable specific to the iOS SDK. Because we did not specify the SDK we wanted to use and as the SDKROOT environment variable was not set, xcrun was not able to find where the executable was stored. Lucky for us, that's an easy fix: we just need to use the --sdk argument.

```
$ xcrun --sdk iphoneos --f PackageApplication
/Applications/Xcode.app/Contents/Developer/Platforms/iPhoneOS.platform/Developer/usr/bin/
PackageApplication
```

The simplest use of PackageApplication only needs a path to the .app package generated at the end of the xcodebuild command but it will also handle edge cases for you, such as resigning the application before packaging it into an IPA file. You can find the path to that package if you look at the end of the command's output, where it shows the code signing process:

```
CodeSign /Users/Palleas/Library/Developer/Xcode/DerivedData/Github_Jobs-
fxohiqkccwdfjbewpeaigyxjxsfd/Build/Products/Debug-iphoneos/Github\ Jobs.app
```

All you need to do is to invoke the PackageApplication command using the path to this package:

```
$ xcrun -sdk iphoneos PackageApplication  /Users/Palleas/Library/Developer/Xcode/DerivedData/
Github_Jobs-fxohiqkccwdfjbewpeaigyxjxsfd/Build/Products/Debug-iphoneos/Github\ Jobs.app
```

The PackageApplication command is pretty quiet by default: if it worked it won't show anything in your terminal but an IPA file will be created near the .app file we've packaged. If you want to make sure something actually happened, you'll need to use the verbose mode with the -verbose argument. You can also use xcrun's --log argument to have details of the command xcrun actually ran.

```
$ xcrun --log -sdk iphoneos PackageApplication  /Users/Palleas/Library/Developer/Xcode/DerivedData/
Github_Jobs-fxohiqkccwdfjbewpeaigyxjxsfd/Build/Products/Debug-iphoneos/Github\ Jobs.app -verbose
```

We won't go so far as to detail each line of the output of the PackageApplication command, but if you look at it you should see the following three main steps. First, the .app package is copied into a Payload folder created in your temporary folder. The path to this folder is available to you through the $TMPDIR environment variable. In our case that is something like: /var/folders/1v/d8vqkw8x23 ndw49f5vs3fzw00000gn/T/. Then, Codesign is invoked with the --verify argument to make sure the .app was properly code signed during the Xcodebuild process. Finally, the Payload folder created earlier is zipped into a new archive with the "ipa" extension.

Choosing the Destinations

Let's take a few minutes to review what we've done. We took the sources of an iOS application and used the xcodebuild command line tool to build the application and create an .app package containing the compiled code and all the assets. Then, we used the PackageApplication command line tool through xcrun to package the application into an archive that can be run on an iOS device.

This process could be enhanced though: having to dig into the output of the xcodebuild command is a pain and hardly automatable! That is why we need to specify where we want the .app package and the .ipa archive.

The destination of the .app package is a build setting you can see if you go back to Xcode, open the build settings of the Github Jobs target and look for the "Per-configuration Build Products Paths" stored as "CONFIGURATION_BUILD_DIR", as shown in Figure 4-5.

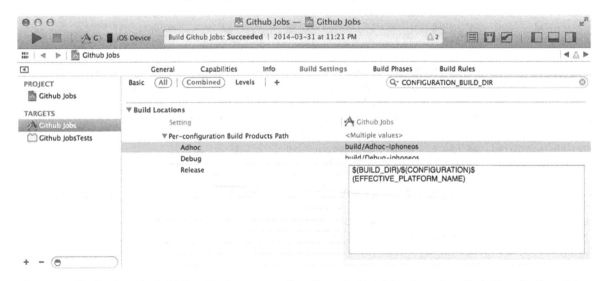

Figure 4-5. The Configuration build dir setting has a per-configuration value that determines where the built application will be stored

You could change the value of this build setting directly from Xcode and use an explicit value but that could be dangerous to your coworker or to your continuous integration tool. The CONFIGURATION_BUILD_DIR build setting is one of those settings you'd rather explicitly pass to the build process when invoking xcodebuild.

```
$ xcodebuild -configuration AdHoc -workspace Github\ Jobs.xcworkspace -scheme Github\ Jobs
CONFIGURATION_BUILD_DIR="/Users/Palleas/Projects/Github Jobs/build" clean build
```

It is very important that you use absolute path for this. You are temporarily overriding a build setting, which means that the CONFIGURATION_BUILD_DIR will be "/Users/Palleas/Projects/Github Jobs/build" for the duration of the build. If you used a relative path such as "./build" the build would simply fail.

Now that we have an .app package and that we know exactly where it is, we can do the same for the IPA file and package the application to a more easily located folder such as the desktop. Fortunately, the PackageApplication tool has an -o (for output) argument.

```
$ xcrun -sdk iphoneos PackageApplication ~/Projects/Apress/Github\ Jobs/build/Github\
Jobs.app -o ~/Desktop/Github\ Jobs.ipa
```

Toying with the Application Manifest

With xcodebuild and PackageApplication through xcrun, we are now capable of taking an iOS application, building it, and releasing it, only from the command line. It means that you could receive a project from somebody from your team and perform this entire process without opening Xcode once! Of course there are things you may want to do, like we've been doing in the previous chapter like changing the bundle identifier of the application, and bumping the bundle version to a new one. What we need is simply to find a way to edit the Info.plist like we have been doing in the previous chapter and that's what the command "PlistBuddy" is here for.

Before we can start messing with it, let's take a few minutes to understand how the property list file format works. The plist file format is heavily used across the operating system that runs on your Mac or your iOS device. It is used to describe applications, much like the Info.plist file of your Xcode project, it is used to store preferences, to cache information. You can use it to store many different types of information:

- String
- Boolean
- Integer and floating points
- Dates
- Binary data
- Array and dictionaries, which would contain one or many values of all these types

One of the numerous advantages of the plist file format is its XML based syntax that makes it easily readable. We've already edited our "Github Jobs-Info.plist" from Xcode but let's take a look add the sources. You can achieve the same result by right clicking on the file and choosing "Open as... Source Code".

```xml
<?xml version="1.0" encoding="UTF-8"?>
<!DOCTYPE plist PUBLIC "-//Apple//DTD PLIST 1.0//EN" "http://www.apple.com/DTDs/PropertyList-1.0.dtd">
<plist version="1.0">
<dict>
        <key>CFBundleDevelopmentRegion</key>
        <string>en</string>
        <key>CFBundleDisplayName</key>
        <string>${PRODUCT_NAME}</string>
        <key>CFBundleExecutable</key>
        <string>${EXECUTABLE_NAME}</string>
        <key>CFBundleIdentifier</key>
        <string>com.perfectly-cooked.${PRODUCT_NAME:rfc1034identifier}</string>
        <key>CFBundleInfoDictionaryVersion</key>
        <string>6.0</string>
        <key>CFBundleName</key>
        <string>${PRODUCT_NAME}</string>
        <key>CFBundlePackageType</key>
        <string>APPL</string>
        <key>CFBundleShortVersionString</key>
        <string>0.1</string>
        <key>CFBundleSignature</key>
        <string>????</string>
        <key>CFBundleVersion</key>
        <string>0.1</string>
        <key>GithubJobsEndpoint</key>
        <string>$(GITHUB_JOBS_ENDPOINT)</string>
        <key>LSRequiresIPhoneOS</key>
        <true/>
        <key>UIMainStoryboardFile</key>
        <string>Main</string>
        <key>UIRequiredDeviceCapabilities</key>
        <array>
                <string>armv7</string>
        </array>
        <key>UISupportedInterfaceOrientations</key>
        <array>
                <string>UIInterfaceOrientationPortrait</string>
                <string>UIInterfaceOrientationLandscapeLeft</string>
                <string>UIInterfaceOrientationLandscapeRight</string>
        </array>
</dict>
</plist>
```

The Plistbuddy executable is your day-to-day tool to interact with property list files easily. It is not in your PATH by default and cannot be found using xcrun because it is not a developer tool per se. We will save you some time, you will be able to find it in "/usr/libexec". Let's add it to our PATH just like we did for xcrun because we're going to use it many times.

```
$ export PATH=/usr/libexec:$PATH
```

The default behavior of PlistBuddy is to work interactively. If you call it without any arguments, it will open a limited, property-list-file-manipulation limited shell in which you're going to be able to run simple commands to display or update existing values and add new ones.

Let's start toying with our Info.plist to achieve a very simple goal: updating the build version and storing the last time update. We will start with the following command:

```
$ PlistBuddy "Github Jobs/Github Jobs-Info.plist"
```

You can retrieve the current bundle version:

```
Command: Print CFBundleVersion
0.1
```

And then bump it to 0.2:

```
Command: Set CFBundleVersion 0.2
```

And finally store the time the application was built at (note the very specific date format):

```
Command: add PCSLastUpdate date "Sat Apr 19 01:14:45 GMT 2014"
```

While this approach is fine from a technical point of view, it is far from being convenient. You can use PlistBuddy in the interactive mode for debugging and manual manipulation purposes - even though opening it in your editor of choice would probably be best - but the PlistBuddy also allows you to run commands directly using the -c argument. In our case that would give us the following commands:

```
$ PlistBuddy -c "Print CFBundleVersion" Github\ Jobs/Github\ Jobs-Info.plist
0.1

$ PlistBuddy -c "Set CFBundleVersion 0.2" Github\ Jobs/Github\ Jobs-Info.plist

$ PlistBuddy -c "Add PCSLastUpdate date Sat Apr 19 01:14:45 GMT 2014" Github\ Jobs/Github\
Jobs-Info.plist
```

We mentioned in a previous chapter that the downside of releasing multiple versions of your application is to have the previously installed versions erased and the only available solution was to change the bundle identifier. Now that we know how PlistBuddy works, the possibilities are pretty much endless. Here is what you could do to release a build of a very specific branch.

The first thing to do is to retrieve the name of the git branch you are currently on:

```
$ git rev-parse --abbrev-ref HEAD
bug-fixing-branch
```

Then, all it takes is the execution of a command using PlistBuddy in non-interactive mode:

```
$ PlistBuddy -c "Set CFBundleIdentifier com.perfectly-cooked.\${PRODUCT_NAME:rfc1034identifier}-
$(git rev-parse --abbrev-ref HEAD)" Github\ Jobs/Github\ Jobs-Info.plist
```

Note that we need to escape the first dollar sign because we don't want it to be evaluated by bash and we still want to use the placeholder with the RFC1034 filter. In our case we could have just hardcoded the "github-jobs" part but we are messing enough already with the application manifest.

You may be wondering why we used the command line to do this (even if the fact that you bought this book tells us you probably aren't). Just imagine an automated build platform that would create a build you could test for each branch your coworker wants you to merge!

Bumping the Build Version Using Agvtool

Updating the build number using PlistBuddy is error-prone and overcomplicated. You have to make sure you update it properly at two different places: the short, marketing version number and the build version number. If your application uses multiple targets, for example an iOS version and an iPad one, you will have to update the version numbers in two Info.plist manifest files. That is four PlistBuddy commands to run! Don't worry though, there is one more tool we need to introduce you to: the Apple Generic Versioning Tool (agvtool).

agvtool is a utility provided by Apple that comes with Xcode and that can be found in its Developers directory just like many of the other tools we've been using so far. Once again, a quick use of xcrun will help you find it:

```
$ xcrun -f agvtool
/Applications/Xcode.app/Contents/Developer/usr/bin/agvtool
```

agvtool can perform different operations but most of them will be useless to us. If you look closely at the documentation, you should see that the "submit" operation will only work if you are an Apple employee. Also, agvtool integrates really well with SVN and CVS. We've already made our case about those two versioning control systems so that's all we'll say on the subject. The operations we care about are what-version, new-version, and next-version.

agvtool is not a simple utility that takes a version number as input and magically returns the next version. In fact, there are a few modifications you need to make to your Xcode project before you can use agvtool. If you try to use it right away, you will get the following error:

```
$ agvtool what-version
There does not seem to be a CURRENT_PROJECT_VERSION key set for this project.  Add this key to your
target's expert build settings.
```

Go back to the "Github Jobs" Xcode project and look for the versioning build settings. The first thing we need to do is to change the "Versioning System" build setting to Apple Generic and set the "Current Project Version" to 1, as shown in Figure 4-6.

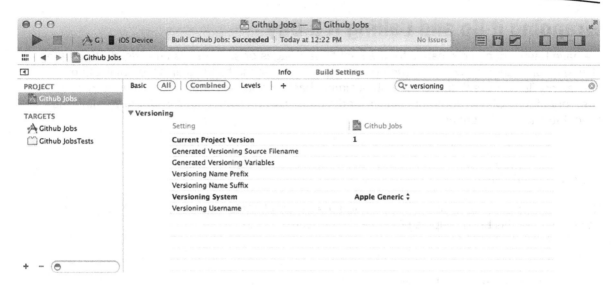

Figure 4-6. The Github Jobs project uses the Apple Generic versioning system and is at its version 1

While we are setting the build version straight, using the application generic versioning system suggests that your "Current Project Version" build setting and the "Build version" property in your application manifest should be synced. Go back to the "Github Jobs-Info.plist" and make sure the "Bundle version" is 1.

We are now able to use agvtool to retrieve the current project's version:

```
$ agvtool what-version
Current version of project Github Jobs is:
    1
```

We can also use it to change the current version in the "Current Project Version" build setting and in the CFBundleVersion property of all the Info.plist file(s) of the project:

```
$ agvtool new-version -all 1.2.3
Setting version of project Github Jobs to:
    1.2.3.
```

Also setting CFBundleVersion key (assuming it exists)

```
Updating CFBundleVersion in Info.plist(s)...

Updated CFBundleVersion in "Github Jobs.xcodeproj/../Github Jobs/Github Jobs-Info.plist" to 1.2.3
Updated CFBundleVersion in "Github Jobs.xcodeproj/../Github JobsTests/Github JobsTests-Info.plist"
to 1.2.3
```

There is one golden rule in the world of continuous integration and that is to avoid messing too much with the application right before it is built. Right now we are in an interactive mode in which we run build commands manually but when we will run them from automated build platforms you will learn that they are a lot less forgiving.

Wrapping it Up and Calling it a Day

We have been writing commands for the past fifteen pages or so, and it is time we start grouping all these commands so we can rerun everything all at once: the building and the application packaging. To achieve that, we will write a simple bash script. Let's start by creating a "bin" directory at the "Github Jobs" project's root directory. By convention, this is where you find the executable tools of a project.

```
$ mkdir bin
$ touch bin/cibuild
$ chmod +x bin/cibuild
```

Note the chmod command we are using to add the executable file mode to our newly created script. The content of this build script is pretty straightforward:

```
#!/bin/bash

WORKSPACE="Github Jobs.xcworkspace"
SCHEME="Github Jobs"
BUILD_DIR="$(pwd)/build"
CONFIGURATION="AdHoc"

ARCHIVE_FILENAME="Github Jobs.app"
IPA_FILENAME="Github Jobs.ipa"

security unlock-keychain -p $PASSWORD $HOME/Library/Keychains/login.keychain

pod install

xcodebuild -workspace "$WORKSPACE" -scheme "$SCHEME" -configuration
CONFIGURATION_BUILD_DIR="$BUILD_DIR" clean build | xcpretty -c

xcrun -sdk iphoneos PackageApplication "$BUILD_DIR/$ARCHIVE_FILENAME" -o "$BUILD_DIR/$IPA_FILENAME"
```

The first line is called a "shebang" and tells the shell that this script should be evaluated using bash. Now the script is pretty simple and doesn't use any shell-specific tools so this part is not really needed, but is a good habit to have.

The next block basically defines a bunch of variables, nothing fancy there and the rest of the script is nothing we haven't covered in the past sections of this chapter beside the "security" command.

The security command is a command line interface to your keychain and all that is security-related. One of the things it can do is unlock the keychain for a small amount of time. When you build your application for the first time, a panel will pop up asking you if you will grant access to your keychain to a specific process. In our case that is "CodeSign", the command that happens at the end of the xcodebuild, that needs access to the private key and the certificates that are stored in your keychain, to sign the build.

Note that hardcoding your password is really not that secure, that is why the $PASSWORD variable is not defined in the script and the script is invoked like this:

```
$ PASSWORD=mypassword bin/cibuild
```

That's not a lot better but at least you can share your script and add it to version control without giving your password away. In the next chapters we will start talking about the integration of this script into automated build platforms that come with secured ways of storing your credentials.

Summary

In this chapter we gave you a little tour of the command line tools available to the iOS developer who wants to be more productive and learn how things work under the hood. Shenzhen, xctool, and xcpretty, are all made by other developers who wanted to leverage the power of the command line and felt like giving back to the community by sharing their work.

We hope we've convinced you that the command line is nothing to be afraid of and can be of great assistance. Using xcodebuild to build the application, xcrun to locate the tools you need, PackageApplication to generate the final ipa file... Apple provides the developer with a lot of tools that will help us set up our continuous integration environment.

The next chapter will be about just that, starting with a continuous integration platform called Jenkins.

Chapter 5

Automatic Builds with Jenkins

It took us almost half of the book to introduce the concept, but it is finally time we start talking about continuous integration. In past chapters, our goal was to give you a tour of the tools at your disposal. Now that we know that Apple provides us with everything we need, let's set up our continuous integration automated build platform using Jenkins.

Before we get our hands dirty, we need to answer the following question: What is an automated build platform, and why do we need one?

Why Do We Need an Automated Build Platform?

An automated build platform runs specialized build processes that we usually call "jobs." A job can perform many actions, from building the application to checking the code style against your team's conventions. A job will be started automatically every once in a while when the project is changed or even manually, sometimes many times a day. Automated build platforms usually come with a user interface to ease the creation of jobs and the exploitation of job execution's results. Put that way, it's basically a glorified web interface over crontab. So what is the added value?

During the lifecycle of a project, you will be integrating pieces of code from your coworker and you need to make sure these pieces of code won't hurt the final product in any way. We've already covered how to quickly build the application from the command line and in the next chapters we will talk about unit testing and quality assurance. The truth is, these tools are useless if you forget to run them, and you will. It may be because you became overconfident in your code-review skills or simply because the deadline is getting too close but relying on a developer to run tools that will annoy him is craziness. The main point of an automated building platform is to maintain a certain level of confidence in the application codebase by building the application as frequently as possible. Continuous integration aims to reduce the pain of integration by increasing its frequency, and that's why an automated build platform will help.

An automated build platform must be running on a neutral environment and definitely not on a developer's computer. Once again, you need to be able to trust your automated build platform. "But I don't understand, the application builds on my computer!" is the kind of discussion you want to avoid.

We will start with a very well-known automated build platform: Jenkins.

Jenkins and Hudson: A Bit of History

Jenkins is a continuous integration platform written in Java that was released ten years ago. It started under the name of "Hudson" in 2004 at Sun Microsystems and was the first viable alternative to CruiseControl, also written in Java.

When Sun Microsystems was acquired by Oracle in 2010, an issue arose in the community and the result was a change of name when Oracle applied for a trademark and Jenkins was born. Oracle, however, announced that Hudson would still be maintained and that the project would continue to evolve. Today, both projects are still alive, even if the Jenkins one seems to have won the popularity contest, according to the latest number of members and public repositories on their respective GitHub organizations.

They both share a common codebase and to this day, each one is considered to be a fork of the other by the respective leaders. Even if we will be using Jenkins in this book, most of the manipulation we will be doing, the configuration we will be tweaking, and the plugins we will be installing, should work on Hudson.

Getting Started with Jenkins

The requirements to run Jenkins on a computer are pretty simple, you only need Java 6 installed. Since Apple stopped shipping OS X with Java pre-installed, we need to make sure Java is available on your computer. Many tools require Java to run even today, so you probably have already installed it without paying much attention. Open a terminal and run the following command:

```
$ java -version
java version "1.7.0_25"
Java(TM) SE Runtime Environment (build 1.7.0_25-b15)
Java HotSpot(TM) 64-Bit Server VM (build 23.25-b01, mixed mode)
```

If the output isn't exactly the same as above, that's okay, as long as it shows a version of Java that is superior to 1.6. If Java isn't installed at all, a message such as, "No Java runtime present, requesting install." should appear. You should then visit the Apple support page to download the Java runtime, which can be found at: http://support.apple.com/kb/DL1572.

Installing Jenkins Using the Command Line

You can install Jenkins using the Homebrew package manager we've talked about in the previous chapters or you could simply use the native package provided on the Jenkins website. From experience, Homebrew is probably the simplest approach since it makes it super easy to update Jenkins when a new version is released (and available via homebrew, of course). To do that, open a terminal and simply run the following command:

```
$ brew install jenkins
```

It will download the most recent version of Jenkins available on homebrew and set up everything you need to be able to start it at launch, as long as you read the whole output of the command. We, on the other hand, won't be using that method in this book. We want to make sure you actually understand how it works under the hood, from downloading Jenkins to actually getting it to build our application. Feel free to jump to the "Having a look around" section if you don't really care about how to run a Java-based web application.

Open a terminal, create a "Jenkins" folder, and change your working directory to the newly created folder. Once this is done, download the latest version of Jenkins using the curl command line tool. Note the -L argument that means, "follow redirects", when you use the "latest" Jenkins URL, you will actually be redirected to the most recent version. At the time we are writing this book, the current version is 1.560.

```
$ mkdir ~/Jenkins
$ cd ~/Jenkins
$ curl -L http://mirrors.jenkins-ci.org/war/latest/jenkins.war -O
```

The installation of Jenkins is nothing if not easy. We just downloaded the latest version of Jenkins in a WAR format, which stands for "Web Application ARchive". This means that everything you need to use Jenkins is in this single file; you can now run Jenkins using the Java command line tool.

```
$ java -jar jenkins.war
Running from: /Users/Palleas/Jenkins/jenkins.war
webroot: $user.home/.jenkins
...
INFO: Started SelectChannelConnector@0.0.0.0:8080
```

If you see a similar output from the Java command, then Jenkins should have started normally. As it says in the last line, your fresh installation of Jenkins is available at the address 0.0.0.0 (which basically means your own IP address) on port 8080. You can customize the HTTP address and the port with the --httpListenAddress and the --httpPort arguments, like this:

```
$ java -jar jenkins.war --httpPort=8908 --httpListenAddress=192.168.1.14
```

Congratulations, you now have your first instance of Jenkins up and running! Open your default Internet browser and load the following address: http://localhost:8080. If everything worked as expected, you should see an empty interface with an old butler (which has nothing to do with the other one from Hudson) in the background and a welcome message asking you to create a job to get started. Don't worry we will get to that in a few moments.

The most amazing thing with Jenkins is probably its design, which most developers would consider "good enough". You will probably think that it is (thinking you won't be spending a lot of time on Jenkins once you've configured your jobs), but that's a lie. In fact, you WILL be spending a lot of time on Jenkins. It may be a couple of minutes every day, but at the end of the week, you'll realize that you've actually spent two hours on Jenkins before you know it. Those two hours are not wasted, don't get us wrong, but that's enough time to assert that Jenkins could be prettier, just like many open-source projects that solved this issue by using the default CSS file provided for by twitter bootstrap.

Loading Jenkins at Startup

Running Jenkins from the command line is fine, to a certain extent. As we mentioned earlier, you don't want to rely on developers to start tools that will annoy them. In fact, you shouldn't be running Jenkins on a developer's computer but on a neutral environment that no one is coding on. Most people and companies usually go for a Mac Mini, which is kind of cheap, in the Apple world. Managing commands that should run at startup is done through the "Launch Daemon" OS X core component. All it takes is to be properly filled up and written in the property list format!. This is a little bit out of the scope of this book so we won't cover it. Note that if you decide to go with Homebrew to install Jenkins on the actual computer that will perform your builds, a launch daemon file will be provided.

Having a Look Around

As shown in Figure 5-1 and as we mentioned earlier, the user interface is pretty simple. You will find on the left, a menu with the main actions available from creating a new job to managing Jenkins and a central area were you will see your jobs and their current status. The section we really care about for now is the one used to configure Jenkins. Click the "Manage Jenkins" link and then, click the "Manage Plugins" link.

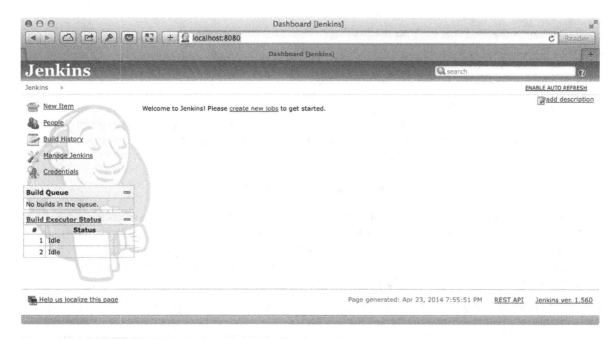

Figure 5-1. A Jenkins instance homepage opened for the first time

Jenkins comes with pre-installed plugins. For starters, there are a few plugins used to manage your user's credentials. The default "credential plugin" will add some basic security features to Jenkins and will store your users' credentials locally, instead of relying on an external system like LDAP (which is also already installed) or a third-party service's OAuth. It also comes with the "Matrix Authorization Strategy Plugin" that will allow you, once configured, to set up more complex authorization strategies.

Jenkins is a tool that started as a continuous integration platform for the Java ecosystem. Because a Java project wouldn't be the same without huge XML configuration files, the standard installation of Jenkins comes with Maven, Ant, and Javadoc support. It can also communicate with remote computers over SSH and DCOM (Distributed Component Object Model) for the ones running Windows and provides plugins to send the build results by e-mail. Finally, Jenkins is nothing if not a community-driven project. That is why Jenkins comes bundled with the "Translation Assistance Plugin" so you can contribute to the translation of Jenkins in your own language.

As you can see, Jenkins comes ready the very moment you run the Java command for the first time. If you're a Java developer with very simple needs. In our situation, we won't need all of these plugins. Only the two SSH related ones will come in handy later in this chapter when we'll talk about building applications on remote computers. For something as basic as Git support so that Jenkins can clone our project, we will have to install a plugin.

Tuning Jenkins

Let's start with an easy modification. The first time you open the "Manage Jenkins" section, you get a message warning you against unprotected installations. If your installation of Jenkins is available on a large network - meaning not only listening on the local host - anyone would be able to start jobs manually on your behalf and access archived, packaged IPA files, for example. Even worse, people would be able to create jobs that would execute malicious shell scripts!

Because that's probably not what you want, let's add simple credentials and secure Jenkins.

1. Go back to the "Manage Jenkins" section and hit the "Setup Security" button that appears right next to the scary warning message. You can also click on the "Configure Global Security" button if you haven't dismissed the warning message before.

2. On the screen that appears, check both the "Enable Security" and "Prevent Cross Site Request Forgery" boxes.

3. In the block that appeared beneath the "Enable Security", select the "Jenkins' Own User Database" and select the "Anyone Can Do Anything" option. Once again, if you start adding multiple accounts to Jenkins, you should consider switching to a dedicated tool such as LDAP.

4. Go back and click on the "Manage Users" link, and finally, click on "Create User".

5. Enter your username, password, full name and E-mail address, as shown in Figure 5-2, and press OK.

Figure 5-2. *Creating a new user*

6. Then, open for one last time the "Configure Global Security" section and select the "Logged-in Users Can Do Anything" option instead of the "Anyone Can Do Anything".

You should be redirected to a login form where you can enter your credentials and we should be ready to install the plugins we need.

At this point, our needs are pretty simple. We need to be able to clone a project hosted in a Git repository hosted somewhere on the Internet. For the consistency with which the whole application is about, let's go for Github. The project should be available for you to download at the following remote URL: git@github.com:Palleas/Github-Jobs.git.

To install the git plugins we need, navigate to the "Available" tab of the "Manage Plugins" section and search for "Git Plugin". You will see only a few results including the "Git Plugin" one. Check the checkbox in the first column. Repeat the same process for the "Xcode Plugin" and click the "Install Without Restart" button, as shown in Figure 5-3.

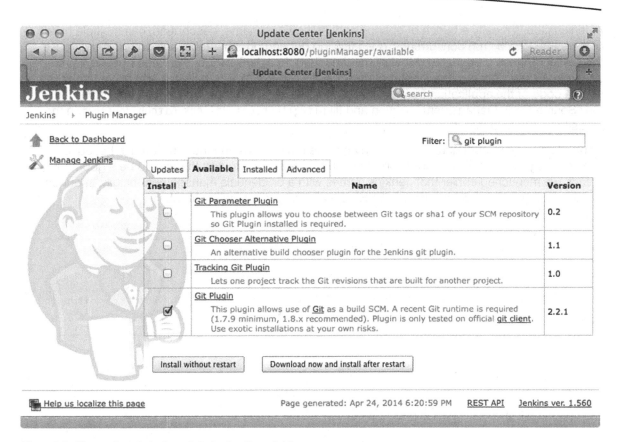

Figure 5-3. You can install plugin and start using them right away

You can think of the "Install Without Restart" feature of Jenkins as the Windows menu to unplug a USB device safely. It would probably be safer to use but nobody does it anyway. More seriously, it is a 100% fine to install plugins without restarting the whole installation. In fact, it was a feature introduced in version 1.442 of Jenkins and now, the only time when you'll need to restart Jenkins would be for plugin uninstallation and upgrades.

There is one more plugin you may want to consider installing called "Green Balls" that will show you how extendable Jenkins really is. It may have taken its author 300 lines of code, but this plugin will show green balls instead of blue ones for successful builds.

Your First Jenkins Job Using the Xcode Plugin

It is time we create our first build. We will start simply with cloning the application, building the app, and generating an IPA file, exactly what we have been doing in the previous chapters. To start creating a build, simply click on the "New Item" in the left menu, enter "Github Jobs for iOS" in the Item Name field, and select "Build a Free-style Software Project". And then press OK.

Even if the job creation process is split in two steps, the job was created when you pressed "Ok" for the first time, but for now it's empty and doesn't do anything.

A Jenkins job is mostly a bunch of options and instructions: name, description, can multiple builds of the same jobs be run concurrently, does this job depend on other jobs, and so on. You can use the default options for this part. Most of the time though, a Jenkins job is created to build a project stored in a source code management platform, such as Git or SVN. We want Jenkins to fetch the source code of the application from a Git repository stored on Github. To do that, select "Git" in the "Source Code Management" section and fill git@github.com:Palleas/Github-Jobs.git in the repository URL field that appeared.

Depending on your configuration, you may get the error shown in Figure 5-4, that's because Jenkins is trying to access a repository it doesn't have access to and that would be a good thing. In fact, we mentioned earlier that Jenkins comes with a credentials management plugin. In our case, we need it to store public and private SSH keys to authenticate with Github.

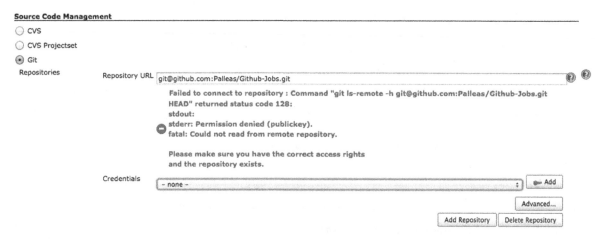

Figure 5-4. *Jenkins cannot access a protected repository*

Creating an SSH key dedicated to Github

The easiest (and probably more secure) way of authenticating with a repository over SSH is to use a private key. To do that, we need to generate a new key, add the public one to our Github account, and give the private one to Jenkins. Open a terminal and generate a new SSH key using ssh-keygen:

```
$ ssh-keygen -t rsa -N "" -f ~/Tools/jenkins.key
Generating public/private rsa key pair.
/Users/Palleas/Tools/jenkins.key already exists.
Overwrite (y/n)? y
Your identification has been saved in /Users/Palleas/Tools/jenkins.key.
Your public key has been saved in /Users/Palleas/Tools/jenkins.key.pub.
The key fingerprint is:
22:69:9f:c0:f8:9c:14:18:ac:47:77:a1:59:d8:a4:33 Palleas@local
The key's randomart image is:
+--[ RSA 2048]----+
|  ..  ++.        |
|   ooo=o         |
```

```
|  o..E.          |
|. .o =           |
| .. B . S        |
|   = = o         |
|    + o          |
|                 |
|                 |
+-----------------+
```

We now have an SSH key stored in our Tools folder that we also stored on the Jenkins archive, thanks to the `ssh-keygen` command.

- The -t argument tells the command to use RSA, a cryptographic communication system used to secure data transmission, invented by Ron Rivest, Adi Shamir, and Leonard Adleman, hence the RSA.

- The –N argument is used to associate an empty passphrase to the key. Most people use empty passphrases out of laziness to avoid typing it in when initiating SSH connections, but in our case it's simply not supported by Jenkins at the time we are writing this book. There is a JENKINS-20879 issue going on though.

Telling Jenkins to use this brand new key is easy thanks to the Jenkins credentials plugin. Go back to the Jenkins homepage and select Credentials from the left menu. Then, select "Global Credentials" and "Add Credentials" from the left menu. Finally, fill the form as shown in Figure 5-5.

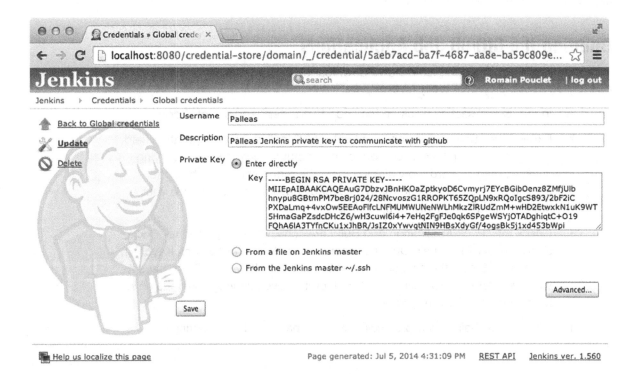

Figure 5-5. Adding a new SSH key so Jenkins can communicate with Github

Note that you can get the content of the private key to paste it into the form by using the following command:

```
$ cat ~/Tools/jenkins.key | pbcopy
```

Then, go to your Github profile and add your public key (the content of the Jenkins.key.pub file) to your profile. If you are wondering how to do that, look at the official Github documentation: https://help.github.com/articles/generating-ssh-keys.

You should now be able to add the Git repository URL to the job configuration, as shown in Figure 5-6.

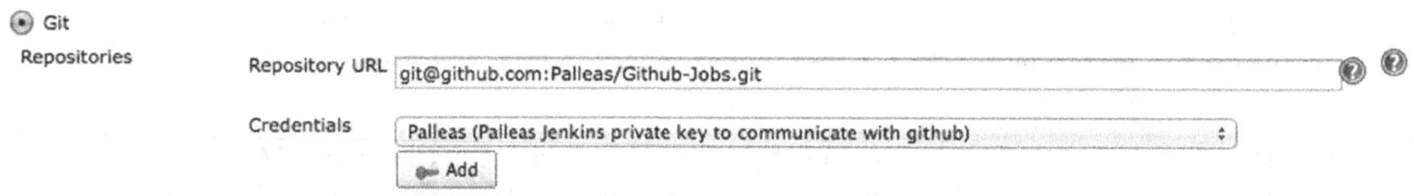

⊙ Git
Repositories

Repository URL git@github.com:Palleas/Github-Jobs.git

Credentials Palleas (Palleas Jenkins private key to communicate with github)

Add

Figure 5-6. Explicitly selecting the credentials allows Jenkins to communicate with the Git repository

"Build Triggers" is not really important right now, and we will only be launching jobs manually and will cover this section in detail later. The third part to a Jenkins job is actually the one that will interest us. It is not enough to simply give a repository of source code to Jenkins, but you have to explicitly tell it what the build will consist of.

Building the Github Job Applications

Fortunately for us, the Xcode plugin we've downloaded earlier makes it pretty easy to describe what building an Xcode project actually means.

1. In the "Build" section, click on the "Add Build Step" and select "Xcode".

2. Expand the "Settings..." panel and enter "AdHoc" in the configuration field. If you are running Jenkins on your own computer because you are trying Jenkins, then you probably already meet the requirements of the code signing process – meaning that you already have the private key in your keychain and the provisioning profile.

3. Check the "Pack Application and Build IPA" checkbox. Expand the "Code signing & OS X keychain Options" section and check the "Unlock Keychain" checkbox. Even if the help section near where the "Keychain Path" says it will use a default value, fill "${HOME}/Library/Keychains/login.keychain" in the text field or it will not work.

4. Fill the "Keychain Password" field with your password and continue.

> **Note**   If you are running Jenkins on a brand new computer, like a fancy new Mac Mini you've just bought for your company, don't worry, we will come back to the packaging process in a couple of sections.

5. If you remember correctly from the previous chapter, we are trying to build a workspace and using a scheme. Expand the "Advanced" section. Fill "Github Jobs" in the "Xcode Schema File" field and "Github Jobs" in the "Xcode Workspace File" field. Do not add the ".xcworkspace" extension or it will look for a "Github Jobs.xcworkspace.xcworkspace" file and the build will fail.

6. Finally, set the "Build output directory" to "${WORKSPACE}/build", where WORKSPACE is an environment variable available during the build that contains the path to the root directory of the project.

You may have already guessed by now but the build won't work as is because we did not add the project dependencies to the project's repository. Click the "Add Build Step" one more time and select "Execute Shell" and drag the block that just appeared above the Xcode one. Fill "pod install" in the text area.

That's basically what our job will consist of for now: installing the dependencies and building and packaging the application. You can have as many build steps as you want, as long as you remember that they are run sequentially and that a failing step will fail the whole build, which makes sense when you think about it.

Archiving the generated IPA

The last part of a build is an optional list of post-build actions, which will be executed no matter what the results of the build. It can be pretty much anything, from generating and publishing documentation to archiving the results of a build. What we want in this situation is to keep track of the IPA files that were created during the build process.

To do that, click on the "Add Post-Build Action" and select "Archive Artifacts", and fill in the pattern of the file you're expecting to be created during the build, in our case the files with the *.ipa file extension, as show in Figure 5-7.

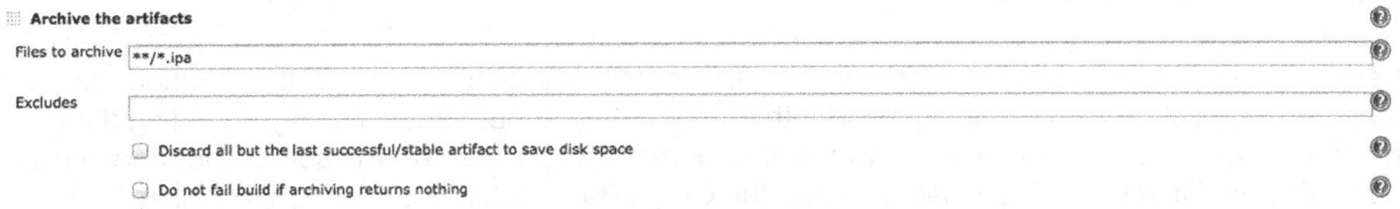

Figure 5-7. Asking Jenkins to find and archive the ipa files at the end of the build

There are some advanced options available with this post-build action, like asking Jenkins to keep only the latest artifact available to save space. That would probably be useful if we were building a very big application but would also prevent building multiple branches of the application and keeping the resulting ipa files. Plus, the last time we packaged the application, the size of the generated package was around 150KB so space should not be an issue for a while.

The job is now properly configured and it is time we trigger a build. Press the "Build Now" button in the left menu to start a build when you are ready and click on the link that appeared in the left menu.

The application is pretty small so the first build shouldn't take more than a minute, including the time it takes to fetch the content from the Github repository. Refresh the page when the build is complete or click the "Enable Auto Refresh" link at the top right of the page. At the end, you should see something similar to what's in Figure 5-8.

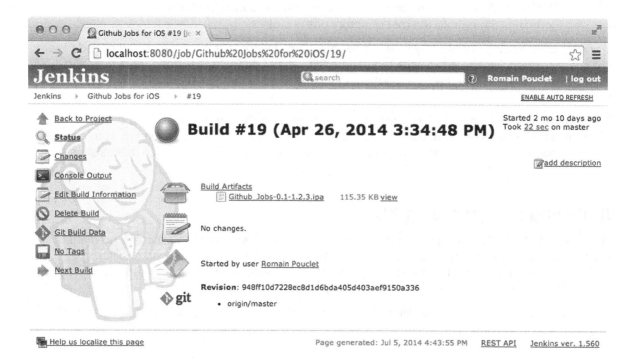

Figure 5-8. A successful Jenkins build

A successful build page contains useful information about what just happened: the duration, the changes that occurred since the last build, other information about the versioning, including the hash the commit at which the workspace is at the time of the build. Of course, the screenshot above may look a tiny bit different if you actually installed the Green Balls plugin that makes everything so much prettier.

What's interesting in this screenshot is the "build artifacts" section that shows the IPA file we wanted Jenkins to archive. With this approach, you can simply build any branch of the application so your tester can visit Jenkins, download the resulting IPA, and install it via iTunes. Of course, we've already been through this, and don't worry, there are much more powerful post-build actions you can install.

The default Jenkins home directory is located at the following path: "~/.jenkins". If you are looking for the path to the archived builds, that is where you will find them:

```
$ find .jenkins/jobs/Github\ Jobs\ for\ iOS -name "*.ipa"
jobs/Github Jobs for iOS/builds/2014-04-26_15-34-48/archive/build/Github_Jobs-0.1-1.2.3.ipa
```

Congratulations, you've made your first steps into the world of continuous integration. There are a few things that can be improved with thought. First, the Xcode Build plugin is good but not great. It gives you control over a lot of things in the build process, sometimes in a pretty confusing way, like the path to the workspace file that doesn't need an extension.

If you take a look back at the script we wrote in the previous chapter, you will see that we don't need so many options. That is why we will be using our script from now on. Plus, it will be much easier to update it. Before we do though, let's have a look at the other features provided by Jenkins.

Jenkins Power User Features

Jenkins is a pretty powerful tool you can learn to use in a couple of hours, even if you've never used a continuous integration platform before. Don't take it for granted though, for it also provides features that will help the power user.

Jenkins REST API

If you look closely, almost every page comes with a "REST API" link at the bottom. The Jenkins REST API allows you to do everything you already did using the buttons and forms, including creating jobs, which can be useful from an automation point a view. You can communicate with pretty much every part of Jenkins. To access the documentation for the available ways to communicate with a specific resource, for example, a job - simply add "/api" at the end of the URL: http://localhost:8080/job/Github%20Jobs%20for%20iOS/api. Don't forget that we secured the access to Jenkins when we installed it. That is why, if you try to fetch content to the comment line, you shouldn't forget to add your credentials. For example, if you are using cURL:

```
$ curl -u romain.pouclet:pwd http://localhost:8080/job/Github%20Jobs%20for%20iOS/api/json
{
  "actions" : [

  ],
  "description" : "",
  "displayName" : "Github Jobs for iOS",
  "displayNameOrNull" : null,
  "name" : "Github Jobs for iOS",
  "url" : "http://localhost:8080/job/Github%20Jobs%20for%20iOS/",
   ...
}
```

Creating and updating a job using the REST API uses a XML-based description of the job. If you look at the content of the config.xml for the Github Jobs for iOS job at the http://localhost:8080/job/Github%20Jobs%20for%20iOS/config.xml URL, you can retrieve the three important sections of a build.

First, the scm section that contains the URL to the git repository we want Jenkins to clone:

```
<scm class="hudson.plugins.git.GitSCM" plugin="git@2.2.1">
    <configVersion>2</configVersion>
    <userRemoteConfigs>
      <hudson.plugins.git.UserRemoteConfig>
        <url>git@github.com:Palleas/Github-Jobs.git</url>
        <credentialsId>5aeb7acd-ba7f-4687-aa8e-ba59c809eb38</credentialsId>
      </hudson.plugins.git.UserRemoteConfig>
    </userRemoteConfigs>
    <branches>
      <hudson.plugins.git.BranchSpec>
        <name>*/master</name>
      </hudson.plugins.git.BranchSpec>
    </branches>
    <doGenerateSubmoduleConfigurations>false</doGenerateSubmoduleConfigurations>
    <submoduleCfg class="list"/>
    <extensions/>
  </scm>
```

Second, the builders section contains the list of build phases we've added. This includes the shell script installing the dependencies using cocoapods, and the Xcode build that builds the app:

```
<builders>
  <hudson.tasks.Shell>
    <command>pod install</command>
  </hudson.tasks.Shell>
  <au.com.rayh.XCodeBuilder plugin="xcode-plugin@1.4.2">
    <cleanBeforeBuild>false</cleanBeforeBuild>
    <cleanTestReports>true</cleanTestReports>
    <configuration>AdHoc</configuration>
    <target></target>
    <sdk></sdk>
    <symRoot></symRoot>
    <configurationBuildDir>${WORKSPACE}/build</configurationBuildDir>
    <xcodeProjectPath></xcodeProjectPath>
    <xcodeProjectFile></xcodeProjectFile>
    <xcodebuildArguments></xcodebuildArguments>
    <xcodeSchema>Github Jobs</xcodeSchema>
    <xcodeWorkspaceFile>Github Jobs</xcodeWorkspaceFile>
    <embeddedProfileFile></embeddedProfileFile>
    <cfBundleVersionValue></cfBundleVersionValue>
    <cfBundleShortVersionStringValue></cfBundleShortVersionStringValue>
    <buildIpa>true</buildIpa>
    <generateArchive>false</generateArchive>
    <unlockKeychain>true</unlockKeychain>
    <keychainName>none (specify one below)</keychainName>
    <keychainPath>${HOME}/Library/Keychains/login.keychain</keychainPath>
    <keychainPwd>keychain-password</keychainPwd>
    <codeSigningIdentity></codeSigningIdentity>
    <allowFailingBuildResults>false</allowFailingBuildResults>
```

```
      <ipaName></ipaName>
      <ipaOutputDirectory></ipaOutputDirectory>
      <provideApplicationVersion>false</provideApplicationVersion>
   </au.com.rayh.XCodeBuilder>
</builders>
```

Finally, the `publishers` section show the artifact archiving post-build phase:

```
<publishers>
   <hudson.tasks.ArtifactArchiver>
      <artifacts>**/*.ipa</artifacts>
      <latestOnly>false</latestOnly>
      <allowEmptyArchive>false</allowEmptyArchive>
   </hudson.tasks.ArtifactArchiver>
</publishers>
```

The config.xml export file is pretty simple to understand and looks a lot like the plist representation of an Objective-C object conforming to the NSCoding protocol. This feature is also convenient because it will allow you to update a job by posting an updated config.xml to the same URL.

Enabling or disabling a job is just as easy with the Jenkins REST API, all you need to do is send a POST request to the /disable and /enable endpoint. What is even more interesting is that you can trigger a build using the /build endpoint, but there are some security issues that you may want to take into account.

When you created the Github for iOS job, you may have noticed a "Trigger Builds Remotely" option in the "Build Triggers" section of the form. This option, as shown in Figure 5-9, allows you to add an authentication token that will be used to secure a call to /build endpoint.

```
$ curl -v http://localhost:8080/job/Github%20Jobs%20for%20iOS/build?token=BewareMyToken
```

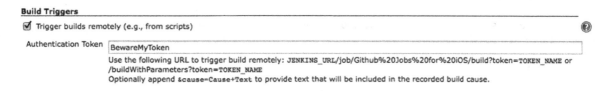

Figure 5-9. Adding a token to secure a call to the HTTP endpoint will trigger a build

You shouldn't rely on this token though, because even if it is still available in the job creation form, it is considered deprecated and may be removed in future releases of Jenkins. Instead, you should use the basic authentication just like you've been doing so far.

```
$ curl -X POST -u romain.pouclet:pwd http://localhost:8080/job/Github%20Jobs%20for%20iOS/build
```

If the build was created, the result should be a response with a "201 Created" status code and the "Location" header should contain the URL of the item that was just created in the queue. The queue is a list of jobs that should be performed. It comes with its own separate API.

The great part about having this API around is that it makes it super easy to interact with Jenkins using a script. We will talk a little more about in the "Getting feedback" section. What you should remember is that you're now aware of a way to trigger the build: manually or calling an HTTP URL. Let's keep going!

Jenkins from the Command Line

If the HTTP REST API didn't make Jenkins "hackable" enough for you, you can also use a command line tool for Jenkins. Written in Java, it will allow you to perform different operations in the simplest approach. To download the Jenkins command line tool, simply visit the "/cli" section of your installation (which would give you something like `http://localhost:8080/cli`) and retrieve the URL to the JAR file. Copy the URL and enter the following commands in your terminal. The first time you will use the command line tool, you will get a warning saying you cannot be authenticated.

```
$ cd ~/Tools
$ curl http://localhost:8080/jnlpJars/jenkins-cli.jar -O
$ java -jar jenkins-cli.jar -s http://localhost:8080 who-am-i
[WARN] Failed to authenticate with your SSH keys. Proceeding as anonymous
```

This time, you won't be able to simply enter a login and password to authenticate against your Jenkins installation, even if you can pass a --username argument to any command to have your password prompted. This method is not recommended. What you need instead is to associate a SSH public key to your profile, available at the "/me/configure" URL, or by clicking on your name at the top right of screen and then click the Configure link in the left menu.

You probably already have a SSH public key stored in your ~/.ssh folder, but we will use the one we generated earlier to communicate with Github. Retrieve the content of the public key stored at ~/Jenkins/Jenkins.key.pub and paste it to the "SSH Public Keys" text area. Press Save, go back to your terminal, and re-run the previous command with the –i option that specifies the private key to use for authentication.

```
$ java -jar jenkins-cli.jar -s http://localhost:8080 -i ~/Tools/jenkins.key who-am-i
Authenticated as: romain.pouclet
Authorities:
  authenticated
```

Of course, using this command with the -s and -i options is a bit annoying, especially if you want to use it multiple times. You can avoid having to specify the Identity file if you use the one stored at ~/.ssh/id_rsa[.pub], which is the default path where ssh-keygen will store the SSH key. Plus, the server option is also a non-issue since, once again, you will be saved by an environment variable, in this situation, the JENKINS_URL environment variable, which you only have to declare once.

```
$ export JENKINS_URL=http://localhost:8080
$ java -jar jenkins-cli.jar who-am-i
Authenticated as: romain.pouclet
Authorities:
  authenticated
```

Just like the REST API, you can export the XML representation of a job:

```
$ java -jar jenkins-cli.jar get-job "Github Jobs for iOS"
```

You can enable/disable a job:

```
$ java -jar jenkins-cli.jar disable-job "Github Jobs for iOS"
```

And, finally, you can trigger a build:

```
$ java -jar jenkins-cli.jar build -w -s "Github Jobs for iOS"
Started Github Jobs for iOS #29
Completed Github Jobs for iOS #29 : SUCCESS
```

As you can see, communicating with Jenkins can be done through multiple different ways, some of which we haven't covered yet. If you don't like starting your command with the java -jar... command, it is also possible to communicate with Jenkins directly via SSH. In fact, if you look at the headers returned by an HTTP call to your installation of Jenkins's homepage, you can see some SSH-related headers in the response that gives you the host and the port on which SSH is listening:

```
$ curl -D - http://localhost:8080 -o /dev/null
...
X-Jenkins-CLI-Port: 52722
X-SSH-Endpoint: localhost:52716
...

$ ssh -p 52716 romain.pouclet@localhost who-am-i
Authenticated as: romain.pouclet
Authorities:
  authenticated
```

We won't be covering the Jenkins SSH endpoint in detail since it is very similar to the way the Jenkins CLI works. There are some obvious advantages for all these access points: HTTP makes it very easy to automate things from scripts and command line tools are powerful ways of communicating with Jenkins manually. The obvious advantage of the CLI is having a list of all the available commands without having to looking for the "REST API" links at the bottom of the pages you'd like to interact with.

What's important to realize is that if you haven't found a way to communicate with Jenkins that suits your needs, you probably haven't looked hard enough.

Getting Feedback

Having a continuous integration platform that builds your application is useless if you forget to run the build, that's why your platform needs to take care of that part for you. Most repository hosting services come with hooks that can call a URL as soon as you've pushed new commits to your remote repository. You can also decide to automatically build your master branch every day at 10 o'clock and create what's called a nightly build. What's important is to keep your job's health report meaningful.

For every job that you create, Jenkins calculates a health report based on the result of the few latest builds and represents it with a little weather icon. As you can see in Figure 5-10, our project is doing great since it's a simple project that has no reason whatsoever not to build successfully.

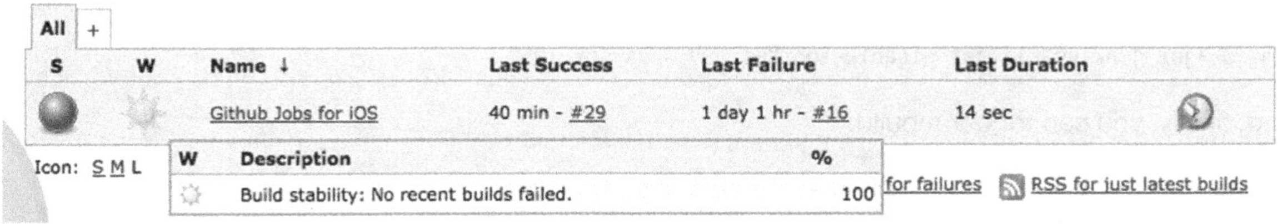

Figure 5-10. If the past builds are all passed, the project is doing great

The health report is based on the result of the previous builds, which is pretty abstract since it only considers the final result: passing or failing. Of course, a passing build does not mean that a job is going great. We will talk more about this in the section about unit testing but consider the following context: a project with a lot of tests failing. Out of laziness, lack of priorities, or a tight deadline, the failing tests have been deactivated and your project sure isn't going great. It is up to you to keep this health report meaningful by adding a bit of context, such as the "Project Health Report Plugin" that can create more detailed reports, as shown in Figure 5-11. By now, you should be able to install it by yourself.

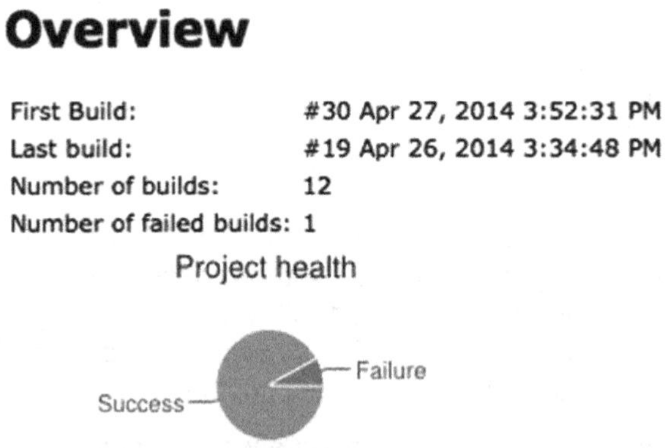

Overview

First Build:	#30 Apr 27, 2014 3:52:31 PM
Last build:	#19 Apr 26, 2014 3:34:48 PM
Number of builds:	12
Number of failed builds:	1

Project health

Figure 5-11. The "project health report" plugin shows a more detailed overview of the project's health

Receiving Notifications and Fixing the Build Right Away

If you want a project to be healthy, there is nothing more important than fixing the build. It's pretty easy to just think, "I'll fix the build later", and forget about it. Even if the application works on your computer and your testing devices, your coworkers may not know that.

To be able to fix the build right away, you need to be notified as soon as the build fails, for example, with a simple e-mail. The default installation of Jenkins will use localhost and a bunch of default settings as the SMTP server to send those e-mails, which is probably not going to work if you haven't got one running. To escape this situation, you can simply use the credentials of your Gmail account, in the E-mail Notifications form that's in the Jenkins system configuration section, which provides a way to test the configuration. Once this is done, all you need to do is add a new post-build action at the end of the "Github Jobs for iOS" job configuration, as shown in Figure 5-12.

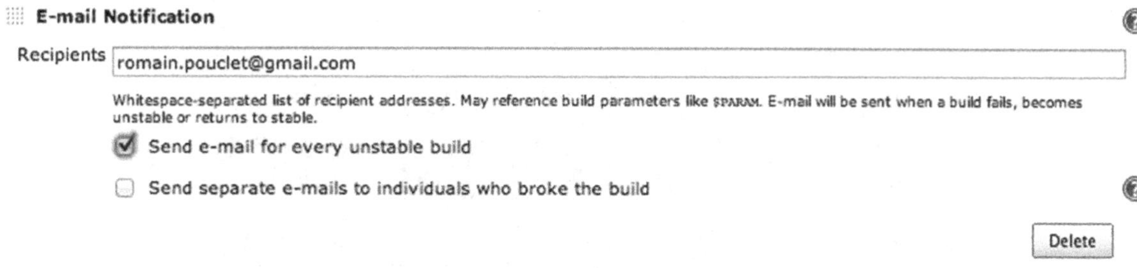

Figure 5-12. *For each unstable build, the user behind* `romain.pouclet@gmail.com` *will receive an e-mail*

Every time a build is failing, someone will be notified with an e-mail containing a direct link to the build. The console output shows exactly what happens so you can slap yourself because you forgot, once again, to share a scheme or to install your dependencies before building the application.

See <http://localhost:8080/job/Github%20Jobs%20for%20iOS/34/>

```
-----------------------------------------
Started by user Romain Pouclet
Building in workspace <http://localhost:8080/job/Github%20Jobs%20for%20iOS/ws/>
Fetching changes from the remote Git repository
Fetching upstream changes from git@github.com:Palleas/Github-Jobs.git
using GIT_SSH to set credentials Palleas Jenkins private key to communicate with github
Checking out Revision 948ff10d7228ec8d1d6bda405d403aef9150a336 (origin/master)
Working directory is http://localhost:8080/job/Github%20Jobs%20for%20iOS/ws/.
...
```

At a time when every once in a while a new startup comes up with a new service that will revolutionize the way you communicate within your company by removing e-mails, it may seem a little bit weird to use them to be notified of a failing build. The thing is, e-mail notifications come free with a standard installation of Jenkins. If you need something that would fit better in your company such as a message in a specific chat room, there probably is a plugin for that. In fact, you should carefully consider the notification type you are going to use. If you hate receiving e-mails, you won't even bother reading the one from Jenkins, you won't fix the builds, and we'll be back to square one.

Watching the State of Multiple Projects

So far the approaches we've covered are useful from a developer's point of view, somebody who can actually do something about the failing build. You don't really want your boss to receive those e-mails (and he probably doesn't either). Plus, these notifications are project specific and sometimes you may want to get a wider look at how things are going.

This is why there are plugins that will show the state of multiple jobs, such as the "Wall Display Plugin". As you can see in Figure 5-13, you can use these kind of plugins to show how a project is going, including the Android version of your application, the backend, and so on.

Figure 5-13. *State of the "Github Jobs" project with all the platforms*

Finally, if you don't like the look or you want something more suited to your needs or integrated in another solution, you can still use the feed available at /cc.xml. When the first version of Jenkins/Hodson was released, CruiseControl was dominating the market of the automated build platform and got to set a standard:

```
<?xml version="1.0" ?>
<Projects>
    <Project activity="Sleeping" lastBuildLabel="1" lastBuildStatus="Success" lastBuildTime="2014-
    04-27T22:06:35Z" name="Github Jobs Backend" webUrl="http://localhost:8080/job/Github%20Jobs%20
    Backend/"/>
    <Project activity="Sleeping" lastBuildLabel="1" lastBuildStatus="Failure" lastBuildTime="2014-
    04-27T21:05:02Z" name="Github Jobs for Android" webUrl="http://localhost:8080/job/Github%20
    Jobs%20for%20Android/"/>
    <Project activity="Sleeping" lastBuildLabel="35" lastBuildStatus="Success" lastBuildTime="2014-
    04-27T21:03:55Z" name="Github Jobs for iOS" webUrl="http://localhost:8080/job/Github%20Jobs%20
    for%20iOS/"/>
</Projects>
```

Now that we know what Jenkins can do for us, let's go back to our Github Jobs for iOS application and update the job so it meets our need.

Integrating Our Build Script

We already covered how to build the Github Jobs application using the Xcode Build plugin that does everything for us, and more. The problem with this kind of plugin is that they act kind of like a "black box", not necessarily in a mean way, since most of them are open-source. The thing is, they abstract a lot of what's happening and add a lot of complexity when we managed to have a build script in about ten lines, including the shebang and the comments. Plus, in case you run into an environment-specific build issue, re-running the build script manually is simply a SSH command away.

With that in mind, go back to the job we created and remove the "Xcode" build phase. Since the script we wrote also handles the installation of the dependencies using Cocoapods, empty the text area of the "Execute Shell" build phase and fill in the following command (don't forget the quotes):

```
"$WORKSPACE/bin/cibuild"
```

If you remember the previous chapter, our script uses xcpretty to make the xcode output more understandable and well, pretty. The problem is that a Jenkins' build console output is plain text, unless you install the AnsiColor Plugin. Once this is done and you've checked the "Color ANSI Console Output" option in the "Build Environment" section, re-run the job and go to the Console Output section of the job. You should see a colorized output, just like the one in Figure 5-14.

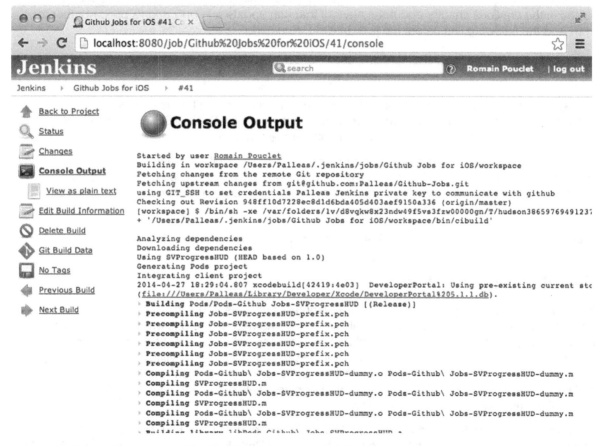

Figure 5-14. The output of the job building the Github Jobs application, with colors

Going back to the script we entered, the $WORKSPACE is yet another environment variable provided by Jenkins for you to use in your build scripts. There are about 15 environment variables available to shell scripts that are listed at "`http://localhost:8080/env-vars.html/`". $JENKINS_HOME and $WORKSPACE are absolute paths, respective to the directory where Jenkins is installed (in our case that would be ~/.jenkins) and to the directory where our repository's content has been stored (in our case /Users/Palleas/.jenkins/jobs/Github Jobs for iOS/workspace). We already used the second one to locate our build script and we could easily find a use for the BUILD_NUMBER one.

Updating the Build Number

Go back to the "Github Jobs" project and open the cibuild script in your favorite text editor. We talked in the previous chapter about the agvtool that can update an application's build number for you. Add the following line before the pod install command:

```
agvtool new-version -all ${BUILD_NUMBER:?"BUILD_NUMBER should be set, are you sure this script is run within a ci job?"}
```

The syntax should not feel strange until the last part. We are using a little bash trick called "parameter expansion". Basically what it means is that if the BUILD_NUMBER variable is not available (or empty), the script will exit with a non-zero return code.

While we are updating the build script and testing that it works well, your Jenkins instance is probably not accessible from the outside so your repository hosting service cannot automatically send a request to automatically trigger a build every time you push. From now on, you should consider running the following command:

```
$ git push && java -jar ~/Jenkins/jenkins-cli.jar build "Github Jobs for iOS"
```

Unlocking the Keychain

In our script, we also rely on a PASSWORD environment variable to unlock the keychain before code-signing the application. It wasn't really secured to hard-code the password in our build script so we found a simple hack where we declared the environment variable right before running the script. That wasn't a whole lot secured, but at least the password wasn't visible in the repository. We won't be able to use the same hack and write the password in the job's configuration form. To keep things secure, we will need to use another plugin called "Mask Password". Go back to the Jenkins' configuration section and install it.

Once that is done, go the "Github Jobs" jenkins job's configuration and look for the "mask passwords (and enable global passwords)" option in the "Build Environment" section. Click the add button and add your password there, as shown in Figure 5-15.

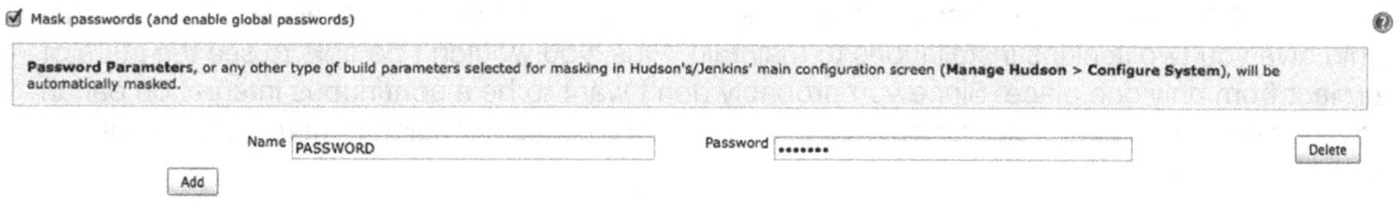

☑ Mask passwords (and enable global passwords)

Password Parameters, or any other type of build parameters selected for masking in Hudson's/Jenkins' main configuration screen (**Manage Hudson > Configure System**), will be automatically masked.

Name `PASSWORD`   Password •••••••   Delete

Add

Figure 5-15. Adding a password as an environment variable to be used in the build script

That's it! Our script should be unlocking the keychain automatically. Don't be afraid about storing your password like this. The password is properly encoded and stored in the config.xml file we mentioned earlier. It will be even safer if you use a global password defined from the Jenkins' administration. Plus, even if you add a new execute shell build step running the following script: echo $PASSWORD, the output of this command (meaning, the password) will be automatically obfuscated by the plugin.

Cleaning up after yourself

There is one final step we haven't mentioned that you really need to think about in this context. Remember that the very first phase of a job is to fetch content from a remote repository and then actually perform some tasks, and one of our tasks consists of updating the build number. This means changing information in multiple places and after running our script, this is the state of our working copy:

```
$ git status --short
 M "Github Jobs.xcodeproj/project.pbxproj"
 M "Github Jobs/Github Jobs-Info.plist"
 M "Github JobsTests/Github JobsTests-Info.plist"
```

That's not good. The next time the new content is pulled from the remote repository, if one of these three files has been modified, a conflict will happen and the build will fail. That is why you need to clean up after yourself. To do that, you have multiple options. The easiest one is to open the "Additional Behaviours" dropdown in the "Source Code Management" section of your build and select "Clean before checkout": it will restore the workspace to a clean state and new content will be pulled safely.

Integrating Xcode Builds into an Existing Jenkins Installation

Sometimes in a company, iOS development may not be the only kind of development that is done. Other mobile developments, such as Android or Blackberry, backend developments using PHP, Java, or Ruby, all of these technologies can be run in pretty much every environment. If iOS development happened later, you may find yourself with a Jenkins already installed on a non-OSX platform that won't be able to run Xcode and build iOS applications.

The easy solution would be to install a new Jenkins dedicated to building iOS applications but that would give you two Jenkins installations to maintain. Plus, you wouldn't be able to see the state of a project from only one place. Since you probably don't want to be a continuous integration pariah and actually want to play well with others, you may want to consider using a more suited solution called "slave nodes".

Slave Node Basics

A Jenkins slave node is basically a lightweight Jenkins instance running on a dedicated node and can be used for scalability purposes, when your instance is building a lot of things and you want to balance the load among multiple builders. The other situation is where you need to build a job on a platform with specific requirements, like being able to run Xcode and the command line tools.

At this point, there is nothing you're about to do that you haven't done before: diving into the manage Jenkins section, adding dedicated credentials, filling text fields, and checking checkboxes.

Anatomy of a Jenkins Slave Node

Open Jenkins' manage section and click on the "manage nodes" link. You should see the master node, meaning the installation of Jenkins you've been running since the beginning of this chapter. Click on the "New Node" link in the left menu. In the form that appears, select the "Dumb Slave" option – which should be the only option available – and fill in the text field a name for the node. Feel free to get creative, but a pragmatic approach would suggest calling it "Xcode builder" for example. Once you've found a name, press OK.

Creating a node is pretty simple. Once you've found the name (and eventually the description), there are a few mandatory fields you need to fill: where the builds will be performed, the labels associated with this node, and how to communicate with this node.

The "Remote FS root" is an absolute path on the slave node of where the jobs will be stored. Think of it as a remote equivalent of the ~/.jenkins/jobs folder on your desktop. Since you will be talking to a remote computer running OS X, you should use the home directory and fill in something like /Users/RemoteUserName/JenkinsBuilds.

The labels are pretty important as well. When you use slave nodes, you don't explicitly tell where you want your build your jobs to be ran. Instead, you set a list of restrictions so Jenkins can find a node that meets those requirements. Fill in the "labels" with "xcode".

Finally, there are multiple launch methods available to start the communication with a slave node, but we are going to use the SSH one. Select the "Launch Slave Agents on Unix Machines via SSH" option from the combo box. In the Host field, enter the IP address of your node. Just like we did to configure the connection with Github, we are going to use Jenkins' credentials storage to authenticate with the remote host. Click on the "Add" link near the combo box and fill in the credentials you use to connect to this computer. It may be a username and a password, or a private key. The former is probably the more secure approach, but the node cannot be accessed from the outside; so a username and a password will do just fine. Note that you will have to enable the remote access from the node if you want to be able to connect to it via SSH.

At the end of this process, your form should look like the one in Figure 5-16.

Figure 5-16. *The node is ready to be created*

The node should be started automatically. If the log shows an error, make sure the credentials you are trying to use are valid, that you entered the proper host and port, that the remote access is activated, and that the computer has a valid java installation. The communication between the master node and the slave one goes through a slave.jar archive that is copied on the slave node via SFTP the first time the master connects to it.

```
$ ssh Camille@192.168.1.14
$ cd /JenkinsBuilds
$ ls
slave.jar
```

If you go back to the "Github Jobs for iOS" and click on the configure link, a new configuration section has appeared so you can tell your job to be run on a computer that runs Xcode. Check the "Restrict Where this Project Can be Run" checkbox and fill in the "Label Expression" field with "xcode", which is the label we entered above, as shown in Figure 5-17.

Figure 5-17. *The application will be built on a slave that can run xcode*

That's all there is to do!

Managing Provisioning Profiles and Private Keys

In this chapter, we've been building and code signing applications multiple times and there is one final thing we haven't covered: what should we do about our provisioning profiles and private keys? The usual answer is simple: there is no magic solution. The provisioning profiles are stored in your Library folder, and you can find them with this simple command:

```
$ ls -l /Users/Palleas/Library/MobileDevice/Provisioning\ Profiles
-rw-r--r--  1 Palleas staff  15799  4 Apr 11:22 0255A8B8-3DD3-4893-8E6E-9F6664DF89B5.mobileprovision
-rw-r--r--  1 Palleas staff  14153 26 Dec 17:06 05A46FE9-236E-4B40-8625-57A857155A7F.mobileprovision
-rw-r--r--  1 Palleas staff  15775  4 Apr 11:22 10F8378B-6638-4A94-AB4B-E505BF562DA9.mobileprovision
-rw-r--r--  1 Palleas staff  15757  4 Apr 11:22 18E20B0C-9446-4A68-A4F2-3483D02624E2.mobileprovision
-rw-r--r--  1 Palleas staff  15846  4 Apr 11:22 1F908F91-7B22-4B31-8629-7D286FE20ECD.mobileprovision
-rw-r--r--  1 Palleas staff  15787  4 Apr 11:22 1FA4FB89-845B-43B9-98DC-07A26B5F3920.mobileprovision
...
```

The private keys are stored in the keychain and we've already used the security command line tools for some basic keychain manipulation but there are other keychain-related methods we haven't covered. You could probably manipulate the keychain on the computer that is running your builds via SSH and install provisioning profiles the same way.

The thing is, even Apple has made huge progress with the management of code signing identities, it remains a complex concept that could be easily solved by plugging a screen into your building computer once and running Xcode manually the first time you want to build an app, making sure everything works smoothly. Once again, there is no silver bullet but we are slowly getting there.

Where Do We Go From Here?

Congratulations, you've set up a pretty decent continuous integration platform. For now, it doesn't do much but in the chapters. We'll use it to deploy the application over the air and update the build process to have a more detailed feedbacks with unit tests and quality assurance tools.

Summary

This chapter was about giving you a tour of the most used continuous integration platform in the world. Now, you will be able to detect if a coworker forgot to check the "Copy Items into Destination's Group" checkbox when he tried to import a new framework into the project (although he or she should have used Cocoapods). We hope you've understood by now why a neutral building platform is important and what you need to do to keep it useful for your team.

The next chapter will cover an alternative solution made by an Australian company called "Atlassian" Bamboo.

Chapter 6

Automated builds with Bamboo

In the previous chapter, we talked a lot about Jenkins, the open source automated build platform. Even if it comes with some issues and weird behaviors, we really hope that at the end of the chapter you realized what a great platform it actually is. We've showed you how easy it is to get it started and described the benefits of having one at home. The question you might me asking yourself right now is "why do we need another one?" That's a good question but before we answer it, let's make one thing clear: this book does not aim to promote Bamboo over Jenkins. This is a simple introduction to how Bamboo will help you in your day-to-day work as an iOS developer.

Bamboo is a commercial product created by an Australian company named Atlassian, also responsible for products like Confluence and, of course, Jira. If you've already been looking for a bug tracker, you've probably run into Jira at least once and may be using it at your company. If that's the case, then you will be happy to know that Bamboo is deeply integrated with Jira, making it super easy to create issues from a failing build, for example.

What is a good enough reason to switch from a free, open source platform to a paying, semi-proprietary one (some of the components are open-source and sources are available for you to hack with the right license)? To be honest, we are not here to give you a reason; we're here to tell you about a different approach Atlassian took when they started working on Bamboo.

At the end of this chapter, we really hope that we will have given you a good look into Bamboo and that you will be able to choose which solution works best for your company.

The previous chapter was kind of a journey that helped you discover Jenkins and the wonderful world of continuous integration platforms. Now that you know everything there is to know to get started, we will use a lot less naïve approach with Bamboo and will try to go as straight as possible to the point: building the Github Jobs iOS application using the bash script we've been working on for the past three chapters. To do that, we will probably have to make some references to the way Jenkins works.

Getting started with Bamboo

If you were expecting software based on a less-bloated platform you will be disappointed: Bamboo is written in Java. If you've been playing with Jenkins as we did in the previous chapters, chances are you will be able to install and configure Bamboo on your computer: Bamboo only requires a valid Java environment.

Let's get started and download a trial version of Bamboo from the Atlassian trial page available at this address: https://www.atlassian.com/software/bamboo/try/. Click on the "Start My Free Trial" button in the "Download section". Bamboo, like most of the Atlassian products, also comes as an "OnDemand" solution, which gives you access to a cloud version of Bamboo. The same solutions are available to you if you chose to stick with Jenkins. For example, Cloudbees (http://www.cloudbees.com) is a cloud platform focused on Java and provides multiple services like installations of Jenkins in the cloud. If these solutions have the neat advantages of leaving the developer and system administrator work to someone who actually likes it, they usually come at a far bigger price than self-hosted solutions.

Once you've clicked on the: "Start my free trial" button, copy the "tar.gz" link, we'll need it in the next section.

Installing Bamboo using the command line

The great thing about Bamboo, just like Jenkins, is that it works out of the box. All you need to do is to download the archive, and run the proper commands. In our case, that would be tar to decompress the archive, and a simple bash script with the proper arguments to keep Bamboo running in the foreground, for now.

```
$ mkdir ~/Bamboo
$ curl -L http://www.atlassian.com/software/bamboo/downloads/binary/atlassian-bamboo-5.5.0.tar.gz -O
$ tar -zxvf atlassian-bamboo-5.5.0.tar.gz
$ cd atlassian-bamboo-5.5.0
$ bin/start-bamboo.sh -fg


Server startup logs are located in /Users/Palleas/Bamboo/atlassian-bamboo-5.5.0/logs/catalina.out
Bamboo Standalone Edition
    Version : 5.5.0
Detecting JVM PermGen support...
PermGen switch is supported. Setting to 256m
If you encounter issues starting or stopping Bamboo Standalone Edition, please see the
Troubleshooting guide at https://confluence.atlassian.com/display/BAMBOO/Bamboo+installation+guide
Using CATALINA_BASE:   /Users/Palleas/Projects/Apress/Bamboo/atlassian-bamboo-5.5.0
Using CATALINA_HOME:   /Users/Palleas/Projects/Apress/Bamboo/atlassian-bamboo-5.5.0
Using CATALINA_TMPDIR: /Users/Palleas/Projects/Apress/Bamboo/atlassian-bamboo-5.5.0/temp
Using JRE_HOME:        /Library/Java/JavaVirtualMachines/jdk1.7.0_25.jdk/Contents/Home
Using CLASSPATH:       /Users/Palleas/Projects/Apress/Bamboo/atlassian-bamboo-5.5.0/bin/bootstrap.
jar:/Users/Palleas/Projects/Apress/Bamboo/atlassian-bamboo-5.5.0/bin/tomcat-juli.jar
May 05, 2014 7:26:38 PM org.apache.catalina.core.AprLifecycleListener init
...
INFO: Server startup in 13062 ms
```

If everything worked as expected, you should see the final "server startup in…" message. If you didn't get this message but an error, check that Java is properly installed running the following command:

```
$ java -version
java version "1.7.0_25"
Java(TM) SE Runtime Environment (build 1.7.0_25-b15)
Java HotSpot(TM) 64-Bit Server VM (build 23.25-b01, mixed mode)
```

If Java is properly installed but Bamboo still isn't starting on your computer, you can always contact Atlassian and get someone to help you with the setup. In fact, that is one of the advantages of working with a paying product: technical support.

Before we jump to the browser and open the bamboo website we've just bootstrapped (available at http://localhost:8085), we need to specify Bamboo's "home" directory (Jenkins simply chose to use ~/.jenkins). Open the bamboo-init.properties file in the /WEB-INF/classes/ folder and look for the commented like containing "Bamboo.home". Uncomment it and enter the path to the directory where you want all your data to be stored. Let's use ".bamboo", so the ".jenkins" home folder doesn't feel lonely.

```
bamboo.home=/Users/Palleas/.bamboo
```

If you're not sure of the directory yet, you will be pleased to know that you can use yet another environment variable:

```
$ BAMBOO_HOME=/Users/Palleas/.bamboo bin/start-bamboo.sh -fg
```

What's important here is the -fg argument that stands for "foreground" meaning that bamboo will be run in the foreground so you can play with it and stop it whenever you like. Note that if you don't use it, there is a stop-bamboo.sh script for you to use to kill a Bamboo instance running in the background.

Open your browser and visit the http://localhost:8085 URL, you should see a form with a big textarea, that is where the fun begins. Even for demonstration purposes, you need to enter a license key that will expire in 30 days. You can ask for a license by clicking on the "contact Atlassian" link that is under the textarea and following a few steps, like creating an Atlassian account. Once that's done, paste the license key in the textarea, as shown in Figure 6-1, and get ready to press "Express installation".

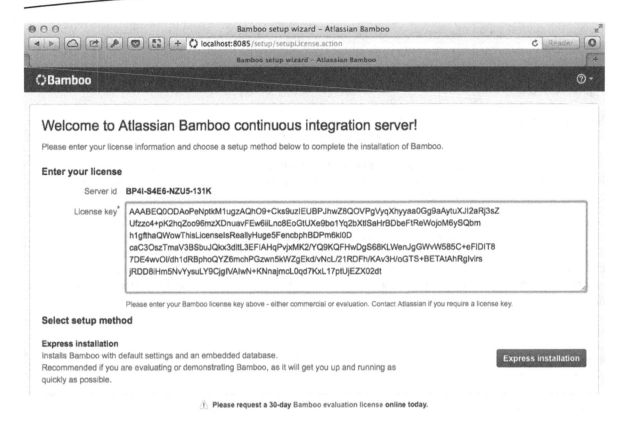

Figure 6-1. Setting up a Bamboo installation using an evaluation license key

Bamboo comes with two different installations, but we will be using the express one that doesn't need you to install a MySQL database and things like that. Instead, the express installation will setup a simpler database stored in files in your BAMBOO_HOME directory.

Press the "Express installation" button. You will be taken to a page where you will fill the administrator's credentials and then to your Bamboo installation's homepage. Congratulations, your Bamboo installation is ready!

Getting ready for production use

Right now we are only playing with Bamboo to give you a tour and show you what it can do, but don't worry. The embedded database can easily be migrated to a more permanent engine such as MySQL, as shown on the following page: https://confluence.atlassian.com/display/BAMBOO/MySQL+5.1. Plus, your data won't be lost if the trial expires, you will simply not be able to build your application, nothing that won't be solved by purchasing a permanent license.

Now that you know that nothing will prevent you from pushing it to production, let's take a look around and see how Bamboo works.

Having a look around: a different approach than Jenkins

Bamboo chose a slightly different approach when it comes to builds. There is in fact some kind of hierarchy where "Plans" are the root level. Click on the big blue "Create" button and select "create a new plan". In the form that appears, fill in "Project name" with "Github Jobs" and "Plan name" with "iOS application", as shown in Figure 6-2. If you look closely at the form, you will notice that there is actually an upper hierarchy level: projects. In fact, if you try to create a new plan, let's say one to build the Android version, you will be able to choose the Github Jobs project from a list. This a neat feature because with the proper credentials, you can give access to all the plans of a project to the members of your team.

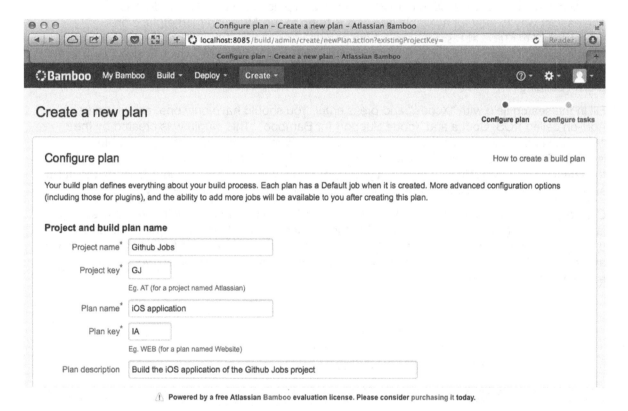

Figure 6-2. *Creating a new plan and implicitly creating a new project as well*

Once this is done, scroll down to the next section where Bamboo wants to know where the code will come from, in our case that would be Github but Bamboo also supports Stash and Bitbucket – both Atlassian products – and raw repositories for the Git, CVS, Subversion, Perforce, and Mercurial systems.

Click on the platform of your choice and fill in your credentials. Also, please note that at the time we are writing this book, the two-factor auth feature that Github deployed to add an extra layer of security to your account is not supported by Bamboo, there is in fact an issue opened on the official Bitbucket page: https://bitbucket.org/site/master/issue/5811/support-two-factor-authentication-bb-7016.

Now that the plan has been created, let's take a moment to understand what a plan actually is.

When you are trying to build an application with sources that are contained in a repository, a plan will be associated to that repository. It can contain multiple jobs, which correspond to a list of instructions to build a project, including the default job that was created when you created the plan. It also contains the instructions about how and when the build should be triggered, who should be notified of the builds' results, and who is allowed to access a plan and its jobs.

Extending Bamboo

Just like Jenkins, it is possible to extend Bamboo with plugins, here called "Add-ons". The easiest way to look for available add-ons is to go to the Atlassian marketplace on `https://marketplace.atlassian.com`, where people can sell their plugins or give them for free. What's important here is that you have a centralized list of all the plugins, which is also available from the "Manage Add-ons" section of your bamboo installation. Let's install a plugin to support Xcode project building.

Fill in the search field with "Xcode" and press enter. You should have only one result for a free Add-on called "iOS, Cocoa and Xcode Support for Bamboo". This plugin was created by the "Atlassian Labs" and will work for Bamboo 5.0. At the time we are writing this, the stable version is 5.5.0. This plugin is semi-official: it was created by Atlassian but isn't formally supported. In fact, the latest version was released almost a year ago. Don't worry, we are only installing the tool for the sake of example, we will actually be using the bash script we created in the previous chapter.

Click on the plugin title and then click on "Get It Now" to download the plugin - which is simply a java archive (JAR) file – and go back to your bamboo installation. In the top-right menu shaped into a wheel, select Add-ons. Click on the "Upload add-on" link, browse to the folder where the Xcode add-on was downloaded and press Upload. If everything worked as expected, you should see something similar to the Figure 6-3.

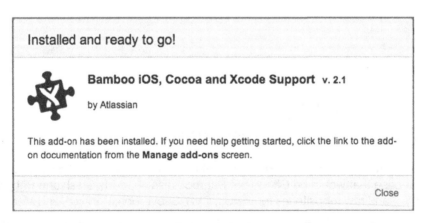

Figure 6-3. The Xcode Add-on for Bamboo was successfully installed

That's how easy it is to install Add-ons with Bamboo but just in case, let see if it actually worked and try to build the Github Jobs application. Remember that we've only created a build plan, which comes with a default build job that does… nothing.

Before we start tweaking our plan, you may be wondering why we made you install an add-on to build an Xcode project when you know we will end up using our script anyway. In the previous chapter, we installed a couple of plugins to render ANSI formatted output properly and mask the password from a build's logs. Unfortunately, we won't be able to do the same this time because adding custom variables, obfuscating the password, and formatting ANSI string are all features that come natively with a standard installation of Bamboo.

From the "Build" top menu, select "All build plans" and then click on the iOS application plan in the list that should only contain one project. Then, in the top right "Actions" menu and select "Configure plan". The "Stages" tab should be selected among an important list of tabs. We will cover a few of them later. The one that really interests us for now is indeed the "Stages" one.

What's a stage? They are simply groups of Jobs, adding a little bit more hierarchy into Bamboo. Every stage can contain multiple jobs that will be run in parallel, that would be useful for example to run unit and functional tests in parallel to save some time. Every stage represents a step within the build process. For now we will only need one: building the application.

Configuration of the default job

Click on the "Default job" in the "Default Stage", you've reached the bottom: that is the lowest level in the hierarchy. This default stage will be the building step of our continuous integration process. If you remember correctly, what we want is: fetching the latest version of the project from the git repository, install the dependencies using Cocoapods and finally build and package the application.

Contrary to the jobs contained in a Stage, steps in a job - actually called tasks - are run sequentially, just like build phases in Jenkins. With Bamboo, fetching the content from the repository is a task itself, a task you can configure if you want. There aren't many options for you to play with, but you can tell Bamboo to remove the content and re-clone the whole project every time you build your application. For an application as small as the Github Jobs one is, that would not make a huge difference but with big projects with huge resources and dependencies, this could significantly increase the duration of the build. You should leave this option unchecked for most of your builds.

In the previous chapter, we lost some time with a failing build because the dependencies where not installed properly. This time we will go straight to the point and start the build process with the installation of dependencies using Cocoapods.

1. To achieve that, click on the "Add Task" button and look for the "Script" kind of build task. Click it once you've found it.

2. In the "Task description" field fill "Installing the dependencies using Cocoapods".

3. Then, make sure the "Inline" choice is selected in the "Script location" list.

4. It is also possible to call existing scripts, which will come in handy when we use our build script but for now, simply enter "pod install" in the "Script body" text field. Finally, press "Save".

5. Now to the final part of our build! Click the "Add task" button and add an Xcode task, which will need a bit of configuration but first, enter "Building the application using xcodebuild" in the "Task description" field. What we need to do now is to add a SDK you want to build your application with.

6. To know which SDK are available, run the following command in your terminal:

```
$ xcodebuild -showsdks
OS X SDKs:
        OS X 10.8                       -sdk macosx10.8
        OS X 10.9                       -sdk macosx10.9

iOS SDKs:
        iOS 7.1                         -sdk iphoneos7.1

iOS Simulator SDKs:
        Simulator - iOS 7.1             -sdk iphonesimulator7.1
```

7. Click on "Add new executable".

8. In the "label" field enter "iOS 7.1" and in the "Path" one, enter the SDK of your choice. In our case, that would be "iphoneos7.1". Note that the help text under the field suggests you to fill in "Path to the Xcode executable including the -sdk argument eg '/Developer/usr/bin/xcodebuild -sdk iphoneos42'", which is wrong on many levels: the developers tools moved from the / Developer directory a while back and the field only wants a value to pass to the -sdk argument of the xcodebuild command. If you were to listen to what the documentation says, you would end up trying to build the application with the following command, since the plugin doesn't check that you've entered a valid SDK:

```
/usr/bin/xcodebuild clean build -sdk /Applications/Xcode.app/Contents/Developer/usr/bin/
xcodebuild -workspace Github Jobs -scheme Github Jobs
```

We suffered so you don't have to. If you try to run the previous command, xcodebuild would throw the following error:

```
xcodebuild: error: SDK "/Applications/Xcode.app/Contents/Developer/usr/bin/xcodebuild"
cannot be located.
```

9. If you entered an invalid SDK, you can add more until you get it right, but in case you want to edit or remove an existing SDK (which are actually executables in disguise), go to the Overview section and in the left menu, select "Executables". You should see a list of the executables available in your Bamboo installation, including the iOS 7.1 one, as shown in Figure 6-4.

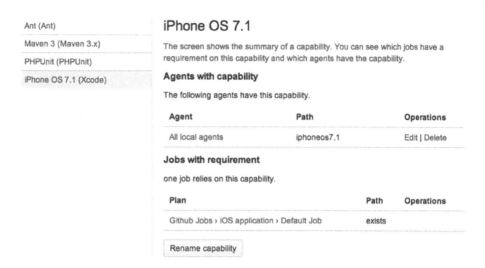

Figure 6-4. *The SDK we added from the Xcode task is now available as an executable*

Don't worry; we will cover how Bamboo manages its executables and why it is actually useful in the next section.

10.   Unfold the "Workspace" section and fill in the Workspace field with "Github Jobs.xcworkspace" and "Github Jobs" in the "Scheme" one. Please note that it gives you a very important advice right under the Workspace field: "First ensure that you share the workspace within Xcode otherwise the build may fail with an error" and that it asks for the actual filename of the workspace, including the "xcworkspace" extension. Your Xcode task configuration should look like the one in Figure 6-5.

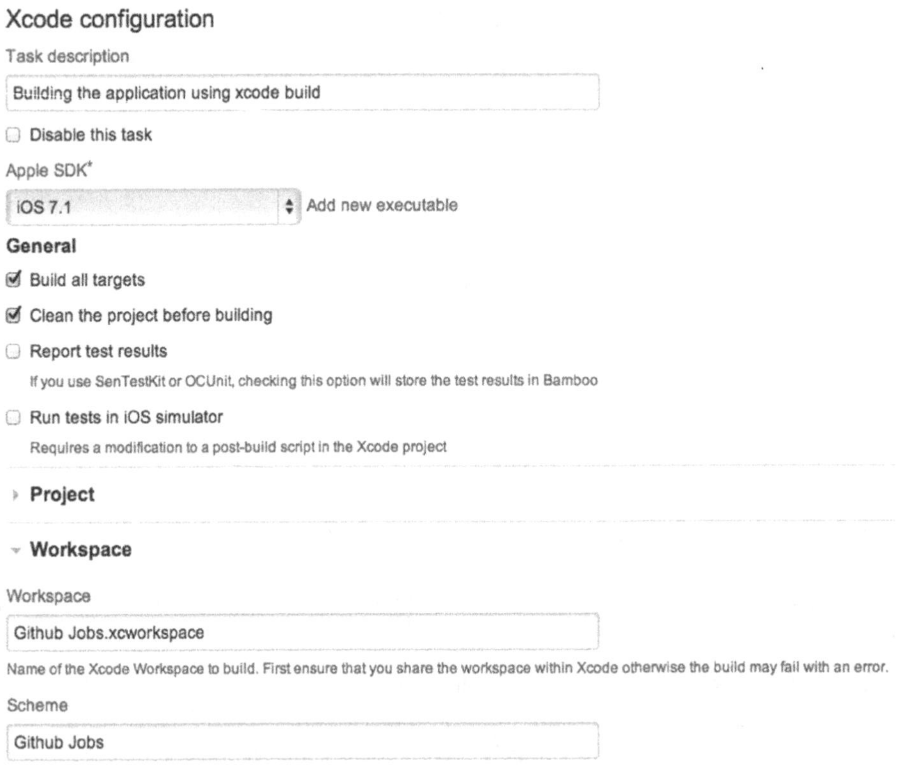

Xcode configuration

Task description

Building the application using xcode build

☐ Disable this task

Apple SDK*

iOS 7.1   ⬍   Add new executable

General

☑ Build all targets

☑ Clean the project before building

☐ Report test results

If you use SenTestKit or OCUnit, checking this option will store the test results in Bamboo

☐ Run tests in iOS simulator

Requires a modification to a post-build script in the Xcode project

▸ **Project**

▾ **Workspace**

Workspace

Github Jobs.xcworkspace

Name of the Xcode Workspace to build. First ensure that you share the workspace within Xcode otherwise the build may fail with an error.

Scheme

Github Jobs

Figure 6-5. Configuration of the Xcode task

Now that the build has been properly configured, it is time to run it. To do that, click on the Run button at the top-right corner of the screen. In the menu that will appear, select run plan. If everything worked as expected, you should see a green message saying the build #1 was successful. Congratulations, you've built an iOS application using Bamboo!

Summing up the Bamboo Basics

Let's sum up what we've just did, because understanding the hierarchy and the pieces that click together is important if you wish to use Bamboo as your continuous integration platform. We created a plan for the Github Jobs for iOS application, part of the Github Jobs project. In this plan, a default stage containing a default job was automatically created. We customized this default job with multiple tasks: fetching the content from our git repository, installing the dependencies using Cocoapods and building the application using xcodebuild.

Once again, if there is something to remember it's that you should not be using plugin for critical parts of your build. In this particular situation, the Xcode plugin hasn't been updated for more than a year. Plus, the wrong documentation really doesn't help.

With that in mind, let's build our iOS application and package it into a valid IPA file. To achieve that, we'll use the bash script we've used in the previous chapter, available at bin/cibuild in our project.

Building the Github Jobs application

Go back to the configuration section of your job and remove all the tasks but the Source Code Checkout and add a new Script task instead. Fill in the description field with "invoking the bash cibuild script" and this time, select "File" as the script location. In the "Script file" field, enter ${bamboo.build.working.directory}/bin/cibuild. Note that you could have simply used bin/cibuild but using an absolute path a) allow us to indicate that multiple global variables are available and b) allow us to make sure we are invoking the right script.

Using environment variables

In order for our script to work, there are two mandatory parameters we need to provide our script: the required password, used to unlock the keychain, and the build number, used to invoke agvtool to bump the build version. We've already used one of the numerous global variables available during the execution of a job in Bamboo: "bamboo.build.working.directory". There is also one available containing the build number named "bamboo.buildNumber". These are not environment variables per se but runtime variables, which mean that when you'll use them, they will be replaced by their actual values during the execution of the job. This is actually a good thing, this way you can choose the list of variable to provide your script with, and avoid risks of potential collateral damages.

In the "Environment variables" field, declare your environment variable using the following syntax:

```
BUILD_NUMBER=${bamboo.buildNumber}
```

Now press "Save", even if the configuration of the task is not over. You could simply add the PASSWORD environment variable using the same syntax but once again, you do not want to show the password in a build's log. That's not very secure. Fortunately, you easily can add new runtime variables at the Plan level, meaning they will be available for all the jobs contained in that plan.

Click on the "Plan configuration" link in the left menu and select the "variables" tab. Create a new variable named "bamboo.keychain.password" and fill in the value field with your password. Note that Bamboo has a pretty clever way of handling those variables: if the name of the variable contains the word "password", the value field will automatically become a password field, and every use of the created variable will be obfuscated so the password doesn't appear in the logs. Press "Add", you should see something similar to what's in Figure 6-6.

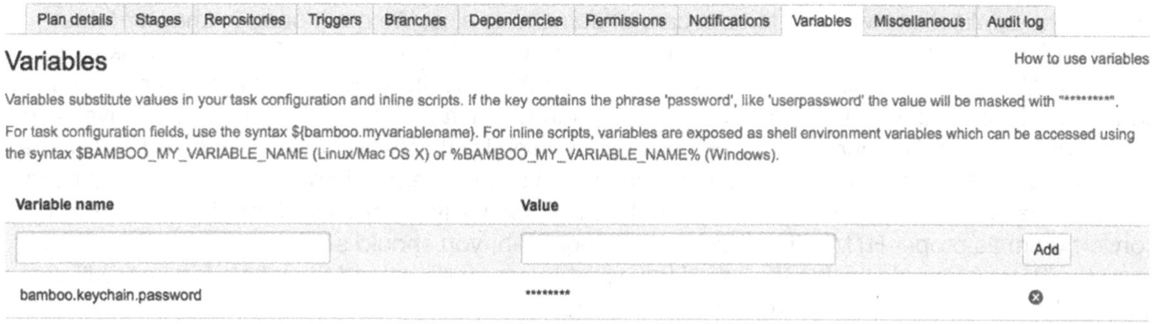

| Plan details | Stages | Repositories | Triggers | Branches | Dependencies | Permissions | Notifications | Variables | Miscellaneous | Audit log |

Variables

How to use variables

Variables substitute values in your task configuration and inline scripts. If the key contains the phrase 'password', like 'userpassword' the value will be masked with "*********".

For task configuration fields, use the syntax ${bamboo.myvariablename}. For inline scripts, variables are exposed as shell environment variables which can be accessed using the syntax $BAMBOO_MY_VARIABLE_NAME (Linux/Mac OS X) or %BAMBOO_MY_VARIABLE_NAME% (Windows).

Variable name	Value	
		Add
bamboo.keychain.password	********	⊗

Figure 6-6. *A new runtime variable is now available for our default job*

Our new variable, let's make it available as an environment variable to our build script using the same syntax that we used before:

```
PASSWORD=${bamboo.keychain.password}
```

Note that if you want to make multiple environment variables available to your build script, all you need to do is to separate them with spaces.

The configuration of our job is complete, as you can see in Figure 6-7, we kept the settings minimal and managed to put all the critical build processes in a simple script that's easy to maintain.

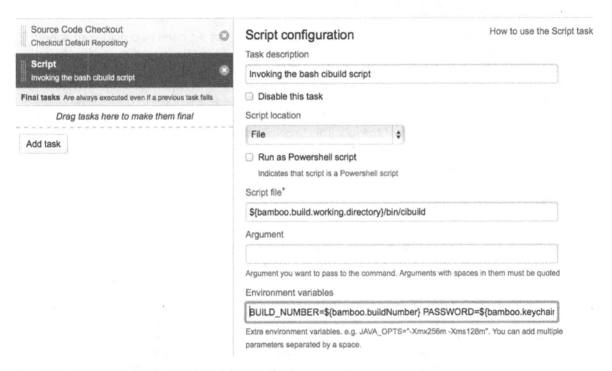

Figure 6-7. The configuration of the script task is pretty simple

Now that the configuration is complete, click "Save" but before you click the "Run" button to re-build the application, we need to take care of something else. We mentioned in chapter 5 that it was important to clean after yourself. To do that, select the "Source Code Checkout" task and check the "Force Clean Build" option. It doesn't clean the repository per se but actually removes the content and reclones everything. Note that this option will increase the build time. Click "Save" and then "Run". Considering our build script has already been battle-tested with Jenkins and that all we are doing is invoking the same build script, you should see the same big green bar saying the build was a success. As we mentioned earlier, Bamboo automatically parse ANSI formatted strings and convert them as proper HTML. If you go to the "Logs" tab, you should see a nice output thanks to xcpretty. There is one downside though, if you want to see or download the whole log, you will get plain text content with the ANSI tags left unconverted.

Archiving the artifacts

Our plan is almost ready, we now have a two tasks that will fetch the latest version of the project from the remove repository and then install the dependencies, build the application and package it into an iPhone archive (ipa) file. The only thing we miss is to automatically retrieve the generated IPA files and store them somewhere safe.

In Jenkins, we used what is called a post-build phase. This approach is fine in many cases but has one major downside: it is actually part of the build. This means that if it fails, the whole build may fail. The approach chose by Bamboo is a bit similar. Based on a pattern, all the files matching a specific pattern will be copied somewhere safe after the build has run. All we need to do is to configure the pattern.

Go back to the default job configuration and select the "Artifacts" tab. In this tab you will manage "artifact definitions," in other words, a list of definitions containing a name, a relative location, and a pattern following the Ant file copy pattern.

> **Note**   Ant? If you've never heard of Ant, Apache Ant is a tool used to automate software build processes, similar to Make. Written in Java, Ant uses an XML-based syntax to describe a build process where make use a pure text file format. If you remember correctly, we mentioned some of the tools that could be used to wrap a build script in Chapter 3. The Ant file copy uses a simple regular expression engine using "*" and "?" symbols to create simple patterns and try to match them against the names of files contained in a directory.

Click on the "Create definition" button and fill the form with the information we gave you before. Fill "Github Job IPA file" in the Name field, "build" in the Location one and "*.ipa" in the "Copy Pattern."

The artifact archiving process doesn't work retroactively; you need to re-run your build to retrieve the IPA file generated at the end of the build. Click on "Create" and then, once again, click on the "Run" button. In the job detail page, click on the "Artifacts" tab. At the end of the build you should see that the IPA file has been archived, similar to what's in Figure 6-8.

Artifacts

Remove artifacts

The following artifacts have been generated by the jobs in this plan.

Job artifacts

An artifact is something created by a job build (e.g. Jar files). Artifact definitions are used to specify which artifacts to keep from a build and are configured for individual jobs. ⑦

Produced in job	Artifact	File size
Default Job Default Stage	🗍 Github Job IPA file	115 KB

Figure 6-8. At the end of the build, the package application has been archived by Bamboo

You or any member of your team with access to this plan can download the archived artifact by clicking on the "Github Job IPA file" link. Once again that is not the most convenient way to share artifacts but we will cover more of that in the chapter about OTA development.

Bamboo Power user features

We covered a very basic use of Bamboo and went a little bit straighter to the point since we've already covered some part of the automatic building process in the previous chapter, when we talked about Jenkins. Bamboo is capable of so much more. Let's have a look at some of the advanced things you can achieve with it.

Rest API

Bamboo wouldn't be a full-featured developer tools without a way for developers to hack their way into most of its core feature. That is why is comes with a REST API to interact with your Bamboo installation, like Jenkins does. Using basic authentication if you haven't activated the anonymous access, it is pretty easy to fetch the current status of your jobs calling the following URL with a simple CURL command:

```
$ curl -s -u romain.pouclet:pwd -H Accept:application/json http://localhost:8085/rest/api/latest/
result | python -mjson.tool
{
    "expand": "results",
    "link": {
        "href": "http://localhost:8085/rest/api/latest/result",
        "rel": "self"
    },
    "results": {
        "expand": "result",
        "max-result": 1,
        "result": [
            {
                "buildNumber": 33,
                "buildResultKey": "GJ-IA-33",
                "buildState": "Successful",
                "id": 1376279,
                "key": "GJ-IA-33",
                "lifeCycleState": "Finished",
                "link": {
                    "href": "http://localhost:8085/rest/api/latest/result/GJ-IA-33",
                    "rel": "self"
                },
                "number": 33,
                "plan": {
                    "enabled": true,
                    "key": "GJ-IA",
                    "link": {
                        "href": "http://localhost:8085/rest/api/latest/plan/GJ-IA",
                        "rel": "self"
                    },
```

```
                "name": "Github Jobs - iOS application",
                "planKey": {
                    "key": "GJ-IA"
                },
                "shortKey": "IA",
                "shortName": "iOS application",
                "type": "chain"
            },
            "planResultKey": {
                "entityKey": {
                    "key": "GJ-IA"
                },
                "key": "GJ-IA-33",
                "resultNumber": 33
            },
            "state": "Successful"
        }
    ],
    "size": 1,
    "start-index": 0
  }
}
```

This is one of many resources available via the API, among with the Project, Build, Report, Queue, Label, and Server information services. Bamboo is much younger than Jenkins: the first stable version that was made public, is barely 4 years old. At that time, CruiseControl's market share was a lot less important than it was when Jenkins was first released. That is probably why Bamboo doesn't come with the semi-standard cc.xml file that you can use to display the status of your projects in third-party clients like CCMenu (http://ccmenu.org).

However, Bamboo does come with a wallboard module that will display the status of your projects in a very similar style to the wallboard Jenkins plugin we installed in the previous chapter.

Wallboards

If we were to add new plans for the Github Jobs Android application and the backoffice, we would have something like the Figure 6-9.

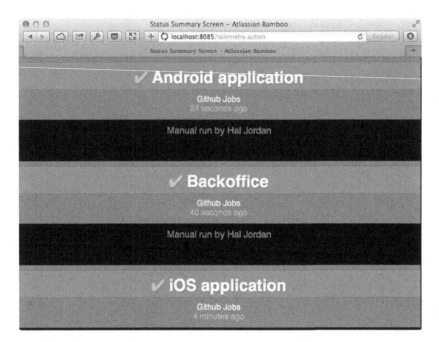

Figure 6-9. *The wallboard shows the status of the plans in our Bamboo installation*

The REST API is not the only way of communicating with Bamboo; its core is extensible enough so you can create your own plugins and add new ones. In fact, the Bob Swift Software company released a very powerful add-on to communicate with Bamboo using the command line, just like Jenkins. The main difference is that this add-on comes with a price: $220 for a maximum of five remote connections. Needless to say, you will need to have pretty important automation needs!

Getting feedback

We are still talking about a continuous integration tool that will build your application and make sure nothing is broken. It is all about feedback being collected and sent to you so can focus on making your application better. Let's have a look at how Bamboo can provide that feedback.

Build multiple branches

When you work on a project involving multiple coworkers, whether you are working on new features or squashing bugs, the safer way to proceed is to use multiple branches. Of course, to do that you'd need to be using a VCS such as Git, but you probably wouldn't have made it this far in the book if it were not the case.

However long the feature may take to be developed, it is very important to know if you've broken anything. Maybe the application won't build, maybe some of the unit test will fail, what's important is to be aware that you broke something and eventually fix it. Yes, eventually. Given you are not working directly on the trunk of the application, it is okay to break the build, as long as you fix it before integrating your work into the master branch. Let's see how we can achieve that with Bamboo.

First, we need to make sure that the Default job in our Default plan only builds the master branch, which is really easy. Open your Plan configuration, go to the "Repositories" section and select the repository that was automatically added when you created your plan the first time. You should only have one. In the "Branch" field that appears on the right when you selected the repository, make sure the content is "master". This means that no matter how the build is triggered (manually, or after a push to your repository), if no changes where made to the master branch, the build job will not run.

It is time we do some work! Go back to your terminal and create a new branch using the following command, unless you've decided to go with a dedicated client, such as Github's official one:

```
$ git checkout -b green-title
```

We are going to perform some crazy update in the application: turn the title in the navigation bar green. As learning Objective-C is not the goal of the book, we needed something very simple to do with the application. Open the "Github Jobs" Xcode project, open the AppDelegate.m file and add the following line in the application: didFinishLaunchingWithOptions: method:

```
- (BOOL)application:(UIApplication *)application didFinishLaunchingWithOptions:(NSDictionary *)
launchOptions
{
    NSString *endpoint = [[NSBundle bundleForClass: [self class]] infoDictionary]
[@"GithubJobsEndpoint"];
    NSLog(@"Endpoint = %@", endpoint);

    NSLog(@"Hi, I'm a sample application for a book.");

    [[UINavigationBar appearance] setTitleTextAttributes: @{NSForegroundColorAttributeName: [UIColor
greenColor]}];

    return YES;
}
```

Now go back to your terminal; commit your changes and push them to the remote repository:

```
$ git commit -am "Make client happy until next Tuesday: green title"
$ git push origin green-title
```

We now have a branch that will need multiple approvals before being merged into master. First we need to make sure we didn't break anything and that the application still builds in Bamboo. Then, we need the approval of the client, making sure the title is as green as he wants it to be. To do that, we need to run the cibuild script we've been using so far and send the generated IPA to the client. Since we've already said that we don't want to jeopardize the stability for the Default job, we need a specific job, just for that branch. This is simply a matter of checking the right checkbox in your plan configuration.

Go back to your plan's configuration in Bamboo, select the "Branches" tab and click on the "Create Branch" button. If you've properly pushed your changes to the remote repository, you should see the green-title branch in the list, as shown in Figure 6-10. Check the "green-title" checkbox and check the "enable branches" one. Then, press "Save". You should see your branch in the left menu, under the branches header section title. If you click on your branch, you should see that the branch is "activated," meaning that Bamboo will build this branch and maintain a build history specifically for this branch. In fact, if you click on the "Run" button; you should start the build #1 for this branch.

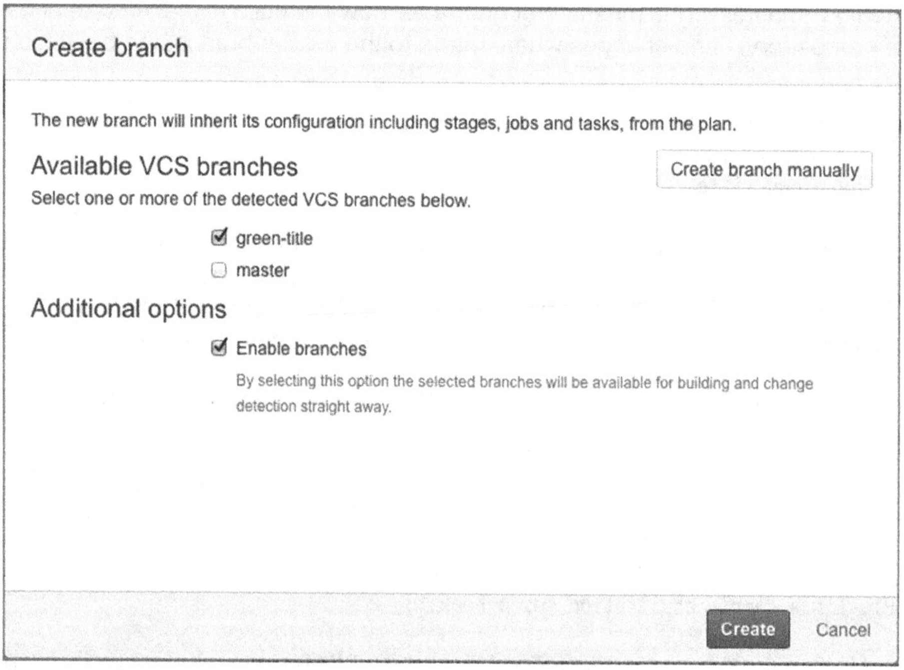

Figure 6-10. Bamboo detected the new branch and is ready to create a job for it

If the job succeeds – and considering the changes that were made, there is no reason it would not – you should find the logs for this specific build in the logs section and the archived artifacts for this branch, ready to be sent to the client.

Of course, you don't need to manually activate a branch in bamboo every time you start a feature, that would be a terrible waste of time. If you open the "Branches" configuration you should see a "Automatically manage branches" checkbox. When checked, the content of the repository will be interrogated every 5 minutes to see if new branches were created. If that's the case, a new job will be created like the one that was created manually for the green-title plugin.

You should not be afraid to create multiple branches, by default, 30-day-old branches are automatically deleted.

That's what CI is all about. Multiple pieces of software that are being built at the same time, integrated in the core of the application (in our case, the master branch) when they are ready. That's in the definition of "ready" that lays all the difficulty.

To be fair, this behavior is easily reproducible on Jenkins, since we've already shown you how to create builds via the API or the command line API. It is much easier with Bamboo though since a) it's native b) having a clear hierarchy of plans and jobs make everything a lot more clear.

Build early, build often

We already talked about how most of the code hosting services (Github, Bitbucket, Stash…) were able to trigger builds based on the endpoint available in Jenkins, also capable of watching your repository for changes and automatically starting builds. Yes, Bamboo is capable of the same things. Being able to build multiple branches in a clean, organized way out of the box probably makes it slightly more powerful, but that's not the topic here. The question you may ask yourself is why should I use these endpoints to start my builds, when should I start looking if I broke something and which frequency should I build my application at. The short answers are: "yes," "as early as possible," and "often."

Relying on your continuous integration platform to watch for changes in your codebase is the default behavior of both Jenkins and Bamboo (with, of course, being able to run the builds manually). It's a good approach but it comes with a few downsides. For starters, if you go to the "Triggers" tab of the Github Jobs iOS application plan, the default repository polling frequency is 3 minutes (180 seconds). This means that if you push a branch you are working on, it may take up to three minutes before the build actually starts. In our case we want to make sure we haven't broken anything and that the application builds on a "neutral" computer. If your build process comes with unit tests and static code analysis, it wouldn't be surprising not to get any feedback before 10 or 15 minutes after you pushed your changes to the remote repository. A lot of things can happen in 10 minutes when you're fixing a bug or implementing a new feature, that's way too long and that is why you need an alternative way of starting the build: a hook.

Setting up a hook with Bamboo

Setting up a hook with Bamboo should feel pretty easy now that you've configured your build and that you've got time to play around in the interface. If you aren't already, open the "Triggers" tab of the Github Jobs iOS application plan and click on the "Add trigger" button. In the description field, fill something like "pushing from <platform>" where platform may be Github, Bithucket, or your homemade code hosting platform. Select "Repository triggers the build when changes are committed" from the type combo box and press "Save trigger".

As we mentioned earlier, most of the platforms come with out-of-the-box support to trigger builds on Bamboo (as well as Jenkins, for that matter. In case your code is hosted on a platform that doesn't, Bamboo comes with a couple of shell and python scripts, you can use to trigger a build. If you go to the folder where you installed Bamboo, you should see a "scripts" folder. There are no scripts dedicated to Git, and for good reason: it would be exactly the same as the one in the "svn-triggers" folder:

```
#!/usr/bin/python
#
# ./postCommitBuildTrigger.py http://bamboo.atlassian.com/bamboo/ myBuildName

import sys
import urllib;

baseUrl = sys.argv[1]
buildKey = sys.argv[2]
```

```
remoteCall = baseUrl + "/api/rest/updateAndBuild.action?buildKey=" + buildKey
fileHandle = urllib.urlopen(remoteCall)
fileHandle.close()
```

> **Note**   We are using the Python script, which is a language available on any standard installation of OS X. On the other hand, the shell script uses wget, a command used to fetch files from the web. It's a pretty powerful command that supports many protocols from HTTP to FTP but that is not available on OSX.

Using this script only requires the base URL of your Bamboo installation, and the build key, which is the concatenation of the build project key and the plan key. In our case, that would be "GJ-IA:"

```
$ ./scripts/svn-triggers/postCommitBuildTrigger.py http://localhost:8085/ GJ-IA
```

All you'd need to do now is edit your git's remote repository "post-receive" hook and call this script from it. Note that the script doesn't need a username and a password to trigger a build. The first reason is that this URL doesn't actually trigger a build, it only asks Bamboo to poll for changes via the "updateAndBuild" URL endpoint, and start a build if, and only if, changes were made. It is also more secure that way, since you won't be giving away valid credentials to some third-party service or hardcoded in a Git hook. Finally, if the anonymous access scares you, you can restrict the access to this URL to a list of IP addresses.

Setting up nightly builds

We mentioned earlier that builds often take time and there is nothing more frustrating than waiting for your build to end. Because of that, and other reasons we'll talk about shortly, you may want to consider setting up a nightly build.

A full-featured build process does not only aim at making sure your application is not broken. Running unit and acceptance tests as well as building the application is one aspect of continuous integration but making sure the collaboration between the member of your team goes smoothly, you will also want to consider generating documentation. That's the kind of thing you don't want to be done for every branch of the project since it will slow down your build, but once a day and only for the relevant branches that will be used by your coworker, usually the master. Not that this rule is also available if you are working alone and your coworker is actually the future you.

EXERCISE SETTING UP A NIGHTLY BUILD

Setting up a nightly build is easier than it may sound: you will need to add a new Job in the current Github Jobs iOS application plan with a triggered configured to start a build every day at midnight or so. Since it is very similar to what we've been talking about in the current chapter, we are making a simple exercise of it.

Setting up a nightly build also comes as a health check for your project and your whole continuous integration platform. Don't make the mistake of believing you won't need one if you're already triggering new builds as soon as you push changes to your repository. Nightly builds and push-triggered builds are not mutually exclusive. Running builds every day at midnight will give you the certainty that your application is not broken and if it is, you will have something to start working on right away.

It is also a way to check that your build machine is behaving as it should be and still capable of building your applications. If it's not, it is better to be aware of it when you start working on your application than when you push changes for the first time of the day, and realize your build machine is down or not working properly.

Integrating Xcode builds into an existing Bamboo installation

Just like with Jenkins, sometimes working on iOS application is only part of your company's activities, and you may have to configure your build in an existing Bamboo installation that cannot build iOS applications. Once again, Bamboo chose to go with a different approach than Jenkins.

In the previous chapter, we had to manage the credentials so Jenkins could connect to a slave node over SSH, and communicate with the slave via a Java archive. This solution is great because it is simple and easy to set up, since you most certainly already are capable of communicating with the slave node over SSH. One downside though is your slave has to be accessible by Jenkins. This is fine in most cases, if your instance of Jenkins is running locally or if you've set up your instances in a way that Jenkins can communicate with the slave node, via a private network of some kind.

On the other hand, Bamboo chose the opposite approach: the remote agent will communicate with the main instance of Bamboo via a TCP connection.

Installing the remote agent

A standard Bamboo installation comes with remote agent support disabled, for security reasons. To enable remote agent support, go to the configuration section of your instance and click on the "Enable remote agent support". If you're worried about the security implication, there is a dedicated page on the Atlassian documentation, also linked in the Agents section of your Bamboo installation: http://docs.atlassian.com/bamboo/docs-055/Security.

Once you've enabled support for remote agent, click on the "Install Remote Agent" button that did appear. On the page that you have been redirected to, you should see a link to download the remote agent installer. Just like Jenkins, it's in a Java archive.

From this moment, we assume you have a remote installation of Bamboo available somewhere. If you haven't, we will be as exhaustive as possible to show you how agents in Bamboo work.

First, download the remote agent installer and start the installation process.

```
$ curl http://bamboo:8085/agentServer/agentInstaller/atlassian-bamboo-agent-installer-5.5.0.jar -O
$ java -jar atlassian-bamboo-agent-installer-5.5.0.jar http://bamboo:8085/agentServer
```

Running the agent-installer will download a lot of java libraries and setup a remote agent in a directory, called the remote agent home. The default path for this directory is "Bamboo-agent-home" in the home directory of the user that started the installation process. You can override this value using the -Dbamboo.home=/path/to/the/home argument.

The bamboo agent directory will contain information about the remote agent, of course, but also the main Bamboo installation. In the "conf" directory you will find a file called "wrapper.conf", among a lot of Java-related settings, such that the maximum amount of memory you're willing to feed this process, you will also find information about the default agent, like its URL:

```
wrapper.app.parameter.2=http://192.168.2.10:8085/agentServer/
```

First, this means that this is where you will have to perform your changes in case you want to tweak the configuration of the remote agent. As we said, this is where you will set the maximum memory allowed and other options. Second, and most importantly, this means that an agent cannot be used for multiple instances of Bamboo. If you thought about sharing a remote agent with multiple instances of Bamboo, think again: it wasn't meant for this.

In this folder, you will also find a shell script that you can use to start manually the remote agent. To use it, simply run the following command:

```
$ bin/bamboo-agent.sh -h
Usage: ./bamboo-agent.sh { console | start | stop | restart | status | dump }
```

The console mode will start the remote agent, make it connect to the main Bamboo installation and more importantly, keep the process in the foreground, so that's good enough for testing purposes. You will eventually have to set up a launched process, like we did for Jenkins and for Bamboo at the beginning, to start the remote agent with the computer. That's one downside with the approach that chose Bamboo: with Jenkins, because the master will connect to the slave, it can easily awaken a slave when needed.

Start the process using the following command:

```
$ bin/bamboo-agent.sh console
Running Bamboo Agent...
Removed stale pid file: /Users/Palleas/bamboo-agent-home/bin/./bamboo-agent.pid
STATUS | wrapper  | 2014/05/13 20:21:46 | --> Wrapper Started as Console
...
```

Now that we have a remote agent that connects to the main installation, as shown in Figure 6-11, it is time to configure the agent and use it to build the application.

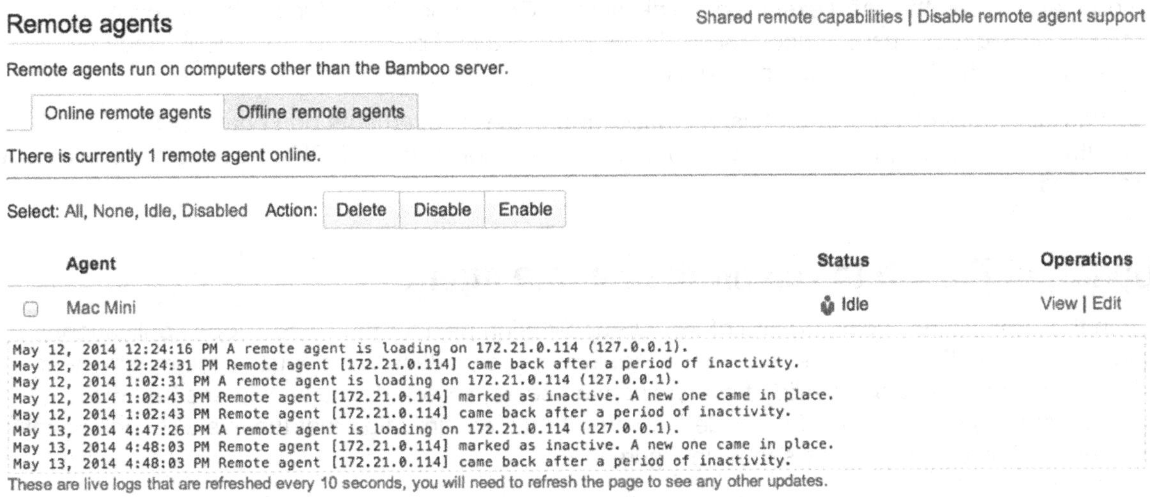

Remote agents   Shared remote capabilities | Disable remote agent support

Remote agents run on computers other than the Bamboo server.

| Online remote agents | Offline remote agents |

There is currently 1 remote agent online.

Select: All, None, Idle, Disabled   Action: Delete   Disable   Enable

Agent	Status	Operations
☐ Mac Mini	👤 Idle	View	Edit

```
May 12, 2014 12:24:16 PM A remote agent is loading on 172.21.0.114 (127.0.0.1).
May 12, 2014 12:24:31 PM Remote agent [172.21.0.114] came back after a period of inactivity.
May 12, 2014 1:02:31 PM A remote agent is loading on 172.21.0.114 (127.0.0.1).
May 12, 2014 1:02:43 PM Remote agent [172.21.0.114] marked as inactive. A new one came in place.
May 12, 2014 1:02:43 PM Remote agent [172.21.0.114] came back after a period of inactivity.
May 13, 2014 4:47:26 PM A remote agent is loading on 172.21.0.114 (127.0.0.1).
May 13, 2014 4:48:03 PM Remote agent [172.21.0.114] marked as inactive. A new one came in place.
May 13, 2014 4:48:03 PM Remote agent [172.21.0.114] came back after a period of inactivity.
```
These are live logs that are refreshed every 10 seconds, you will need to refresh the page to see any other updates.

Figure 6-11. An agent called "Mac Mini" is connect to our main Bamboo installation

Configuring the agent

The main point of using remote agent to build your application is not so much to scale the huge amount of builds your continuous integration platform has to handle but actually to be able to run jobs on agents with very specific capabilities. In our case, that would be an agent with the xcodebuild command available.

Click on the settings button at the end of the top menu and select the "Agents…" item. In the Remote agents section, you should see the remote agent you've set up, as shown in Figure 6-11. This picture was taken a little too early, but when you click on the "Edit" link, you can actually give a name to this agent. In our case, we named it Mac Mini because we really lacked imagination on this.

Click on the name of your remote. This is where you will see the information about your agent, as shown in Figure 6-12. What's important here is the "Capabilities" section. The "Agent-specific capabilities" is where you will add capabilities about your agent. For example, we want to specify that our build can run xcodebuild commands.

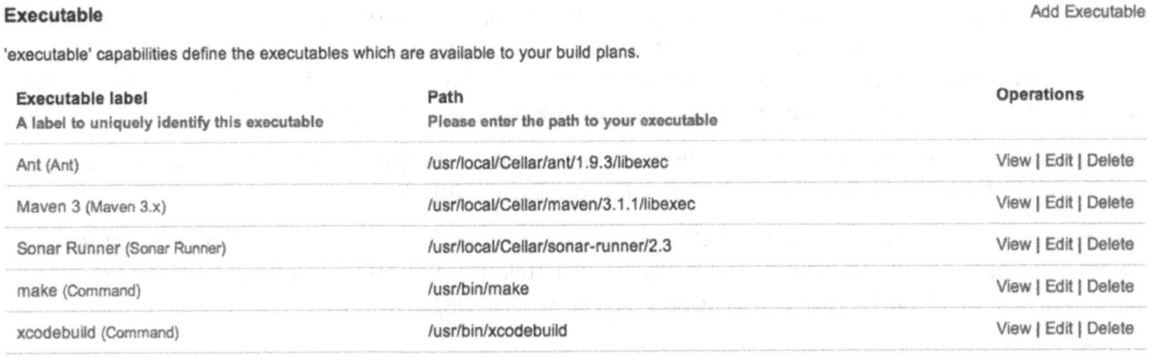

Executable   Add Executable

'executable' capabilities define the executables which are available to your build plans.

Executable label A label to uniquely identify this executable	Path Please enter the path to your executable	Operations
Ant (Ant)	/usr/local/Cellar/ant/1.9.3/libexec	View	Edit	Delete
Maven 3 (Maven 3.x)	/usr/local/Cellar/maven/3.1.1/libexec	View	Edit	Delete
Sonar Runner (Sonar Runner)	/usr/local/Cellar/sonar-runner/2.3	View	Edit	Delete
make (Command)	/usr/bin/make	View	Edit	Delete
xcodebuild (Command)	/usr/bin/xcodebuild	View	Edit	Delete

Figure 6-12. The Remote agent we've connected to the main Bamboo installation has many capabilities

To do that, click on the "Add executable" link, select "Command" in the type field, fill xcodebuild in the label field and "/usr/bin/xcodebuild" in the path field and press Add. You should see the requirement in the list, as shown in Figure 6-12.

You can add as much requirement as you need, and these requirements don't have to be a list of executable commands. It can be version of the Java Development Kit (JDK) or even simple key/value properties.

Updating the job to run on the remote agent

Open the "Default job" configuration of the iOS application plan for the Github Jobs application, and click on the "Requirements" tab. In the requirement list, select "Xcodebuild", the requirement we created earlier, and press Add. If everything worked as expected, you should see that the requirement has been successfully added, along with the confirmation that there is a list one agent capable of running your job, as shown in Figure 6-13.

Figure 6-13. There is one agent capable of running our job since we need xcodebuild

In case you are wondering, yes we could have been more specific on the requirements, since our build script requires tools like bash to run, xcpretty to make the output pretty, and xcrun to package the application, but we decided to keep things simple.

Summary

The goal of this chapter was to give you a tour of an alternative to Jenkins, because nothing is more dangerous than sticking with your favorite toys without looking at the alternatives. Once again, we didn't want to tell you that one was better than the other; in fact both solutions come with pros and cons. By now, you should be able to choose which solution suits you best.

Bamboo is a full-featured product maintained by a profitable company that comes with a nicely designed interface, powerful add-ons, and well-organized build plans.

This book will also cover the new tool released by Apple to set up continuous integration for your project but because you probably need a break from building platforms, the next chapter will cover an equally important part of the build process: Over The Air deployment!

Chapter 7

Over-The-Air distribution

In the previous chapters we covered how to build the application manually or by using the continuous integration platforms Jenkins and Bamboo. We mentioned earlier that the question that usually follows a successful build is whether or not to send it to your quality assurance team. No matter how many tools you've added to your build process (automated testing, static code analysis, etc.) you will still need feedback from actual users to know if your application is ready to be released. In this chapter we will talk a little bit about Over The Air (OTA) distribution and how people decided to create a business based on a product that would ease the process of distributing applications. Then, we'll integrate with one of these services: TestFlight. Finally, we'll see how it actually works and develop our own, homemade, continuous integration platform.

What is Over The Air distribution?

Distributing software is an old problem developers had to solve years ago and is not limited to mobile applications. There was a time that the problem faced when releasing new or updated software was how to ship a few thousand CDs containing the software for users to install. With the advent of the Internet, the problem of distributing mobile applications became how to distribute these applications via Wi-Fi or cellular network. In the end, OTA is simply a fancy term referring to the way the application is distributed.

What does it have to do with continuous integration?

A common misconception with continuous integration is thinking it is solely about building an application every day or so and releasing beta versions when it's ready. That is not continuous integration but actually continuous delivery. As we've shown in the previous chapters, it's a more complex process.

That being so, the concept of continuous integration is never far from the one of distribution because being able to release a build of your application and retrieve feedback from the users is yet another feedback helping you to decide if you should integrate a feature or a bugfix, or not.

iOS app distribution: a valid business model

As mentioned in previous chapters, releasing an iOS application is a complex process. Code signing the application and using the proper provisioning profile is a task most of the iOS developers struggle with. It took a long time before Apple actually started providing a way of releasing beta versions of your application without using the App Store. At the time of writing this book, distributing beta versions via Apple is still in beta. Of course, you can always install the application manually on your testers' device, but you don't want to be that guy.

With the release of iOS 4, Apple introduced Ad-Hoc provisioning profiles that allow you to install applications on an iOS device without the help of Xcode. An Ad-Hoc provisioning profile is pretty much similar to a standard distribution profile you use to submit your application on the App Store. The main difference is that it contains the unique device identifier (UDID) of all the devices allowed to run the application. At this time, you can register up to 100 device identifiers, including your own. That's usually enough to send your application to a small number of testers, but these slots have to be used carefully: you can only remove a device id once a year, when your Apple developer account is renewed.

Once you've generated your Ad-Hoc distribution profile (we'll come back to that part later), it is actually possible to install an iOS application on a device without plugging it into a computer, simply using a webpage. After all, that's what the App Store application on your device does. To do that, all you need is a server and a couple of files accessible from your iPhone's browser. Additionally, you probably don't want your website to be "free for all" and let anybody download your application, you will need a security layer. All of this will take you time and knowledge you don't necessary have nor do you want to learn it. This is how third-party services were born.

TestFlight (`testflightapp.com`) and HockeyApp (hockeyapp.net) are services that were born out of the need to ease this process for developers and beta testers. Create an account, build your application with the proper provisioning profile, and that's it. The authorized users are ready to download beta versions of your application. Both services used to work for the Android and iOS platforms but in February 2014, Burtsly, the company behind TestFlight, was acquired by Apple, who removed the support for the Android platform.

Since Apple made TestFlight the encouraged way of distributing beta versions of your application by acquiring it, we will be using it to release a beta version of the Github Jobs for iOS application.

Distributing the app using TestFlight

The next part will be about distributing a build manually using TestFlight. If you're already familiar with the service, you will probably not learn anything new. Feel free to jump to the next section where we'll submit the build automatically via Jenkins and Bamboo, before writing our very own simple distribution platform!

Visit TestFlight's registering page (`https://testflightapp.com/register/`) and create an account, we will need it later when we have a functional build we want to send to our users. First, let's create an Ad Hoc provisioning profile and use it to package our Github Jobs for iOS application.

To do that, gather a few unique device identifiers from your team or your testing devices and add them to Apple's developer portal, then:

1. In the left menu, select the "Distribution" link under the "Provisioning Profile" section and then clink on the plus sign at the top right of the screen. Chances are you've already visited this section to generate a Development provisioning profile or a distribution one to submit your application on the App Store. This time though, select the "Ad Hoc" distribution and press the "Continue" button.

2. Select your application identifier, in our case that would be something like UBSUPPBORX.com.perfectly-cooked.github-jobs. Press the continue button.

3. From the list that appears, check the list of iOS device you want to distribute the application to, as shown in Figure 7-1.

 Select devices.

Select the devices you wish to include in this provisioning profile. To install an app signed with this profile on a device, the device must be included.

☑ Select All	4 of 4 item(s) selected
☑ Beta tester iPhone #1	
☑ Beta tester iPhone #2	
☑ Beta tester iPhone #3	
☑ Beta tester iPhone #4	

Figure 7-1. The beta version of the iOS application will be sent to four beta testers

That's the kind of process you should do very carefully. Remember that a) you've a limited number of slots and b) every time you want to add a new beta tester, you have to update your provisioning profile and generate a new build.

Actually, that's not completely true. Apple also proposes an enterprise program that you can use to release applications outside the App store to a more important number of users. It is not meant to replace the app store but to help deploy in-house applications. In fact it is not possible to use such an account to release applications on the App Store. However, it comes in handy when in those situations because you don't have to select a list of unique device identifiers. This plan really targets companies and comes at a price: around $300 a year.

Once you've selected your devices, perform the following steps:

1. Give a name to your provisioning profile. Don't hesitate to make it an obvious one, such as "Github Jobs Ad Hoc Distribution". The future will thank you when you get to a gigantic amount of provisioning profile to manage.

2. Once it's ready, press the continue button. You will now have a choice: download the generated provisioning profile and add it manually or from Xcode's preferences panel, navigate to the Accounts tab, click on the View details button and hit the refresh button. In both cases, you should see it in the list, as shown in Figure 7-2.

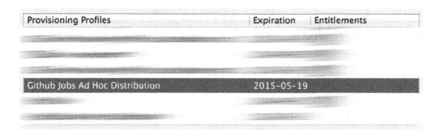

Figure 7-2. The provisioning profile is available in Xcode and can be used for the Github Jobs application

3. From Xcode, open the Github Jobs project, navigate to the build settings of the Github Jobs' target and look for the provisioning profile section. You should be able to select the "Github Jobs Ad Hoc Distribution" one from the list for the Adhoc configuration, as shown in Figure 7-3.

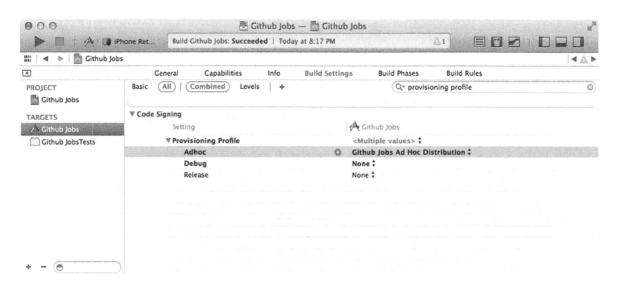

Figure 7-3. The application built with the Adhoc configuration will use our new provisioning profile

Now that everything is properly configured, let's build and package the application. At this point in the book, you should be able to choose from running the continuous integration building script at "bin/cibuild" in your project's folder or simply using Xcode, for now. Don't worry; we'll automate everything in the next section.

Open your browser and log into TestFlight with the account you created earlier. You should be prompted to create a new team. Click on the "create a new team" button and fill in the team name field with "Github Jobs beta testers" for example. Make sure to choose an explicit name, it will be easier for you later when you'll manage multiple teams.

In TestFlight, teams are lists of users that can be used to setup permissions easily. For example, you may want a team of users dedicated to security whom you will send builds that fix major security breaches to first, before releasing a new version to your "regular" beta testers. Press the save button. You should be redirected to the page dedicated to uploading a new build. If you're not, from the dashboard, click on the "Upload a build" button.

Open a finder window, drag and drop the IPA file you've just built in the zone created for this purpose and fill in the text area what's new with this version. If you've read this book in the right order, at this point the major change coming with this version would be "Turning the titles green in the navigation bar". This is a very simple app so, there is indeed not much to say in the release notes, but in a real-world context, you should take extra care when you write those notes. Nobody likes a simple "Bug fixes and new features" release notes, your user want details and that could not be more true when people are curious and motivated enough to use the beta versions of your application.

When you're ready press the upload button, check the authorized users in the list and press "Update and notify", which means that the user allowed to install the applications that registered into TestFlight will get an e-mail containing a link to download the new version of the application. You can also simply send them the link manually.

That's pretty much all you need to do to send a beta version of your application to your beta testers. Of course gathering unique device identifiers from them so you can generate a new provisioning profile is a bit tedious but overall you'll admit that TestFlight did a great job of easing the process of over the air distribution. If everything worked, you should see the build in the App section of your TestFlight Dashboard, as shown in Figure 7-4.

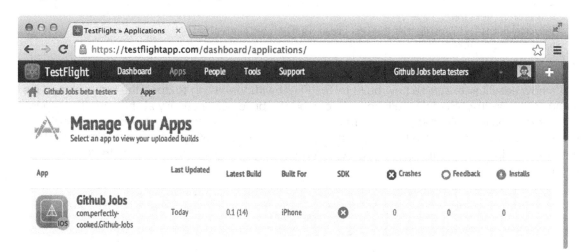

Figure 7-4. The application is visible in the TestFlight dashboard, showing the latest uploaded build

TestFlight for the power user

The process we've just explained has one big downside: it's 100% manual, and that's what we've been trying to avoid when you set up Jenkins or Bamboo, depending on which solution you choose. Fortunately for us, TestFlight is a tool for applications developers and comes with a REST API!

1. Click on your profile at the top right of the screen and select "Account Settings".

2. In the left menu, select "Upload API": this is where you will find the token required to make authenticated calls to the API.

3. Click on the "Github Jobs beta testers" in the top menu and click on the "edit info" button: this is where you will find the team token, needed to actually authenticate you when you'll update a new build.

The rest of the process is a simple curl command away. After navigating to the build folder where the generated IPA file was stored, run the following command:

```
$ cd ~/Projects/GithubsJobs/build
$ curl http://testflightapp.com/api/builds.json \
-F file=@Github\ Jobs.ipa \
-F api_token=Nx4b86M2NM1c2SfjM2SOD6xM9Og3fN7Oc1c8xNAeeo7oEaefD64NccDEOfywM72zj2O2Ai4_DeMf \
-F team_token=zNwS5M3_A4I4S7jb63ON7AbN3OI28xa4Cxz6MNa5o6Mx4Oazec8NS7gd1EdMDa5826joy2ONy1D3 \
-F notes='Turning the titles green in the navigation bar'

{
    "bundle_version": "0.1 (14)",
    "install_url": "https://testflightapp.com/install/5fU8cO83f9fTebaMd3d342edD2Mz4dc-
    47z65cMEdxUa/",
    "config_url": "https://testflightapp.com/dashboard/builds/permissions/10335151/",
    "created_at": "2014-05-19 22:39:21",
    "device_family": "iPhone",
    "notify": false,
    "team": "Github Jobs",
    "minimum_os_version": "7.1",
    "release_notes": "Turning the titles green in the navigation bar",
    "binary_size": 108686
}%
```

That's how easy it is to send a new build to TestFlight without having to open the browser, and it's because of this simplicity that we'll be able to send the build automatically at the end of a Jenkins or a Bamboo build. Note that for this command to work, you need to navigate (using the "cd" command) to the folder where the IPA file is stored. Also check that your file is actually named "Github Jobs.ipa". If one of these two criteria is not met, you'll get a "curl: (xx) couldn't open file "Github Jobs.ipa".

Uploading the app to TestFlight at the end of a Jenkins build

The previous section gave you a tour of how you can use TestFlight to distribute a beta version of your application. It was a manual process and even if the user interface is really intuitive that's a task that can end up to be time consuming really quickly. Fortunately, the REST API makes it possible to automate this process and submit the packaged application at the end of a build from your favorite continuous integration platform. Let's start with Jenkins. Even if you chose to go with Bamboo, we suggest you read this section, as we'll cover a wider topic than simply uploading a build to TestFlight at the end of the build process.

If you remember correctly, the build process we set up in Jenkins was pretty simple: clone the application and run a bash script that takes care of everything else. At the end of the build process, we added a post-build phase that would archive the generated artifacts and keep them safe.

Well, our needs have changed and being able to download the packaged application from Jenkins is not enough anymore. Fortunately for us, Jenkins has a really great community. In situations like this where you need to integrate a very popular service such as TestFlight, chances are somebody has already developed a plugin for it. Let's install the TestFlight plugin for Jenkins.

Installing the TestFlight plugin for Jenkins

Open the "manage Jenkins" section and navigate to the "Manage plugin" page. In the "available" tab, look for TestFlight. Check the install checkbox on the left and press the Install without restart button. If you remember correctly, we mentioned earlier why it was safe to install a plugin without restarting your instance.

Now we need to fetch our credentials, the API and the team tokens, and store them securely in Jenkins: we don't want anybody with access to the Jenkins build to be able to retrieve those tokens and we don't want these tokens to appear in the build log.

While in the "manage Jenkins" section, navigate to the configure System page and scroll to the bottom of the page where you should see a configuration section dedicated to "TestFlight". Press the add button to add a new pair of API and team token and give it a name, such as "Github Jobs for iOS", as shown in Figure 7-5.

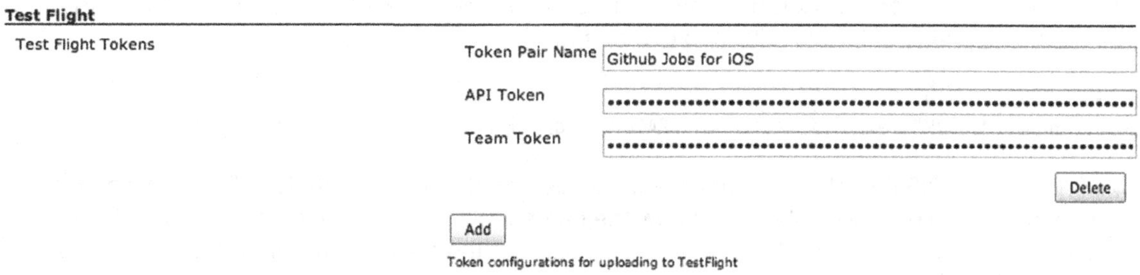

Test Flight

Test Flight Tokens		
	Token Pair Name	Github Jobs for iOS
	API Token	••
	Team Token	••

Delete

Add

Token configurations for uploading to TestFlight

Figure 7-5. We've added the required credentials to upload a build via the REST API

Press "Save" when you are ready. Note that this manage section only manages the credentials, which means that it will only permit you to add, edit, and delete as many credentials as you need. This means that you won't be able to know if your credentials were properly entered until you've run a successful build and tried to send the generated IPA to TestFlight.

Configuring the Github Jobs for iOS jenkins job

Navigate to the dashboard, click on the "Github Jobs for iOS" job and select "Configure" in the left menu. Scroll to the bottom of the page where the post-build actions are declared, and click the Add post-build action. In the list, select " Upload to TestFlight".

Check the "Token Pair". Make sure you've selected "Github Jobs for iOS". It should be the case if you've just installed the plugin and only added one pair of tokens. The two next options shall contain the ant patterns Jenkins should use to retrieve the IPA and (potential) dSYM file. These patterns rely on the same syntax we've used before to archive the artifacts: ant patterns. The default value for the IPA is "**/*.ipa", which will work for us because the build is stored in a build folder relative to the workspace. On the other hand, the dSYM file must be zipped before it is uploaded to TestFlight. In fact, the plugin won't look for dSYM file but related '-dSYM.zip' or '.dSYM.zip' files.

We already mentioned in Chapter 2 what the dSYM file was and what it is used for: it contains the debug symbols of your application. Without this file, the crashlogs collected by testflight are useless because they cannot be transformed into proper, useful stack traces for debugging. Before Apple's acquisition of the company behind TestFlight, Burstly, TestFlight came with an official SDK that would collect crashlogs but to do that, it actually needed the dSYM file to symbolicate the logs the SDK would collect and send. So why are we mentioning this if the SDK is no longer available? Simply because Apple announced that collecting crash logs would be available later next year, in 2015. By then, retrieving and sending dSYM files using a command line instruction should be easy for you. Let's see how it can be done.

We know that the dSYM file is generated when the application is built, which means during the execution of the xcodebuild command. We could update our cibuild script and zip it right after the xcodebuild command, but that's not recommended: we want to keep our build script as neutral as possible. On the other hand what we can do is use a dedicated build phase that will find the dSYM file and zip it.

Scroll up a bit, press for the "Add build step" button and select "Execute shell" in the list. In the textarea that appears, enter the following command:

```
cd "$WORKSPACE/build"
find . -name "*.dSYM" -exec zip -r "$WORKSPACE/build/Github Jobs.dSYM.zip" {} \;
```

It will find all the "*.dSYM" files and for all of these file add them in the created ZIP file. Since we know how the IPA file will be called, we know the name the zipped dSYM file should have to be found by the TestFlight plugin. We could also explicitly set the name of the zipped dSYM file in the field provided for that purpose.

We mentioned earlier how important the release notes are, especially in the context of beta testing applications. In fact, the TestFlight REST API will throw an error if you try to upload a new build without release notes:

```
$ curl http://testflightapp.com/api/builds.json \
-F file=@Github\ Jobs.ipa \
-F api_token=<API_TOKEN>  \
-F team_token=<TEAM_TOKEN>
```

You must supply api_token, team_token, the file, and notes (missing notes)

The plugin we are using has two ways of setting the release notes: a manual one and the automatic one. The manual one uses the content of the "Build Notes" text area. Let's be honest, this one doesn't make much sense unless you are willing to update it before each build. The second uses the changelog from the version control system, in our case Git.

If the release notes are important for your users, the changelog are just as important to the developers. By writing explicit commit messages, meaning no "fix this" or "fix that", the TestFlight plugin will automatically generate proper release notes for the users. Check the "Append changelog to build notes" option and press "Save".

Building the application and sending the resulting IPA to TestFlight

On the Github Jobs for iOS job page, press the "Build Now" link in the sidebar. Once it's started, click on the build and navigate to the "Console Output" section. There are a few sections in the output that interest us, especially after the execution of the cibuild script.

```
$ /bin/sh -xe /var/folders/1v/d8vqkw8x23ndw49f5vs3fzw00000gn/T/hudson65668607800036881.sh
+ find '/Users/Palleas/.jenkins/jobs/Github Jobs for iOS/workspace/build' -name '*.dSYM' -exec zip
-r '/Users/Palleas/.jenkins/jobs/Github Jobs for iOS/workspace/build/Github Jobs.dSYM.zip' '{}' ';'
  adding: Users/Palleas/.jenkins/jobs/Github Jobs for iOS/workspace/build/Github Jobs.app.dSYM/
(stored 0%)
  adding: Users/Palleas/.jenkins/jobs/Github Jobs for iOS/workspace/build/Github Jobs.app.dSYM/
Contents/ (stored 0%)
  adding: Users/Palleas/.jenkins/jobs/Github Jobs for iOS/workspace/build/Github Jobs.app.dSYM/
Contents/Info.plist (deflated 52%)
  adding: Users/Palleas/.jenkins/jobs/Github Jobs for iOS/workspace/build/Github Jobs.app.dSYM/
Contents/Resources/ (stored 0%)
  adding: Users/Palleas/.jenkins/jobs/Github Jobs for iOS/workspace/build/Github Jobs.app.dSYM/
Contents/Resources/DWARF/ (stored 0%)
  adding: Users/Palleas/.jenkins/jobs/Github Jobs for iOS/workspace/build/Github Jobs.app.dSYM/
Contents/Resources/DWARF/Github Jobs (deflated 66%)
```

At the end of the build process, but **before** the post-build actions, the script we added before is run. As you can see in the output, it found a dSYM file, created a zip archive with its contents (hence the -r option) and named it "Github Jobs.dSYM.zip".

```
Uploading to testflight
File: /Users/Palleas/.jenkins/jobs/Github Jobs for iOS/workspace/build/GithubJobs.ipa
DSYM: /Users/Palleas/.jenkins/jobs/Github Jobs for iOS/workspace/build/GithubJobs.dSYM.zip
```

```
TestFlight Upload speed: 741.05Kbps
TestFlight Install Link: https://testflightapp.com/install/jdiejdi787b13dec113902b4ii343a1-
MTExNTY5NzA/
TestFlight Configuration Link: https://testflightapp.com/dashboard/builds/permissions/11129470/
```

Once the build is complete, the post-build actions are run in sequential order. The TestFlight one we added in the past section shows that it found the IPA file and deduced the path to the zipped dSYM file. With this information, we sent an upload request to TestFlight using the REST API and got a valid payload in response, containing the URL to the configuration page, where you can go and select the users that should receive this build and the installation URL we've used before that you can send to user so they can install the application.

If you go back to testflight and open the Github Jobs for application app from the Apps section of the top menu, you should see your build, as shown in Figure 7-6.

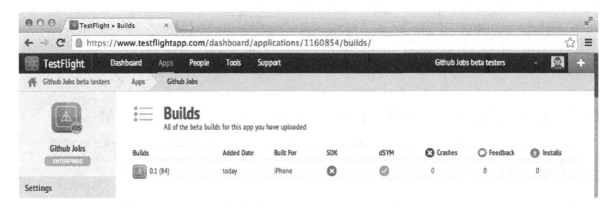

Figure 7-6. The build #84 was successfully uploaded to TestFlight

Click on this build and navigate to the "Build Information" section from the left menu. In this section, you will see all the information about your build including, as shown in Figure 7-7, the release notes that have been retrieved from the commit history.

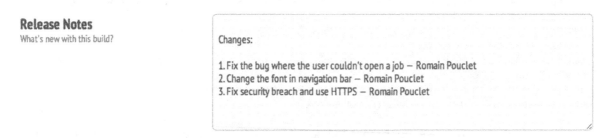

Figure 7-7. The build's release note were created via the repository history and includes the name of the author

As a bonus, the page presenting the Github Jobs for iOS job has been updated, as shown in Figure 7-8 and contains the information we've just mentioned, so you don't have to look for your build once back in TestFlight.

Figure 7-8. *The job page was updated with information about the latest build*

Let's sum up what we've done. We created and set up a TestFlight account so we could have access to an API token and a Team token, which are required to perform an authenticated call to TestFlight Upload API. With this information, we went back to Jenkins and installed the TestFlight plugin, so we could update the Github Jobs for iOS job and upload the packaged application at the end of the build. But because we wanted to add the dSYM file and that folder needs to be sent as a ZIP archive to testflight, we first updated the job and added a "Run script" build phase that would take care of the compression process. Finally, we added a "Upload to TestFlight" post build action that would upload the artifacts generated during the build instead of simply archiving them like we were doing before.

You may be wondering why we didn't update our build script and simply add the compressing action and the upload to TestFlight and simply run one script once and for all. That's because sending the build to TestFlight is not part of the build process, per se. We want our continuous integration architecture to provide us a valid and meaningful feedback. That's why a job failing because of a build that doesn't work won't be treated the same way that a job that fails because there was an issue during the upload to TestFlight. Separation of concern is, in fact, a design principle that applies here. By splitting the build phases into small sections, it's much easier to detect the points of failure and fix them before they endanger the stability of the whole build.

Now that we know how to upload the build at the end of a Jenkins build, let's see how to do the same with Bamboo.

Uploading the app to TestFlight at the end of a Bamboo job

If you skipped directly to this section thinking that you don't need to read about Jenkins because you chose to go with Bamboo well, you may find it hard to follow. As with the previous chapter, there actually are going to be some small comparisons with the way Jenkins works.

Open Bamboo and navigate to the configuration section of the Github Jobs for iOS section. There are a couple of steps we need to take care of before being able to upload the build generated during the execution of the Bamboo plan we set up in the previous chapter.

Once again, the approach chosen by Bamboo is a bit different from Jenkins'. We no longer have a single job but a plan, with multiple stages, with multiple jobs and multiple tasks. In the "Stages" section, you should see a "Related deployment projects" subsection with a "Create deployment project" button. This is indeed what we are going to use: a deployment project.

Deployment projects are linked to build projects and communicate through "shared artifacts", which means that this project will need the generated IPA file and, that's right, the zipped dSYM file. Once again if you don't know about the zipped dSYM file, have a look at the Jenkins section of this chapter.

Updating the Default Job configuration

First, we need to update our build to compress the dSYM file into a zip file we can send to TestFlight. Click on the "Default Job" link, then click on the "Add task" button and select the script tasks. In the description field that appears, fill "Zipping the dSYM file". Select "inline" as the script location and paste the following command in the textarea:

```
cd ${bamboo.build.working.directory}/build
find . -name "*.dSYM" -exec zip ${bamboo.build.working.directory}/build/GithubJobs.dSYM.zip {} \;
```

This is pretty much the same command that we used for Jenkins, only the environment variables are different. This command will create a ZIP of the dSYM file, to make this dSYM archive available to the deployment plan, we'll need to archive it as an artifact, just like we did for the IPA file in the previous chapter. Press "Save" and select the "Artifacts" tab, where you should see the "Github Job IPA file" artifact definition already configured.

Create a new definition. Fill in the "Name" field with "Github Job compressed dSYM file", "build" in the "Location" one, and "*.dSYM.zip" in the "Copy pattern" one. Press "Create" when you're done. You should now have two artifacts definitions, as shown in Figure 7-9.

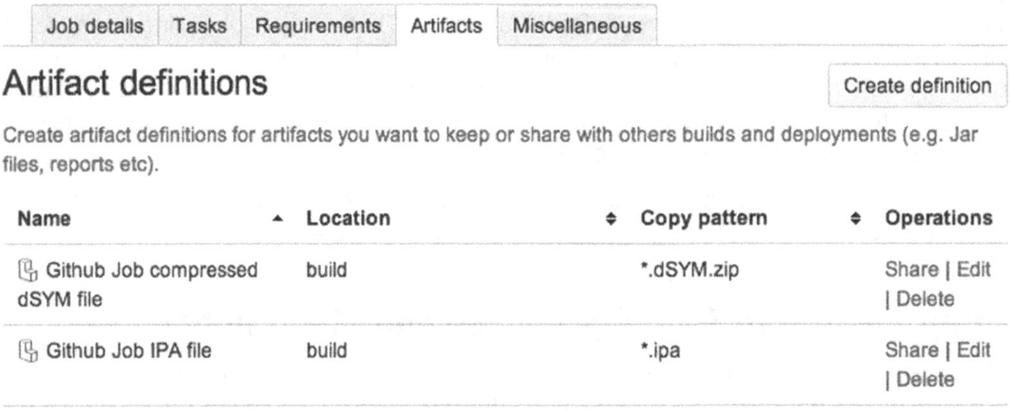

| Job details | Tasks | Requirements | Artifacts | Miscellaneous |

Artifact definitions

Create definition

Create artifact definitions for artifacts you want to keep or share with others builds and deployments (e.g. Jar files, reports etc).

Name	Location ▲	Copy pattern ⬍	Operations ⬍
🗍 Github Job compressed dSYM file	build	*.dSYM.zip	Share | Edit | Delete
🗍 Github Job IPA file	build	*.ipa	Share | Edit | Delete

Figure 7-9. We configured two artifacts definitions

The default behavior for the archived artifacts of a build is to remain private. If you need them for another Job, say for a deployment one, you need to share them. To do that, press the Share link for both the IPA and the dSYM zipped folder. Note that we could have shared them right away when we created them. We are now ready to create the deployment job.

Creating the deployment job

Go back to the Github Jobs for iOS configuration and while in the "Stages" section, click on the "Create deployment project" button. In the description field of the "Deployment project details" section, fill "Sending the build to testflight", because that's what we are trying to achieve.

Leave the other default options: since we haven't talked about a proper Git workflow we will build the master branch or the iOS application plan in the Github Jobs project. Press the "Create deployment project" button.

The next thing we need to do is create an environment, which is a configuration of where the application must be deployed. In our case we need to create a "beta" environment that will send the build to TestFlight, but we could have a production environment that sends the build directly to the App store, for example. Press the "Add environment" button, fill in the "Environment name" with "Beta" and press the "Continue to task setup" button.

Configuring a deployment job is very similar to configuring a standard job: you need to configure a list of tasks that will be run sequentially. The deployment job already comes with two tasks: one that will clean the working directory and one that will download the artifacts in the working directory. The working directory is the location when the deploy process will happen.

Contrary to Jenkins where we added the deploy process at the end of the job, the way Bamboo works is a bit different, as deploying and building jobs are two different things. In total fairness we could achieve the same behavior with Jenkins as a job can be triggered at the end of another job. We could totally have a build job that would trigger a deploy job.

Click Save and go back to the deployment project - even if we haven't added any tasks yet – and press Deploy. A deploy build is based on a branch (in our case, we want to deploy the result of the build run against the master branch) and a build number, usually the last one. Finally, the deployment needs a name. The default value for this field the name of the build plan with the number of the build you want to deploy, for example "iOS application-26". Press the "start deployment" button, and wait a few seconds.

For now the only time-consuming task performed is the download of the artifacts. The duration depends on the location artifacts are coming from but in most situations, they are simply copied from one place on an agent to another. This means that by the time you've finished reading this sentence, the deploy job should be over.

If you look at the log, you should see something similar to the following:

```
24-May-2014 15:10:44 Build Deployment of 'release-2' on 'Beta' started building on agent
Default Agent
24-May-2014 15:10:44 Build working directory is /Users/Palleas/.bamboo/xml-data/build-
dir/2981890-3145731
```

Opening your terminal and displaying the content using the command tree (available via homebrew, for example) of this build directory should give you the following output:

```
$ cd /Users/Palleas/.bamboo/xml-data/build-dir/2981890-3145731
$ tree
.
└── build
    ├── GithubJobs.dSYM.zip
    └── GithubJobs.ipa

1 directory, 2 files
```

This means that these two files are available for us to use the way we want to, and we want to upload them to TestFlight!

If you go back to the tasks list management of your deployment job, click on "Add task" and look for a task which name contains "TestFlight" you should actually find one. Its full name is "Upload iOS application to TestFlightApp.com configuration" and is available because, in the previous chapter, you installed the Xcode plugin for Atlassian. It works pretty much the way the one for Jenkins does but at the time we are writing this book, the latest version of this plugin doesn't work very well with the latest version of Bamboo and causes the job to fail for some Java dependency injection error. Once again, that is the downside of using with a semi-supported plugin. But fear no more, for we have a solution! Remember that little gem called Shenzhen we mentioned in Chapter 3? Well it comes with a helpful command to upload ipa files to TestFlight, so that's what we are going to use instead.

Uploading a file to TestFlight using Shenzhen is super simple. The syntax looks like this:

```
$ ipa distribute:testflight -help

  Usage: ipa distribute:testflight [options]
  Options:
    -f, --file FILE .ipa file for the build
    -d, --dsym FILE zipped .dsym package for the build
    -a, --api_token TOKEN API Token. Available at https://testflightapp.com/account/#api-token
    -T, --team_token TOKEN Team Token. Available at https://testflightapp.com/dashboard/team/edit/
    -m, --notes NOTES Release notes for the build
    -l, --lists LISTS Comma separated distribution list names which will receive access to the build
    --notify Notify permitted teammates to install the build
    --replace Replace binary for an existing build if one is found with the same name/bundle version
```

Contrary to the Jenkins plugin, there is no way to automatically fetch the Git history and use it as the release notes. You could probably hack something during the execution of the build process and store the result as a text file artifact that you would retrieve and use during the deployment job, but that's a bit out of scope. Just know that it can be done.

Clear the search field while still in the "Add Task" panel and once again, look for the "Script" one. In the Task description field fill "Using Shenzhen to upload the file to TestFlight", select "Inline" from the script location combo box and in the script body text area enter the following command:

```
ipa distribute:testflight \
-f "build/Github Jobs.ipa"
-d "build/Github\ Jobs.ipa-dSYM.zip" \
-T 17a2c80c77933a14e002c369560b73ee_MzgyNjAzMjAxNC0wNS0xOSAyMjo0Njo1MS4yNjE2MzA \
-a 4d219661d922badbc7489b2173791483_MTg2MDU0NzIwMTQtMDUtMTkgMjI6NDA6MzEuOTE3NDU4 \
-m "Changed stuff, like a lot"
```

Finally, press the "Save" button and then the "Back to deployment project" one. When you're ready, hit the deploy button. Unless you've been running builds in the background while you were reading this book, this time you shouldn't be asked for the branch, the build result and the name to use for this deployment. That's the default behavior of Bamboo. You want to keep each release meaningful and what is the point of creating a new release to deploy the exact same build result? Press the "Start deployment" button.

You should see the following output at the end of the job's logs:

```
24-May-2014 17:06:58    Build successfully uploaded to TestFlight
24-May-2014 17:06:58    Finished task 'Using Shenzhen to upload the file to testflight'
24-May-2014 17:06:58    Finalising the build...
24-May-2014 17:06:58    Stopping timer.
24-May-2014 17:06:58    Build 2981890-3145731-3637262 completed.
24-May-2014 17:06:58    Finished processing deployment result Deployment of 'release-5' on 'Beta'
```

The build has been successfully uploaded to TestFlight, so that's a victory, but there is one thing that we need to fix. The deployment job now relies on a third-party tool, Shenzhen, to send the build over the air. Of course, as we showed you earlier, we could have used curl, but that wouldn't have given us the opportunity to talk about remote agents one last time.

When we set up our default job that would build the application, we used the agent matrix compatibility to let Bamboo decide which agent the build should be run on. Our needs were pretty simple: we needed a computer with the xcodebuild command. A deployment environment can also be run on a specific agent. The small difference here is that it doesn't use the agent compatibility matrix. This time, you need to explicitly set the agent you want to run the job on. Go back to the deployment job configuration panel, select the "Beta" one we created earlier, and press the "Agents" button. In the list, select the agent or the agents that are allowed to deploy your app. Note that it doesn't have to be an agent with the capability of running the building tasks. After all, Shenzhen is written in Ruby, which works pretty much the same on every platform. You may want to run a deploy job from an agent which is explicitly allowed to upload things to a server because of its IP address or a private authorization key.

Finally, there is one final step missing in our plan: we are still running the deployment jobs manually! From the same environment configuration panel, press the "Triggers" button. Press, the "Add trigger" button and, as shown in Figure 7-10, select "After successful build plan" from the "Trigger type" combo box and make sure the "Use the main plan branch" is checked: you probably don't want to build every feature branch that builds successfully. Press the "Save Trigger" button.

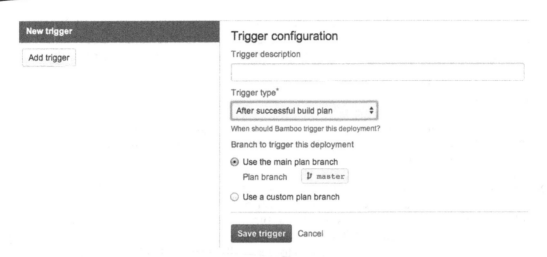

Figure 7-10. A successful build of the master branch will automatically start a deployment job

To make sure everything worked, go back to the "Github Jobs iOS application" plan and hit the build button.

EXERCISE: OBFUSCATE THE TOKENS

Now that you're really starting to master Bamboo, you may not feel confortable that we hardcode the API and team tokens in the shell script that calls Shenzhen's ipa command. To make sure you understand how everything works, make sure those token don't appear anywhere without being obfuscated.

Hint: A bamboo deployment job can use build environment variables just like a regular job.

TestFlight and HockeyApp are great products but the downside with putting everything in the cloud, besides the obvious fact that when Amazon is down you basically can go home and call it a day, is a matter of privacy. Some people don't like not to be able to see where their data is stored or simply want to hack their own distribution platform. This is exactly what we are going to do in the next section!

Writing your own distribution platform

Guiding you through the steps required to develop and deploy a full-featured tool such as TestFlight would take a lot more than a couple of pages. Plus, only a few of these pages would be about iOS and iPhone applications. Because web development is not the goal of this chapter, we are going to focus of the distribution process, and let you work on the remaining part of the apps using the web technology of your choice.

A distribution platform needs to be able to store the built application and a couple of other files we'll cover in the next section.

Understanding the provisioning profile

A provisioning profile is, once again, a file using the property-list format that Apple loves so much. In the previous section, we helped you to generate a distribution provisioning profile that you downloaded from Apple developer portal and installed using the iPhone Configuration Utility. The more Xcode evolves, the more this process gets easier and you can now ask Xcode to automatically download all the provisioning profiles you're entitled too. Still, we only wanted to cover this subject a little so we can tell you more about those provisioning profiles now.

If you're an iOS developer that has already been working on an application and released an application on the App Store, you probably already have struggled with the code-signing process of your application. "Valid signing identity not found", "The executable was signed with invalid entitlements"... These errors are far too common to the community of iOS developers and the solution often suggested is to remove all your provisioning profiles and start fresh. Of course that usually works, but let's have a look at the provisioning profile. Hopefully, you will be able to diagnose these issues and fix them without deleting everything, uninstalling Xcode, and throwing your computer through the window.

Your provisioning profiles are stored in your ~/Library folder, you can either look for all of them using the iPhone Configuration Utility, as we've shown in Figure 7-2, or simply using your terminal. Open a terminal window, navigate to the proper directory and list the files available.

```
$ cd ~/Library/MobileDevice/Provisioning\ Profiles
$ ls -hal
total 1337
drwxr-xr-x  56 staff   1.9K 19 May 20:05 .
drwxr-xr-x   5 staff   170B 31 Mar 19:36 ..
-rw-r--r--   1 staff    15K  4 Apr 11:22 220C65F1-0BAF-4A6F-AE5A-B96F5600DBA8.mobileprovision
-rw-r--r--   1 staff    14K 26 Dec 17:06 05A46FE9-236E-4B40-8625-57A857155A7F.mobileprovision
-rw-r--r--   1 staff    15K  4 Apr 11:22 10F8378B-6638-4A94-AB4B-E505BF562DA9.mobileprovision
-rw-r--r--   1 staff    15K  4 Apr 11:22 18E20B0C-9446-4A68-A4F2-3483D02624E2.mobileprovision
-rw-r--r--   1 staff    15K  4 Apr 11:22 1F908F91-7B22-4B31-8629-7D286FE20ECD.mobileprovision
...
```

The one that really interests us is the first one, that appeared magically at the top of the list because we needed it to. We created it at the beginning of this chapter and used it to distribute the application via TestFlight. We mentioned earlier that a provisioning profile was using the property-list file format. Using your favorite text editor, open your provisioning profile and look at its content.

The file is pretty much human readable but contains weird characters at the beginning:

```
0<82>^\õ^F *<86>H<86>÷^M^A^G^B <82>^\æO<82>^\â^B^A^A1^KO ^F^E+^N^C^B^Z^E^@O<82>^L»^F
*<86>H<86>÷^M^A^G^A <82>^L¬^D<82>^L¨<?xml version="1.0" encoding="UTF-8"?>
<!DOCTYPE plist PUBLIC "-//Apple//DTD PLIST 1.0//EN" "http://www.apple.com/DTDs/PropertyList-
1.0.dtd">
<plist version="1.0">
```

And at the end of the file:

}o¾^@*Ì!YëÿI¬nu^Yè<9a>z^CÑ<86>öçö°^NKIú£·Aº×ÑãV¡}<83>«<97>®øQJ&Á<85>B^S&<8d>^CTf^P^`<84>^E^R1+kTÀ
ÈA¼T^^çT^S^@ÒJÇ»Á<8a>¯<81>^H<8e>ðF
¿'¦¾ÜÏ9:<80>p^Y#2£kf]<9e>M¨GI2{EmQ3§tg N¶loH÷,13^EDkE¾tKo2<86><91>´>%(%<9e>3ÂQ<86>üOå¯;ª»D,^AIât34ú
Dï^TÂ^Qò-^Y^ZQ<89>Ó^HJAlXVÞ<9b>:á^EWåbÏÒ^Oo<82>^Eº0<82>^D¢ ^C^B^A^B^B^A^A0^M^F *<86>H<86>÷^M^A
^A^E^E^@0<81><86>1^KO ^F^CU^D^F^S^BUS1^]0^[^F^CU^D
^S^TApple Computer, Inc.1-0+^F^CU^D^K^S$Apple Computer Certificate Authority1)0'^F^CU^D^C^S
Apple Root Certificate Authority0^^^W^M050210001814Z^W^M250210001814Z0<81><86>1^KO
^F^CU^D^F^S^BUS1^]0^[^F^CU^D
^S^TApple Computer, Inc.1-0+^F^CU^D^K^S$Apple Computer Certificate Authority1)0'^F^CU^D^C^S Apple
Root Certificate Authority0<

Only a few pieces are understandable: "Apple Computer Certificate Authority". The provisioning profile that was generated by Apple is code-signed using the PCKS#7, a public-key cryptography standard. The 7th version is the one that is used to sign messages and is called the Cryptographic Message Syntax (CMS) Standard.

These weird characters are a way to check that the provisioning profile file was not altered after Apple generated it. Remember that Apple only gives you a hundred slots of devices? That would be a shame that you could simply add new Unique Device Identifier by modifying an easy to read Plist file.

If you navigate through the content of this XML file you should see a few key pieces of information, like the name of this provisioning profile:

```
<key>Name</key>
<string>Github Jobs Ad Hoc Distribution</string>
```

A Universally Unique Identifier (UUID) that was generated by Apple:

```
<key>UUID</key>
<string>227G45F1-0BAF-4A6F-AE5A-B96F5825DBA8</string>
```

And the list of iOS Unique Device Identifiers that you added when you generated this provisioning profile:

```
<key>ProvisionedDevices</key>
<array>
    <string>THIS-IS-A-DEVICE-UDID</string>
    <string>THIS-IS-ANOTER-DEVICE-UDID</string>
    <string>THIS-IS-A-THIRD-DEVICE-UDID</string>
    <string>THIS-IS-A-FOURTH-DEVICE-UDID</string>
    <string>THIS-IS-A-FIFTH-DEVICE-UDID </string>
</array>
```

The UUID is important. You've probably already seen it if you changed the code signing settings of your application and wanted to commit these changes through git or another VCS. If you go back to Xcode filter the build settings on "UUID", you should only see the provisioning profiles section, as shown in Figure 7-11. That's because the provisioning profile you want Xcode to use is actually identified by its unique identifier, while you only see its name.

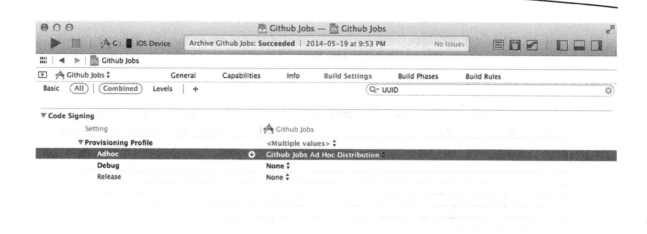

Figure 7-11. Looking for "UUID" will show you the provisioning profile section of you're application's build setting

The provisioning profile also contains information about the entitlement of your application, like if you're going to use iCloud or Apple Push Service (aps). When you run into an inexplicable issue where Xcode is not able to build your application because of one of the errors mentioned above, you might want to take a look at the content of the provisioning profile you are trying to use.

iTunes Music Store XML manifest to the rescue

Now that you know more about the provisioning profile, let's set up our own distribution platform. We will need a simple HTML page, a packaged application, and a XML file that we will call the manifest. In the Android ecosystem, distributing an Application without using the Play store is easy: all you need to do is to show a direct download link to your application that a user will click via the mobile device's browser. If you were to try to do the same on an iPhone, the user would get an error message from iOS saying that it doesn't know what to do with this IPA file. This is a bit annoying and we all know that it is not true.

Sharing an IPA file is a more complex process that requires a proper URL scheme and, as we mentioned earlier, a XML manifest. This information is required so iTunes understand what to do with the file.

Creating a simple HTML page

For the sake of the example, our own distribution platform will contain a single HTML page with a title, a capture of the application, and a download button. From the folder of your choice, create an index.html file with the following content:

```
<!doctype html>
<html>
    <head>
        <title>Download Github Jobs for iOS</title>
    </head>
```

```
    <body>
        <h1>Github Jobs for iOS</h1>
        <a href="<URL>">Click here to download the application</a>
    </body>
</html>
```

Ruby comes with a bundled HTTP server that we can use to share this page on our local network. Open a terminal, navigate to the directory where you stored the index.html file and run the following command:

```
$ ruby -run -e httpd -- --bind-address 0.0.0.0 --port 5000 .
[2014-05-25 16:43:51] INFO  WEBrick 1.3.1
[2014-05-25 16:43:51] INFO  ruby 2.1.1 (2014-02-24) [x86_64-darwin13.0]
[2014-05-25 16:43:51] INFO  WEBrick::HTTPServer#start: pid=46428 port=5000
```

If you open your browser and navigate to the URL localhost:5000, you should see a page similar to the Figure 7-12.

Github Jobs for iOS

Click here to download the application

Figure 7-12. Our very distribution platform looks really great

The manifest

Now that we have our pretty good looking HTML page, let's talk about the XML manifest we need to create so you can download your application. If you remember correctly, the first time we packaged the Github Jobs for iOS application into an IPA file, we used Xcode's organizer. When the organizer asks you where you want to post the generated file, there is a small check box with the label "Save for Enterprise Distribution". When selected, a form appears and asks you some information. Under the hood this information will be stored in a Plist file similar to the one we are about to write.

Go back to your text editor and create a github-jobs.plist file near the index.html, one with the following content:

```
<?xml version="1.0" encoding="UTF-8"?>
<!DOCTYPE plist PUBLIC "-//Apple//DTD PLIST 1.0//EN" "http://www.apple.com/DTDs/PropertyList-
1.0.dtd">
<plist version="1.0">
<dict>
    <key>items</key>
    <array>
        <dict>
```

```
                <key>assets</key>
                <array>
                    <dict>
                        <key>kind</key>
                        <string>software-package</string>
                        <key>url</key>
                        <string>http://<YOUR-LOCAL-IP>:5000/GithubJobs.ipa</string>
                    </dict>
                </array>
                <key>metadata</key>
                <dict>
                    <key>bundle-identifier</key>
                    <string>com.perfectly-cooked.Github-Jobs</string>
                    <key>bundle-version</key>
                    <string>0.1</string>
                    <key>kind</key>
                    <string>software</string>
                    <key>title</key>
                    <string>Github Jobs for iOS</string>
                </dict>
            </dict>
        </array>
    </dict>
</dict>
</plist>
```

Make sure to replace <YOUR-LOCAL-IP> with your actual local IP address and ensure that the bundle-identifier and the bundle-version are the one of your application. Then, copy the latest version of your application – or even better, download it from the artifacts section of your latest Jenkins or Bamboo build – and store it at the same level as your index.html and your github-jobs.plist.

Open your index.html file from your text editor and use the following URL as the href attribute of the download link:

```
itms-services://?action=download-manifest&url=http://172.16.43.115:5000/github-jobs.plist
```

Finally, open Safari mobile from your iOS device (one that is authorized to execute this application, of course) and navigate to your website using your local IP. If you don't know your IP address, open the Network section of the System Preferences where it should be displayed. Remember we used 0.0.0.0 as the binding address so your "website" is accessible on your local network and not only your own computer. Click on the download link. You should be asked if you really want to download the application.

Congratulations, you've set up a very simple distribution platform!

EXERCISE: SEND THE NEW IPA FILE AT THE END OF A JOB

In case you're also interested in web development, here is a simple exercise for you. At the end of a Jenkins or a Bamboo job, send the new IPA file to your webserver so you can always download the latest version of your build.

Bonus: setting up ACL using the provisioning profile

There are a few things that don't work with our own platform: the design, the manual editing of the index.html and github-jobs.plist files, and of course the security! Right now, anybody with access to your local network could easily install the application and use it. If you were to upload this small platform to the cloud, basically anybody could download and install your application.

It is, in fact, really easy to check if a user is authorized to download your application, once again using the application. Even if you wanted to add a simple login/password authentication process to your application, you would still have to check if the user is allowed to install the application. Fortunately, you already specified that when you created the provisioning profile. Let's use it one more time!

Decoding a provisioning profile

We mentioned earlier that an IPA file was nothing but a code-signed ZIP archive containing the application. Well this application itself contains the provisioning profile. In fact, if you unzip the archive and look into the Payload folder, you should see a file named "embedded.mobileprovision". Using your terminal, navigate to the folder (using the "cd" command) that contains the generated IPA file and run the following command:

```
$ unzip Github\ Jobs.ipa
$ cd Payload/Github\ Jobs.app/
Github Jobs.app|master ⇒ ls -hal
total 1032
drwxr-xr-x  13 Palleas  staff   442B 20 May 20:03 .
drwxr-xr-x   3 Palleas staff   102B 20 May 20:03 ..
-rw-r--r--   1 Palleas staff    74K 20 May 20:03 Assets.car
drwxr-xr-x   3 Palleas staff   102B 20 May 20:03 Base.lproj
-rwxr-xr-x   1 Palleas staff   397K 20 May 20:03 Github Jobs
-rw-r--r--   1 Palleas staff   1.4K 20 May 20:03 Info.plist
-rw-r--r--   1 Palleas staff    15K 20 May 20:03 LaunchImage-700-568h@2x.png
-rw-r--r--   1 Palleas staff     8B 20 May 20:03 PkgInfo
-rw-r--r--   1 Palleas staff   150B 20 May 20:03 ResourceRules.plist
drwxr-xr-x   5 Palleas staff   170B 20 May 19:49 SVProgressHUD.bundle
drwxr-xr-x   3 Palleas staff   102B 20 May 20:03 _CodeSignature
-rw-r--r--   1 Palleas staff    12K 20 May 20:03 embedded.mobileprovision
drwxr-xr-x   3 Palleas staff   102B 20 May 20:03 en.lproj
```

The embedded.mobileprovision file contains a list of authorized devices to run the application. If you were to set up a real-life application, simply associate one or many devices identifiers to a user's account and use the information contained in the latest build to see if you should show him the download link. Of course, this is highly theoretical but that should be enough to get you started.

Summary

At the WWDC 2014, Apple announced what they are planning to do now that they had acquired the company behind TestFlight. Internal testing teams, beta distribution up to a thousand of users, crash reports, and user feedbacks are among the planned tasks. Most of these features are still in a beta at the time we are writing this book and will be limited to iOS 8. Some others, like the crash reporting, should be released later in 2015. You can't expect those solutions to be perfect just yet, but that's really something most developers are happy about. What's important here is that you know pretty much how everything works, from using an existing distribution platform to developing your own.

This chapter was about over the air deployment. We introduced you (or not) to a very famous solution called TestFlight that was recently acquired by Apple. This solution is really powerful since it will help you manage your application and multiple teams of users so you can send beta versions of your application without the hassle. We showed you how to send those builds to TestFlight using the command line and even doing so automatically at the end of a build process, using your favorite continuous integration platform.

Now that we've given you a break from the continuous integration platform, you should be ready to discover a new tool that was released by Apple last year: Xcode Bots.

Chapter 8

Day-to-day use of Xcode bots

We mentioned in the first chapter that this book was going to be like a journey. We started with giving you a tour of the tools at your disposal and we set up a simple but powerful continuous integration architecture using multiple platforms. By now we hope you've made a choice between Jenkins and Bamboo but if you haven't, here is a chapter to make it even harder for you to make a decision.

The previous chapters covered the tools from a time when Apple didn't care very much about continuous integration. Fortunately for everyone, clever people found ways to adapt the existing tools to the new technologies and thanks to Jenkins and Bamboo, you should end up with pretty decent continuous integration architectures.

Xcode 5's release was not only about giving you a hint of what OSX 10.10 may look like and allowing you to merge storyboard files without headaches. It comes with major improvements that you will be able to use: OS X server's Xcode service and Xcode bots. Of course it wasn't perfect; we have yet to find an Apple developer tool that was perfect on day one. Some would say Apple doesn't care but we stand with the ones that think they actually do. Xcode bots were more than welcomed the day they were announced. However, at WWDC 2014 Apple announced changes and improvements that make Xcode Bots must-use tools for the iOS and OSX developers.

We'll start with a quick description of why we need to have a look at yet another continuous integration tool and then move to OS X Server, with a little bit of Apple history. Next, we'll move to Xcode 5 and how to integrate it with OS X Server to manage our git repository and be able to create a fancy new bot. Finally, we'll use this bot to build the Github Jobs for iOS application every night and see how it works with a non-officially supported 3 tool: Cocoapods.

Why do we need yet another continuous integration tool?

After we covered how to setup the continuous integration platforms Jenkins and Bamboo, we kind of broke the flow by covering a different subject: over the AIR application deployment. Right now you may be wondering why we would need another continuous integration platform, since everything you know at this point is more than enough to automatically build and deploy an application.

The thing is, Xcode bots are not meant to replace your Jenkins or Bamboo installation. Not yet anyway. At this point, Xcode bots are very promising but also really flawed. In this chapter, we will show you how to install, set up, and use these new features, and how they will fit in your day-to-day workflow.

Let's call this chapter the final quest on your journey to the ideal continuous integration platform. Once we have covered in detail how it works, we will use the remaining chapters to talk about automated testing and quality assurance.

Without further ado, open the Mac app store with a credit card ready and let's dive in.

OS X server

Before we start talking about how the OS X Server works, we need to understand the process that led to the very first release of this tool.

A bit of history

Before OS X Lion, Mac OS X and Mac OS X server where two separate operating systems, the latter was similar to the desktop version but came with additional administrations tools. The server version was meant for rack-mounted server computers called Xserve which have now been replaced by the Mac mini server and the Mac Pro server.

When OS X Lion was released, Mac OS X and Mac OS X server merged into a single operating system called OS X. The server-related components are now released in a separate packaged application that you can download form the Mac App Store. Note that Mac Pro and Mac Mini computers can be bought with OS X preinstalled but as we are going to show you, setting up OS X Server on a computer is pretty trivial.

Installing OS X server on your computer

OS X server will cost $20, and you won't be able to use Xcode's continuous integration features if you don't install it. To run the latest version of OS X server, you will need at least OS X Mavericks and the latest version of Xcode. We are using the third beta of Xcode 6 and version 3.1.5 of OS X Server. Open the Mac App store, search for "OS X Server" and install it on your computer.

Once it's installed, launch it to start the installation process, which will require root privileges. Don't worry though: it will not erase the contents of your computer. At the end of the installation process, you should have an overview of the services available to you through OS X server, similar to Figure 8-1: calendars, messages, mail, time machines, and Xcode, of course.

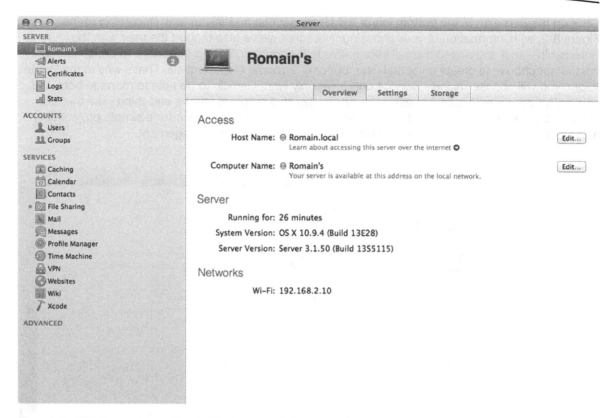

Figure 8-1. OS X Server comes with out of the box support of many services

As you can see, in a couple of clicks we have a server almost ready to work for us where it took a few more steps to do the same with Jenkins or Bamboo. This is one of the reasons a continuous integration platform using OS X Server makes sense: it relies on tools you're already familiar with - like the app store - and it looks and feels like an OS X application.

The service we really care about for now is Xcode, which is disabled by default. Let's activate it so we can get started. Select the Xcode item in the left menu. Toggle the switch in the top-right corner and when the file panel opens, navigate to your Application folder and select the Xcode application. Once the Xcode setup is complete, you should see more information about your newly activated Xcode service.

The first thing to know is that your Xcode server is automatically made available on your local network, in our case that would be "romain.local", which is the default generated hostname of the computer based on its name.

Second, the Xcode service comes with a default permission scheme where only the authenticated users can create Bots and everyone can see them, as long as they are on the same network, of course. OS X server use the same database of user that the operating system. If you go to the Users section from the left menu, you should see all the users present on your computer. Let's say that an intern will join your company next summer, but you don't want to create him a full access to the computer that hosts your OS X server. Let's create an account.

Click on the plus sign at the bottom left of the Users section and fill the form according to the Figure 8-2, with information of your choosing. Note that we've also tagged the user with the "internship" label and added a small informative text about her. What's important to notice is that we did not choose to create an actual user, but only a couple of credentials. That's why in the Home folder, you will choose "None – Service only": we only want Camille to be able to manage bots. We could also use a similar panel to assign our new user to a group of interns and things like that but a) that's a bit out of the scope of this book and b) that would be too much for a simple project such as ours. Press the "Create" button and go back to Xcode's service management.

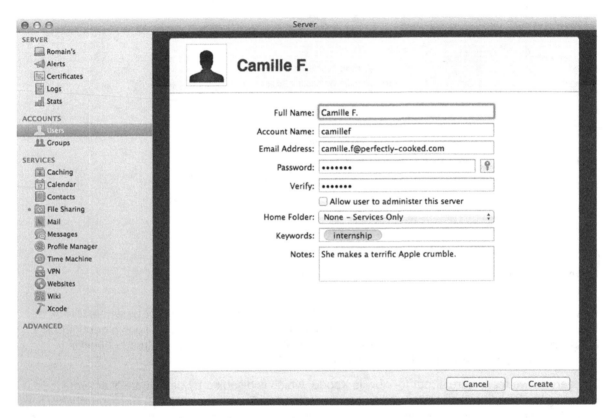

Figure 8-2. Camille the intern will be able to use her credentials to access some of the services

Let's tweak the permissions and make it so only administrators and our intern can create bots, and that only logged in users can view all the bots. To do that, click the edit button next to the permissions section. Select "only some users" in the first combo box, hit the plus sign and search for Camille in the field that appears. Also, check the checkbox button at the bottom of the panel and select "only logged in users" in the combo box next to it. Finally, press OK.

Under this section is more information about how the builds will be performed. The first thing you see is the version of Xcode that will be used to build the application. If you remember correctly what we talked about in Chapter 3, that it is possible to switch between developers directories using xcode-select or the DEVELOPER_DIR environment variable. This is pretty much what this section is here for, only here you have a user interface and a little bit more confusing error message when you try to select an invalid Xcode app: "This application cannot be used with OS X Server."

The Xcode service can also use credentials to connect to your existing Apple developer account so it can automatically download code signing identities and provisioning profiles. Click on the "add" button near to the Developer teams section and fill in your credentials. If this Apple identifier is linked to multiple teams, select the one you want to use with this installation of OS X server. If you're a member of only one team, simply confirm that you really want to add this server to your team.

Last but not least, the Xcode service for OS X server will be able to run tests on multiple devices at once. Even if we'll cover unit testing in the next chapter, plug one of your devices into the computer that runs OS X server and wait until it detects it.

We've made an Xcode service available on our local network, set up basic permissions, configured the developer directory where it will find all the tool it needs to build the application and finally we configured our Apple developer account and plugged a device. At the end, your service configuration should look like Figure 8-3.

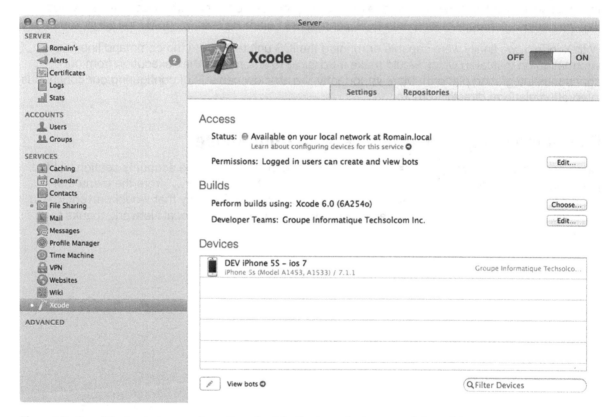

Figure 8-3. Everything has been properly configured and the Xcode service is now ready to work for us

One of the great features in this new release is that OS X Server is now capable of hosting Git (and SVN, but…) repositories as well as connecting to existing ones, as you can see in the "Repositories" tab in the top menu, but we will cover this part in the next section. It is time to leave OS X Server for now and see how things work on the Xcode side.

Xcode 6

Xcode 5 was a very important release for many developers. It came with a lot of upgrades and fixes for interface builder, especially for Auto Layout. What's even more important is that it came with integration with OS X server, thanks to the Xcode service we configured earlier. At the WWDC 2014, Apple announced a new version of Xcode, which is even better.

Just like iOS 7.0, the beginning of the communication between Xcode and the OS X server were a little rough. This section will cover how to setup a continuous integration architecture for your project using only Apple technologies.

Continuous integration

Being able to run unit tests from a single keystroke or compiling, archiving, and packaging an application using a couple of steps is nothing new. The first one has the downside of taking time that you don't necessarily have and most of the time the developer will forget to do so, which would make your test suite pointless. The second one is a boring process. To fix that, we discovered a few tools that we could use directly or wrap into build scripts, like Facebook's xctool or Marin Usalj's xcpretty.

With Xcode 5, we finally were capable or running the iOS unit tests from the command line (more information on that later) which would make it possible to automatize their execution from our continuous integration platform. More importantly, we are now capable of configuring our continuous integration platform directly from Xcode.

Communicating with Xcode service from Xcode

Open Xcode's preferences (or hit "⌘ + ," with Xcode open) and select the accounts section. Hit the plus sign at the bottom-left corner of the window and select "Add server..." from the menu that appears. If everything is working as expected and you don't have a proxy that would prevent it, you should see that your server has been automatically discovered on your local Network, thanks to bonjour, as shown in Figure 8-4.

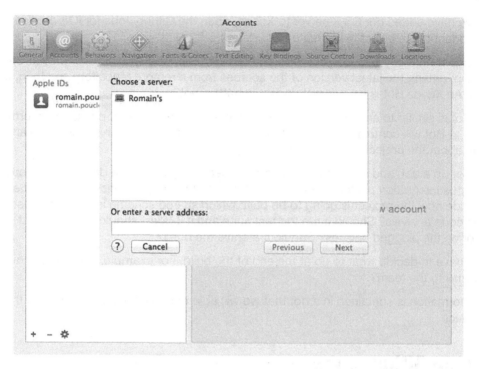

Figure 8-4. The instance of OS X server we've set up is automatically discovered on the local network

> **Note**   Bonjour: Bonjour is Apple's implementation of the zero-configuration networking group. Originally called "RendezVous", Bonjour can be use to locate other computers using multicast Domain Name System (mDNS) service record.

Note that a similar behavior could be achieved with Jenkins, as it will respond with an XML based message containing information about the installation if you send an UDP broadcast on your network, as shown in the following command:

```
$ echo "Hey Jenkins" | nc -u 0.0.0.0 33848
<hudson>
        <version>1.560</version>
        <url>http://localhost:8080/</url>
        <server-id>990ad56b5659020020aee81d644db8ca</server-id>
        <slave-port>57621</slave-port>
</hudson>
```

This is useful if you want to make sure that your instance or instances Jenkins master and slaves are reachable from one to another.

Select your OS X Server from the list and press the Next button. In the window that appears, enter the credentials you've chose for the intern and press OK. Note that a Guest access is available but since we've configured it this way, it won't be able to access the existing bots, let alone create one.

Now that we have added our OS X server to Xcode, open the Github Jobs for iOS application and from the Product menu select the "Create Bot…" item.

If you remember correctly how our jobs worked both with Bamboo and Jenkins, they all started with a simple step: getting the latest version of the sources from a remote repository and then, the build could start. An Xcode Bot is no different. In fact, what's a bot?

An Xcode Bot is similar to an Xcode scheme in that they both are a set of packaged information and instructions. A Bot will contain a reference to a remote repository that he has access to and other information about the project to build: when, how, and what then.

When you set up a bot, and we'll cover this part in a second, you have to decide, like pretty much any continuous integration platform, when you want to build a project. Once this is decided, you have to decide how the project is going to be built: which shared scheme is it going to use? Should it run static code analysis? Should it run the test suite and if it does, should it run the tests in the simulator or on the plugged devices? Should it archive the build?

Finally, you have to decide what to do at the end of the build. For example, if it failed, should you send an e-mail to the team?

All of this information is contained in a bot that we will able to build the application from the OS X Server instance.

Setting up Github Jobs

A great feature of the new OS X server is the ability to host git repositories, which makes it technically a viable replacement for third-party services such as Github or Bitbucket. Of course, that is not entirely true since these services do not only provide hosting but also pull requests, release management, and things like that. In this section, we'll see how to create our very first bot, give access to our remote repository to Xcode server and see what can be done to manage the dependencies.

Nightly build of Github Jobs for iOS using Xcode bots

A bot is capable of different things: running tests, using code static analysis and archiving the application. Because we are saving the best for the end of this book, we will only create a bot that will archive the build every night.

We mentioned earlier that the information provided by an Xcode Bot was the scheme that should be used to build the application. If we use the command line to get a quick look at the available schemes, here is what we get:

```
$ xcodebuild -list
Information about project "Github Jobs":
    Targets:
        Github Jobs
        Github JobsTests

    Build Configurations:
        Debug
        Adhoc
        Release
```

If no build configuration is specified and -scheme is not passed then "Release" is used.

Schemes:
    Github Jobs

The only scheme available if the Github Jobs scheme we used in our script to build the application via Bamboo or Jenkins. Open the "Manage Scheme" panel from Xcode, open the details of this Scheme and uncheck, if needed, the Shared checkbox. Close the "manage schemes" window and go back to the Bot creation window. If you try to use that scheme to build the Github Jobs for iOS application, a "Share scheme" checkbox will be automatically checked, as shown in Figure 8-5 and if you try to uncheck that scheme, the OK button will be disabled.

We already covered the scheme-sharing problem in Chapter 3 and we mentioned how easy it was to forget about this option. That's yet another advantage of using a tool dedicated to Xcode project: you simply can't create an Xcode Bot based on a non-shared scheme.

Fill in the Name field with a dedicated name to your nightly build bot. Feel free to get creative, after all what is the point of using tools referencing robots if you can't give them awesome name? We'll call ours "Klaus".

Make sure the server selected is the one you set up in the past section and, as shown in Figure 8-5, make sure the "Commit changes and integrates immediately" option is checked.

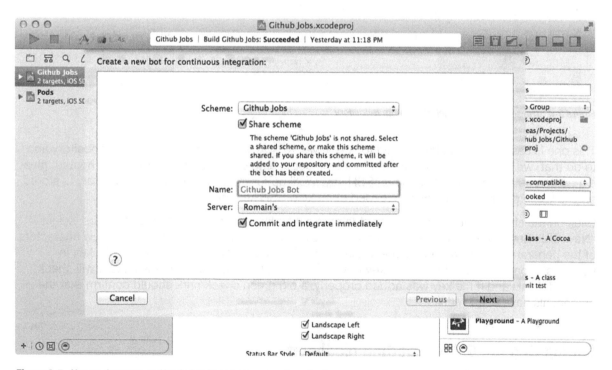

Figure 8-5. *You can't create an Xcode bot based on a non-shared scheme*

Granting access to the remote repository on GitHub

The next step of the configuration of this bot will search your working copy for a remote the server has access to. Unfortunately, it has access to none and you will get a warning, as shown in Figure 8-6.

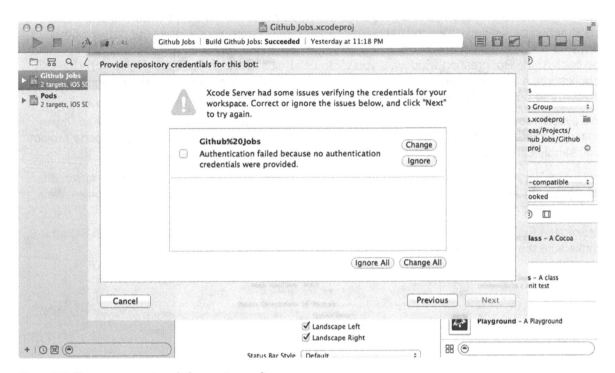

Figure 8-6. *The server cannot reach the remote repository*

This one is easy to fix, we simply need to find a way to give the server access to our repository and to do that, we have exactly two different options, depending on where the repository is hosted: give it a username and password or use an SSH key. We'll go for the SSH key as our repository is stored on GitHub, a company that has succeeded at making SSH key management a breeze.

Click on the change button on the right side of this warning and in the menu that appears, select "New SSH Key". Leave "git" as the username and click on the little gear near the first few characters of the generated public key. In the menu that appears, select "copy" to store the public key in your pasteboard and add this public key to your account. Once it's done, press next. It will check the credentials and if the key was added properly, a big green checkmark should confirm that the credentials have been verified.

Configuring the Bot and getting feedback

In the next window, select "Periodically" in the schedule combo box and make it a Daily build that will happen at 1 AM every day. Then, uncheck "Perform analyze action" and "Perform test section": for now we only want to build the application like our continuous integration script has been doing in the past chapters. Finally, press "Next".

This last screen is pretty important. We mentioned earlier that an Xcode bot was a simple container of information about how and when to perform very specific actions. Well, this panel will also allow you to configure the things that should happen before and after these actions. The default configuration of this screen is to send mails to the committers in case of failure of the build or the analysis. These committers are identified by their name and e-mail every time a commit is made:

```
$ git show 1e93f4d83499660e63fc9ec21cbd16803f7f4268
commit 1e93f4d83499660e63fc9ec21cbd16803f7f4268
Author: Romain Pouclet <palleas@gmail.com>
Date:   Sat May 31 18:38:52 2014 -0400

    Fix script and scheme and stuff
```

This also means that if you decide to build an open-source library you found on GitHub via an Xcode Bot, the authors might get e-mails about failing builds. Think before you integrate!

We'll go back to this screen in a few moments so simply click the "Create " button and wait for the magic to happen. It is in fact an awesome feedback to start working in the morning and know right away if anything is wrong with the project.

In the last screen, select both "committers" checkboxes so everyone who contributed to the project that is being built will be aware of the result of the nightly build.

> **warning/caution**   For some reason, Xcode may not be able to automatically open the commit panel. If that's the case, select Source Control > Commit and commit your changes manually. It is important if the scheme is not properly scheme, the Xcode service will not be able to build your application.

When you're ready, navigate to the log navigator, which is the last tab in Xcode's file explorer. This is the panel where you'll find a list of all the actions that we performed. If it hasn't started already, right-click on your Bot and select the "Integrate Now" item so you can immediately see the results of your integration, which probably failed with an error related to your Podfile. Hang in there, we'll fix it in the next section. First, let's take a look at the feedback available directly in Xcode. The first section, as shown in Figure 8-7, sums up was happened during the build: the actual errors, the warnings, the results of the static analysis, and the results of the unit tests.

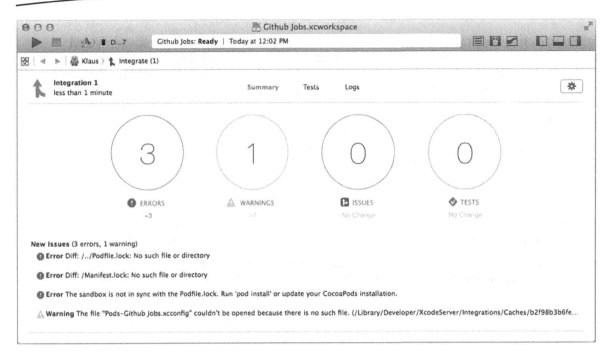

Figure 8-7. The integration failed with three errors and one warning

Note that the issues visible on this figure are listed under an "Unresolved Issues" section. Because this is actually the first integration ever performed by this Bot, these issues are marked as new.

The second section, as shown in Figure 8-8 shows the list of commits involved in an integration that happened later. When a new integration is performed, the bot will fetch the new commits on the remote repository. In case of build failed, you can easily see when the error might have been introduced.

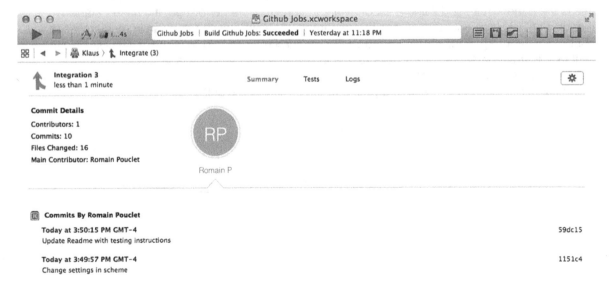

Figure 8-8. The second section of the integration detail shows the list of committers involved

> **Note** Git alone is capable of locating where a regression was introduced thanks to the `git bisect` command by performing a "binary" search. More information on this page:
> http://git-scm.com/book/en/Git-Tools-Debugging-with-Git#Binary-Search

Let's have a look at why the integration is failing now. If you look at Figure 8-9, you can see errors obviously related to Cocoapods: the PodFile.lock and the Manifest.lock files cannot be found, nor can the xconfig file and we are seeing an error about the sandbox not in sync.

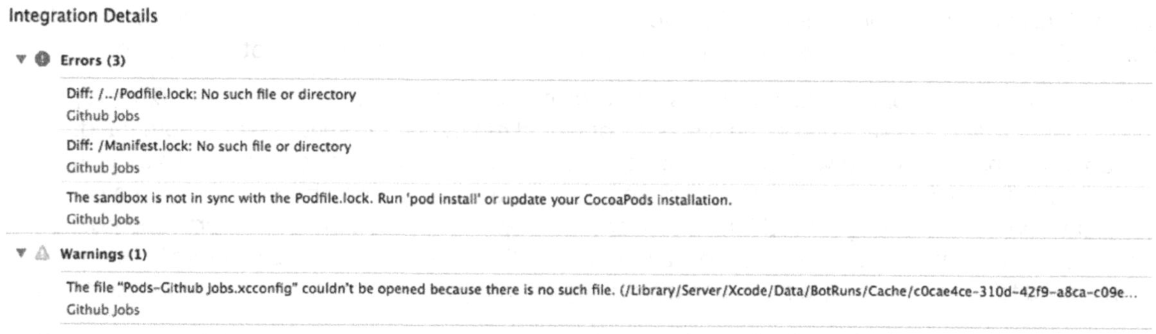

Integration Details

▼ ⓘ **Errors (3)**

    Diff: /../Podfile.lock: No such file or directory
    Github Jobs

    Diff: /Manifest.lock: No such file or directory
    Github Jobs

    The sandbox is not in sync with the Podfile.lock. Run 'pod install' or update your CocoaPods installation.
    Github Jobs

▼ ⚠ **Warnings (1)**

    The file "Pods–Github Jobs.xcconfig" couldn't be opened because there is no such file. (/Library/Server/Xcode/Data/BotRuns/Cache/c0cae4ce-310d-42f9-a8ca-c09e...
    Github Jobs

Figure 8-9. The integration still fails for some reason related to CocoaPods

To understand this error, you must first remember what we mentioned in Chapter 2, about all the tools at our disposal to setup our continuous integration platform. One of these tools was the "Run script build phases" that you can add to your build process and that will run arbitrary shell scripts.

Navigate to the "build phases" tab from the details of the Github Jobs target, you should see a phase called "Check Pods Manifest.lock" running the following script:

```
diff "${PODS_ROOT}/../Podfile.lock" "${PODS_ROOT}/Manifest.lock" > /dev/null
if [[ $? != 0 ]] ; then
    cat << EOM
error: The sandbox is not in sync with the Podfile.lock. Run 'pod install' or update your CocoaPods
installation.
EOM
    exit 1
fi
```

This script uses the PODS_ROOT, a user-defined build setting that was added by CocoaPods the first time you ran the pod install command, to locate both Podfile.lock and Manifest.lock files. This file contains information about your dependencies, so that the next time you or one of the people working with you need to install the latest version of your project, the dependencies will be installed at the same versions. With the two paths to those files, it then uses the diff command to compare those files. If they don't match, it means that the dependencies currently bundled with your project are not at the proper version. You fix this problem by running the pod install from your project's directory.

This script fails because the Manifest.lock file does not exist, nor does the Pods folder containing your dependencies. That would probably necessitate adding the Pods folder to your main repository but we really don't want to do that. What we want to do is installing our dependencies before the build actually starts.

Installing the dependencies during an integration performed by an Xcode Bot

The first solution that should come to mind would be to add yet another run script build phase, but that causes a few issues. A build phase is stored at the target's level and in our case we would be tweaking the "Github Jobs" target. This also means that every time we build the application from Xcode, the script will run. We could simply add an if condition in the script that would exit if it wasn't performed by the "_teammserver" user, but that would not be a very stable and trustable solution. We could also duplicate the target but that would mean managing two targets, one for the day-to-day work and one for the continuous integration. Tweaking the target is definitely not the solution.

In Xcode 5, installing your dependencies was a tedious process, to say the least. You had to use a pre-build scheme action that would execute a script that would run the famous pod install command. This approach had several downsides: because this script was stored at the scheme level, you wouldn't get any output from the execution of the script and had to manually redirect this output to some file. The great news is we no longer need this hack, because Apple introduced in Xcode 6 pre- and post-integration triggers. We've already seen how a post-integration trigger can send the committers e-mail when a build fails, let's see how we can use a pre-integration trigger to invoke the cocoapods executable.

From the integration screen, click on the setting gear at the top right of the screen, it will allow you to edit the settings of your Bot. Click next until your reach the "Configure bot triggers" section. Click the "Add Trigger" button under the "Before Integration" header and select "Run Script". In the field that appears, enter the following script:

```
export LC_ALL="en_US.UTF-8"
PODFILE=`find . -type f - name Podfile`
cd `dirname $PODFILE`
pod install
```

This script is pretty straightforward. The first thing it does is to define the current locale. This is requirement from Cocoapods, otherwise you'll get the following error:

```
CocoaPods requires your terminal to be using UTF-8 encoding. See
https://github.com/CocoaPods/guides.cocoapods.org/issues/26 for possible solutions.
```

Then, it uses the find command to locate the PodFile. When this script is executed, the current directory is not your project root directory. Once this file is located, the dirname command is used to retrieve the path to the directory containing this file and navigate to this directory. Note that we could have hardcoded the path to this folder, but this way is probably cleaner in case you change the name of your project, for example.

Once we've navigated to this folder, we run the pod install command to install the dependencies. The Pods folder is created with the Manifest.lock file in it and the xcconfig file that contains extra information needed for Cocoapods to behave normally. For example, this is the one that was generated for our project:

```
GCC_PREPROCESSOR_DEFINITIONS = $(inherited) COCOAPODS=1
HEADER_SEARCH_PATHS = "${PODS_ROOT}/Headers" "${PODS_ROOT}/Headers/SVProgressHUD"
OTHER_CFLAGS = $(inherited) -isystem "${PODS_ROOT}/Headers" -isystem
"${PODS_ROOT}/Headers/SVProgressHUD"
OTHER_LDFLAGS = -ObjC -framework QuartzCore
PODS_ROOT = ${SRCROOT}/Pods
```

What's important here is the PODS_ROOT that is declared to contain the path to the Pods directory. When this file can't be loaded, the PODS_ROOT build setting is not available during build time. This also means that the path to the Manifest.lock file cannot be computed, hence the integration fails we've been having.

It may seem surprising that Apple released a tool that requires so much work to make it behave properly but remember that we are using a third-party tool that isn't affiliated with Apple whatsoever. In all fairness with Xcode and the OS X Server Xcode server, if we weren't relying on Cocoapods to manage our dependencies, we could have set everything up in a few minutes. From creating the project, to building it using a bot as well as hosting it on the OS X Server.

If you try to start an integration now the errors related to Cocoapods should no longer happen and be listed under the list of resolved issues, as shown in Figure 8-10.

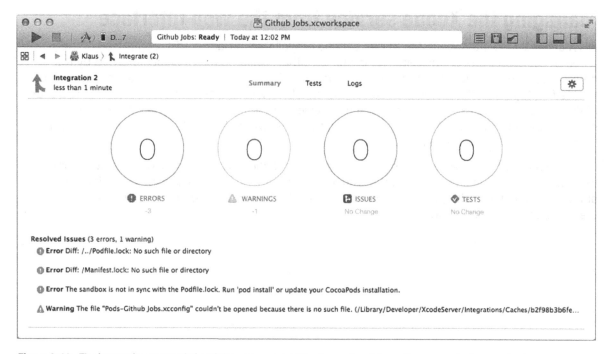

Figure 8-10. The integration succeeded and the errors we had the in previous integration are marked as resolved

When we used Jenkins or Bamboo to build the application, both platforms had in common the ability to restrict the build to a specific branch of the application. We haven't seen this feature with the Xcode Bot, but that does not mean it's not there.

When you create a bot from Xcode, it will retrieve the name of the branch your project currently uses and restrict the Bot to this specific branch. If you want to change the name of the branch, you'll have to edit the Bot from the log panel and without changing anything, simply click your way through the few steps of the process. We'll admit that this is not a very good process but that's only because Xcode has limited control over the parameters of a Bot. The Xcode integration is meant to be very simple process: you are working on a feature and want to know if you've broken anything. Once your feature is done, delete (or update) the Bot and move on.

To be honest, you could probably not find a worse name than Klaus for your bot; we've only used it so we have a reason to change it later. You should always use self-explanatory names so you can quickly know their purpose. For example, our bot should probably be named "Github Jobs (Nightly)", that would make more sense and be easier to find in the list of bots. To do that, as well as to change the branch the integration will be run on, simply go back to the setting panel using the gear button at the top right of the screen we used earlier to add a pre-integration trigger.

The only way to have better control over your OS X server continuous integration platform is to use a different interface that communicates directly with your server: the web interface. Since we've covered pretty much everything there is to know about the bots, Xcode side, let's move on to the web interface. Note that in Xcode 5 there was a way to edit directly a Bot's settings from the web interface but as of the latest beta of the Xcode server, this feature seems to be gone.

Managing the Xcode service from the web interface

OS X server's web interface to the Xcode service is available through a URL composed of the name of your computer on the network, in our case that would be romain.local followed by the path component "xcode", which gives us: `http://romain.local/xcode`. You can guess the URL by yourself or, from the OS X server Xcode service panel, click on the "View bots" button at the bottom of the screen. You can also click on the settings wheel at the top right of the Xcode screen and select "View Bot in browser". Of course, this last solution will open the details about a bot, not the "homepage" of your Xcode service.

OS X Server will not show you an error if you aren't authenticated but because we've configured it this way at the beginning of this chapter, you'll have to authenticate if you want to see information about the currently existing bots, as shown in Figure 8-11.Fill in the credentials of the user you created earlier, and press "Log In".

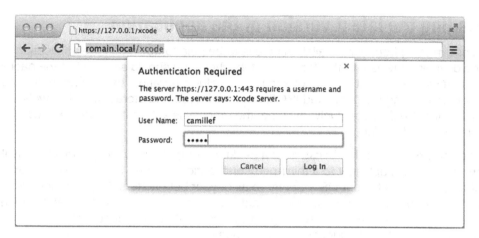

Figure 8-11. *The web interface comes with a log in form*

The main interface shows information about the latest integration and the next one to happen, as well as a list of the latest available download. Beneath these blocks is the list of all the currently existing bots with their status and the time of the latest integration. Click on the name of your Bot from this list to show more details.

The web interface is very similar to what we've seen in Xcode, as shown in Figure 8-12. You have the list of the past integrations on the left, and the current status of the bot on the right, focused on the results of the latest integration.

Figure 8-12. *This webpage shows the detailed information about Klaus the bot*

Downloading the latest version of the application

The final piece missing from our installation here is to be able to download the application and install it on testing devices. Navigate to the "Archives" tab where you should see a list of the packages application that was created at the end of each successful integration. Every time, both the archived version of the project and the generated IPA file were retrieved and stored here, like we've been doing with Jenkins and Bamboo. Only this time, the process is automatic since it knows exactly what pattern of file to look for.

If you click on one of the "Product" links from a desktop computer, you will be able to download it so you can, for example, upload it to a third-party distribution platform like Testflight. After all, you don't want to give access to your OS X Server to all of your beta testers. On the other end, if you try to click on this link from an iOS device, you will actually be able to download this application and run it on your device! That's the kind of advantages that come with a continuous integration platform dedicated to one technology. In our case, that's Xcode projects.

Using the big screen feature to get live feedback

We mentioned earlier that the crucial part of a continuous integration platform was being able to get instantaneous feedback to know if you've broken your application or if you're hurting the product in any way. That's why both Jenkins and Bamboo come with solutions to display the current status of an installation. OS X Server and its Xcode service are now different. If you click on the first icon in the menu at the top of the screen, it will open the "Big screen", a web page dedicated to, well, big screens such as TVs. As shown in Figure 8-13, this interface will automatically update to show the details on the latest integrations.

Figure 8-13. The "big screen" mode provides a more suitable way to display results about builds

Summary

It took a while but Apple is finally stepping up to the world of continuous integration. Even if we are still far from a tool capable of replacing our installation of Jenkins or Bamboo, it really shows the advantages of using a tool dedicated to a platform. Forget about scheme sharing and complex processes to get a nightly build, with OS X server and the Xcode service, you're a couple of clicks away from creating a project, hosted on your server automatically building every time you push a commit to your remote.

We've showed you how to install and get started with OS X Server and how to be able to use it even if you're not working the way Apple suggests by using your own provisioning profile and relying on a third-party tool to manage your dependencies.

We haven't covered all the features provided by this tool, it is in fact also capable of running your test suites and that's exactly what the next chapter will be about.

Chapter 9

Adding Unit testing to the mix

We are approaching the end of this book, which means you should have learned a few things about continuous integration by now. We've covered the major solutions to setting up a continuous integration environment: The free and open-source solution that is Jenkins; the enterprise one with an opinionated workflow that is Bamboo; and finally the official one, the Xcode Bots. It will take some time before the Xcode Bots become the de-facto solution for continuous integration of Xcode projects, but the previous chapter showed that we are slowly getting there.

Although we covered a few different solutions, in the end all we did was build the application. Of course we also had to fetch the latest version of the source and install the dependencies while making sure the keychain was accessible so we could codesign the application. As complex as this process may be, it's only a small part of the feedback that can provide a continuous integration platform. An application that builds properly doesn't mean an application that works as expected.

This chapter will cover another kind of feedback that can help you detect that your application doesn't work as it should: automated unit testing.

The first part will be about automated testing, what it is and it is important. Even if automated testing is not the core topic of this book, most people only see the time-consuming part of writing tests and when a project's deadline starts to look difficult to meet, they usually are the first things to go. Then, we'll go deeper into the subject and write our first unit tests for the Github Jobs for iOS application, talk about how they work, best practices, and how to run them. More importantly, we'll cover how to run them from the command line so we can make them a part of our continuous integration process, along with the one that builds the application.

Automated Testing

In the software world, automated testing is the use of a dedicated tool that can repeat a predefined number of testing scenarios. For each scenario, the resulting outcome is compared to the expected one. If they are equal, then the test is marked as passing. If they are not, the test is marked a failed. The main advantage of most of the available testing tools is to be able to re-run failed test cases until "all is green".

Reasons to test

There are many reasons to test, the most obvious one being that you need to make sure everything works as expected. It doesn't matter which kind of test you are writing, this is a common pattern for all of them: starting with a couple of initial parameters, apply a few specific modifications to those parameters, and make sure the final outcome matches the expected one. In the case of unit testing, it would mean comparing the result of a method invoked with specific parameters to a final, fixed value.

A lot of people think that testing is reserved for some kind of elite developer with special skills that help them understand what an assertion is. It may be true for some of the more obscure technologies out there but it's definitely not the case for iOS and OSX applications, especially now that Apple made automated testing a first-class citizen in the development process. Your application automatically comes with a testing target and running your test suite is only a keystroke away. There was a time when unit testing an iOS project was hard, but Apple made sure that time is over.

Once you've reached a stable version of your product, let's say the first version that made it to the store, you may be lucky enough to have some time dedicated to cleaning and refactoring. We all know how that works and everybody has once had to cut some corners and use the more pragmatic approach to meeting a deadline. It's in those situations that you should force yourself into writing a test case for the hack you're currently writing. When you have to get back to these pieces of code, knowing how they should behave will help you rewrite it and your test suite will help you detect that you've broken something. That's the beauty of automated testing: the implementation does not matter (much) as long as the end result meets the expectations.

Bad project managers commonly think that one solution to making a project go faster is to simply throw developers at it until it's done. We all know that it couldn't be less true. That's especially problematic when the current developers need to spend time teaching how the project works to a new developer joining the team. We're not saying that you should be rude to new developers but once your project has reached a certain point in terms of the test suite, this will start acting as the best documentation for your project you could ever write. Test cases describe various parts of the application. A new developer will simply have to navigate through the different scenarios to have a better understanding of the project. Note that the new developer could be a metaphor for the future you, when you will have to go back to this project six months from now. Do you not overlook the test scenarios in your application: nobody likes writing documentation.

Last but not least, there is an intense feeling of satisfaction from watching the execution of a test suite where no failure happens. If this quest for the "green bar" can quickly become addictive, being able to come back home after a hard day of work knowing that you have digital proofs of the well-being of your application is priceless. How many of us already had trouble sleeping because of a feature in an application that went live when we knew it wasn't truly stable?

Reasons not to test

With a little experience, it becomes difficult to find reasons not to test, especially because of all the advantages we listed in the previous section.

We mentioned earlier that during projects with hard-to-meet deadlines, automated tests are usually the first thing to go. Don't worry; you will go back to them during the next iteration. Only you won't. If you didn't take the time back then, chances are you won't take the time now either. Plus, the longer you wait, the more tests you'll have to write or update so they pass. Automated testing can take a lot of stress off knowing that even if you're late, the features that are implemented work as expected.

To be honest, the only acceptable situation in which not writing tests make sense is for very simple projects. At the beginning of this book we mentioned that you have to be pragmatic with your continuous integration platform. It goes the same way for unit testing. Don't write test cases for the sake of testing, do it because it helps you create a better product.

Unit testing

In software programming, unit testing is a method used to test small pieces of the software's source code. When you think within the Oriented-Object-Programing paradigm, a unit usually means a class and each test case means a scenario that runs against methods in the class.

The concept of unit testing is language-agnostic and each language usually comes with is de-facto unit testing framework: JUnit for the java ecosystem, PHPUnit for the PHP one, and of course, XCTest for Objective-C. This framework was released to the public with Xcode 5 and was a replacement for SenTestingKit, an old testing framework bundled with Xcode since Xcode 2.

We mentioned earlier that unit tests were now first-class citizens in an Xcode project. The Github Jobs for iOS application is a really small application, but since unit testing is not the core topic of this book, that's more than enough to introduce you to it and let you work on your own. Of course, if you're already an accomplished developer with strong experience in writing unit tests, feel free to jump to the part where we run our test suite from the command line and integrate it into Bamboo, Jenkins, and the Xcode Server.

Xcode unit testing integration

Open your Xcode project, make sure the Navigator panel is open and select the 5th tab in the top menu, that's the "test navigator". As you can see in Figure 9-1, this is where you will see the list of all the available unit tests in your project. Because we used Apple's default template, a testing target was generated, with a first failed test case.

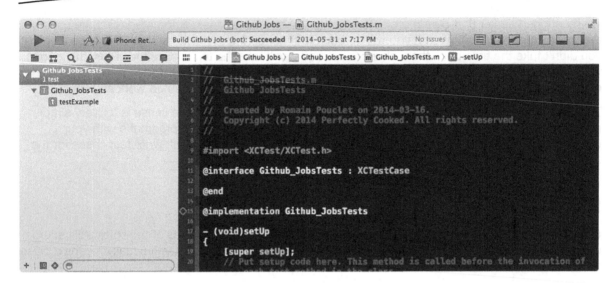

Figure 9-1. *The default project template comes with a testing target and a failing test case*

To have a test case class show up in this navigator, it has to inherit from XCTestCase, a class of the XCTest framework, although the implicit convention would be to give your class a name ending with "Tests" so it will be easier for you to find your tests classes later. The same goes for the test case methods, your method name must start with "test" and must not return anything. These are the conditions to have the integration with Xcode working.

As you've seen, our project is not very big so there isn't much to be tested but we will find something simple. We want each job offer returned by the web service to be wrapped into a dedicated class, just in case we get greedy and want to add other job offers service providers.

Adding tests for the PCSJobOffer class

In case you don't remember, here is the format of a job offer returned by the Github Jobs api:

```
{
  "url": "abced-fghij-klmnop-1234567",
  "company_logo": "http://github-jobs.s3.amazonaws.com/abced-fghij-klmnop.png",
  "company_url": "http://our-company.com",
  "id": "abced-fghij-klmnop-1234567",
  "created_at": "Wed Jun 04 20:06:50 UTC 2014",
  "title": "iOS developer",
  "location": "Bay Area, CA",
  "type": "Full Time",
  "description": "Our company is awesome.",
  "how_to_apply": "Email your resume to jobs@company.com",
  "company": "Company, Inc."
}
```

Of course we don't need all these fields because our application only displays a title and a company. For the sake of the example, our PCSJobOffer class will contain the following fields: title, location, date, and URL.

Creating the test case class

Go back to Xcode and create this class. Click on "File", and then select "New ➤ File". Select Objective-C class, call it PCSJobOffer and save it to your project. In the PCSJobOffer.h file, add the properties we mentioned earlier, as shown in Figure 8-2.

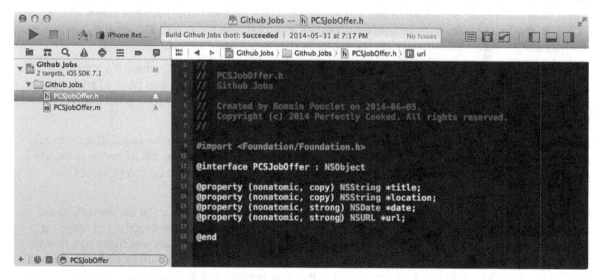

Figure 9-2. The PCSJobOffer class with the main properties

We don't have to do anything else for now, the class exists with its first properties declared, which would be almost too much if we wanted to follow the Test-Driven-Development method (TDD). We only created the implementation file before the test case class to avoid an unnecessary "file not found" and "Use of undeclared identifier 'PCSJobOffer'" errors in Xcode.

> **Note** The Test-Driven Development method (TTD) is a well-known way of developing an application. Basically, it consists of writing the test cases before anything else, and then implementing the required code to make those tests pass while working on the actual implementation. If you want to know more about Test-Driven Development in iOS, Graham Lee (a.k.a. @secboffin) wrote an awesome book on the subject, available at the following URL:
> http://www.amazon.com/Test-Driven-iOS-Development-Developers-Library/dp/0321774183.

We are now ready to create the associated test case class that will make sure that the PCSJobOffer class, when fed with the proper JSON dictionary, will extract the title, location, date, and URL properties and store them properly. Let's create the PCSJobOfferTests. Click on the File menu and select "New ➤ File". From the template panel, select "Objective-C test case class". Call it "PCSJobOfferTests", make sure it's a subclass of the XCTestCase class, select the "GithubJobs Tests" folder when asked for the path to store the file and press the "Save" button. While you're at it, remove the "Github_JobsTests.m" file, as it's a failing test case anyway. Note that there's no header file for your test cases for these classes, as they will never be called directly.

In this class, we will only have one test case to make sure the content of the JSON dictionary given to the PCSJobOffer class initializer will end up in a properly mapped object. We mentioned earlier that in the OOP paradigm, a test case was actually a **method** in a test case **class**. In the PCSJobOfferTests.m file, remove the "testExample" method that came with the file and create a test method called "testThatDictionaryIsProperlyMappedToProperties" instead.

There's no such thing as a too verbose test class, especially in Objective-C where it's not rare to meet 100 characters long method signatures. When you write a test case, you have to imagine that you or somebody else will probably read those tests later. They have to be so explicit that you can understand exactly what is being tested.

A working test case will feed a known input to a unit of code and compare the result of a method's execution to an expected result. In our case, the known input would be the JSON we've showed earlier containing the information about the job and the unit of code would be the PCSJobOffer initializer.

First we need to retrieve the JSON payload. The input we feed to the class must be something we know. Because of the obvious latency and the impossibility of predicting the exact list of resulting job offers, we have to store this JSON in a file that will be loaded before each is actually run. Select File ➤ New ➤ File, choose "Empty" form the "Other" section. Name the file "job.json" and save it in the Github JobsTests folder, so we can load it in the next section. In the job.json file, paste the JSON payload we mentioned earlier. Note that if you're reading the paper version of this book, this may be a little hard. Simply remember that the project is available on Github and that you can fetch the content from here: https://github.com/Palleas/Github-Jobs/blob/master/Github%20JobsTests/job.json

Notice that each test case class comes with a "setUp" and a "tearDown" method. These methods will respectively be called before and after every test case. This means that our test file will be loaded every time. This may seem like a waste of resources to you but that's really not your concern in this particular situation. Add an NSDictionary "jobPayload" property to the PCSJobOfferTests class and in the setUp method, write the following code:

```
- (void)setUp
{
    [super setUp];

    NSString *path = [[NSBundle bundleForClass: [self class]] pathForResource: @"job" ofType: @"json"];
    NSData *content = [NSData dataWithContentsOfFile: path];
```

```
    NSError *jsonError = nil;
    self.jobPayload = [NSJSONSerialization JSONObjectWithData: content options: 0 error:
&jsonError];
    XCTAssertNil(jsonError, @"The Job payload should be loaded without error, got %@", jsonError);
    XCTAssertNotNil(self.jobPayload, @"The job payload should be properly loaded");
    XCTAssertTrue([self.jobPayload isKindOfClass: [NSDictionary class]], @"Job payload should be a
dictionary");
}
```

What are we doing here? First, we retrieve the path to the JSON file using the NSBundle method. Note that we are not using the *[NSBundle mainBundle]* singleton because, in this particular context, we are not trying content from the main bundle, which is your application. In our case, everything that is about our test case is contained in a different bundle, that's why we use the bundleForClass: method. Then, we load the content of this file into a variable of type NSData named "content" and we use the NSJSONSerialization class to turn these bytes into a valid NSDictionary.

In this situation we're actually loading the JSON payload by hand but in case you wanted to test objects wrapping the call to the network, there are really good libraries such as OHHTTPStubs (available at https://github.com/AliSoftware/OHHTTPStubs) that will intercept the actual networking call.

What's next is more interesting though. These functions starting with "XCT" are called assertions and if a certain condition is not respected (object actually nil when it shouldn't be, condition evaluating to true when it shouldn't...), an exception will be thrown, marking the assertion and the test case as failed. If we are using these assertions right now, it's because we want the test to fail early. There is nothing worse than a test failing because of an initial condition declared incorrectly.

In the tearDown method, add the following code:

```
- (void)tearDown
{
    self.jobPayload = nil;

    [super tearDown];
}
```

Nothing fancy here, we are simply resetting the content of the jobPayload property to nil before the next test case is run, even if we know that it will be overridden in the next execution of the setUp method. We are now ready to write the actual test.

In the testThatDictionaryIsProperlyMappedToProperties method, add the following code:

```
- (void)testThatDictionaryIsProperlyMappedToProperties {
    PCSJobOffer *offer = [[PCSJobOffer alloc] initWithPayload: self.jobPayload];
    XCTAssertEqualObjects([NSURL URLWithString: @"http://jobs.github.com/positions/abced-fghij-
klmnop-1234567"], offer.url, @"URL should be http://jobs.github.com/positions/abced-fghij-
klmnop-1234567");
    XCTAssertEqualObjects(@"iOS developer", offer.title, @"Title of the job offer should be
\"iOS developer\"");
    XCTAssertEqualObjects(@"Bay Area, CA", offer.location, @"Location of the job offer soulld be
\"Bay Area, CA\"");
}
```

Note that the "initWithPayload" initializer doesn't exist for the PCSJobOffer class, so create an empty one for now:

```
- (instancetype)initWithPayload:(NSDictionary *)payload {
    self = [super init];
    if (self) {
        // Here we'll add something
    }

    return self;
}
```

We are now ready to run the tests.

Running the test

We mentioned earlier that the Xcode integration of the unit test could be seen in the "test navigator" in the left sidebar. This is not a simple visual indication because the integration actually goes deeper than that. If you look at the narrow column where the line numbers are displayed and where you usually add breakpoints, there are small squares near the @implementation symbol and near the test case method, as shown in Figure 9-3.

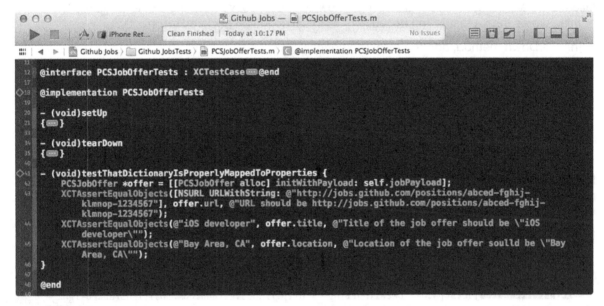

Figure 9-3. *Xcode automatically recognize test case class and test case methods so you can easily run specific tests*

These shapes are actually buttons that you can press to run a specific test case or all the test cases of a class. Since we only have one test case class with a single test case in it, we can run all the tests. These buttons will come in handy when you'll have only one failing test case you want to re-run until it passes.

Open the Product menu and select "Test", or hit ⌘ + U. As expected, the tests should fail and the failing assertions should be highlighted in the main editor and listed in the test navigator, as shown in Figure 9-4.

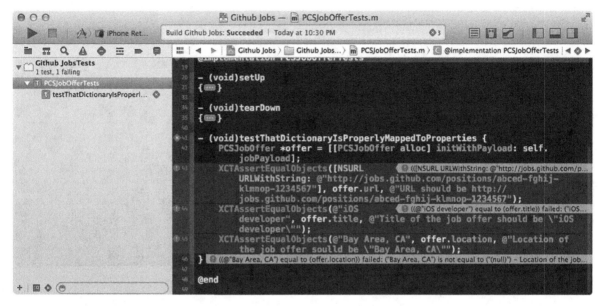

Figure 9-4. *The failing assertions are highlighted in the main editor and the failing test method is shown in the test navigator*

Our situation is pretty easy to explain. Since our class initializer is empty, nothing is actually done with the provided NSDictionary instance when the object is initialized. This means that the properties still contain their default values, which is nil. We are using the XCTAssertEqualObjects assertion to compare those objects, note that we could have started with XCTAssertNotNil and move from here.

We mentioned in Chapter 2 that Xcode 5 came with a new kind of navigation allowing you to open the associated test case class form another class of your project. Open the PCSJobOffer.m file. With your cursor on the initWithPayload method, click on the "related files" button at the top-left corner of the editor and select "Test Callers ➤ [PCSJobOfferTests testThatDictionaryIsProperlyMappedToProperties]" with the alt key down to have both test and implementation file visible on the same screen.

Finally, implement the content of the initWithPayload method with the following code, and re-run the failing test case:

```
- (instancetype)initWithPayload:(NSDictionary *)payload {
    self = [super init];
    if (self) {
        self.title = payload[@"title"];
        self.url = [NSURL URLWithString: payload[@"url"]];
        self.location = payload[@"location"];
    }

    return self;
}
```

Now that we have actually implemented the content of the `initWithPayload` initializer, the test should pass and a visual mark should be visible near test case and the `@implementation` symbol of the test case class, as shown in Figure 9-5.

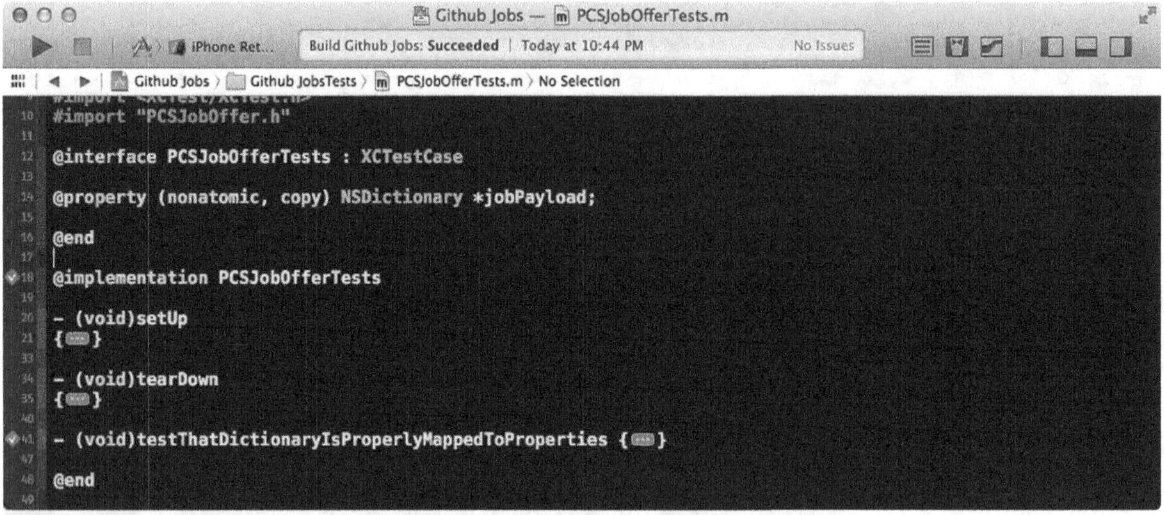

Figure 9-5. Xcode is showing the passing test cases with green symbols

This section gave you a simple introduction to unit testing. We created a class that will wrap the JSON description of each job offer so we use beautiful objects instead of unpredictable NSDictionary instances. We wrote the test case first, so we know how we wanted our initializer to behave and then we wrote the actual implementation.

> **Note**   Mapping libraries: This example is typical of the redundant things developers have to do. That's why if your application is working a lot with remote objects and mapping a lot of descriptions to plain old Objective-C objects, you should consider taking a look at libraries such as Mantle (https://github.com/Mantle/Mantle) or KZPropertyMapper (https://github.com/krzysztofzablocki/KZPropertyMapper).

Congratulations, you just wrote the beginning of a trustworthy test suite that you will be able to improve every time you'll want to add features to your application. Simply remember that now that you've built the foundation of your test suite; you no longer have an excuse not to write the test first and then the implementation.

Note that we haven't updated our code in the main view controller to use the PCSJobOffer class instead of the dictionary. That's pretty easy to do though. Open the PCSViewController.m file and update the content of the NSURLSessionDataTask completion handler. Instead of the following:

```
self.jobs = [NSJSONSerialization JSONObjectWithData: data options: 0  error: &jsonError];
```

Use:

```
NSArray *results = [NSJSONSerialization JSONObjectWithData: data options: 0 error: &jsonError];
NSMutableArray *jobs = [NSMutableArray array];
[results enumerateObjectsUsingBlock:^(NSDictionary *jobPayload, NSUInteger idx, BOOL *stop) {
        [jobs addObject: [[PCSJobOffer alloc] initWithPayload: jobPayload]];
}];
```

Don't forget to update the content of the tableView:cellForRowAtIndexPath: method, or you'll get an error:

```
- (UITableViewCell *)tableView:(UITableView *)tableView cellForRowAtIndexPath:(NSIndexPath *)
indexPath
{
    PCSJobOffer *offer = self.jobs[indexPath.row];
    UITableViewCell *cell = [tableView dequeueReusableCellWithIdentifier:@"Cell"
forIndexPath:indexPath];
    cell.textLabel.text = offer.title;

    return cell;
}
```

Note that we could have wrapped all these processes into a dedicated class that would abstract the whole process of fetching the job offers and unit test this class. This would have required that we introduce the concept of mocking and stubbing objects to tweak the way the payload is retrieved, so we don't actually call Github job's endpoint. Remember that we need to be able to trust the data we are getting. That would be way out of this book's scope. Once again, you should consider buying Graham Lee's book that covers all of these notions and more.

A good test suite must have the following qualities:

■ It must be easy to read, so you can understand in one quick look what unit is currently being tested. There is nothing worse than test suites that you can't understand, especially if they don't pass properly.

■ It must be fast to run. You won't take the time to run all your tests if you know it's going to cost you an hour. Of course as we mentioned earlier, it is possible to use Xcode to run specific test cases. If, on the other hand, the test suite takes an hour to execute, then by the time you get the results about a feature you are working on, this feature may already be obsolete.

These qualities are important but even if you follow them closely, you still have to run your test suite. That's what your continuous integration platform is for. It will automatically run the test suite for you but to do that, we need to be able to run them from the command line.

Running the tests from the command line

Before Xcode 5, the xcodebuild tool was only able to run the tests of OSX projects. This was a huge problem for iOS developer but fortunately, the Facebook iOS team fixed this issue when they released xctool the first time:

```
$ xctool test -sdk iphonesimulator
[Info] Collecting info for testables... (2471 ms)
  run-test Github JobsTests.xctest (iphonesimulator7.1, application-test)
    [Info] Installed 'com.perfectly-cooked.Github-Jobs'. (11709 ms)
    [Info] Launching test host and running tests ... (0 ms)
    ✓ -[PCSJobOfferTests testThatDictionaryIsProperlyMappedToProperties] (12 ms)
    1 passed, 0 failed, 0 errored, 1 total (12 ms)


** TEST SUCCEEDED: 1 passed, 0 failed, 0 errored, 1 total ** (27536 ms)
```

This was before Xcode 5, which makes sense if you think about it. This release came with the first version of the XCode Bots, which are capable of automatically running your test suite for you, as we'll cover later in this chapter.

Running your tests from the command line using the official xcodebuild command line tool is done using the following instruction:

```
$ xcodebuild -workspace Github\ Jobs.xcworkspace -scheme "Github Jobs" -sdk iphonesimulator7.1 test
...
Test Suite 'All tests' started at 2014-06-06 22:17:00 +0000
Test Suite 'Github JobsTests.xctest' started at 2014-06-06 22:17:00 +0000
Test Suite 'PCSJobOfferTests' started at 2014-06-06 22:17:00 +0000
Test Case '-[PCSJobOfferTests testThatDictionaryIsProperlyMappedToProperties]' started.
Test Case '-[PCSJobOfferTests testThatDictionaryIsProperlyMappedToProperties]' passed
(0.019 seconds).
Test Suite 'PCSJobOfferTests' finished at 2014-06-06 22:17:00 +0000.
Executed 1 test, with 0 failures (0 unexpected) in 0.019 (0.019) seconds
Test Suite 'Github JobsTests.xctest' finished at 2014-06-06 22:17:00 +0000.
Executed 1 test, with 0 failures (0 unexpected) in 0.019 (0.019) seconds
Test Suite 'All tests' finished at 2014-06-06 22:17:00 +0000.
Executed 1 test, with 0 failures (0 unexpected) in 0.019 (0.022) seconds
** TEST SUCCEEDED **
```

This command is nothing we haven't covered already. It takes a path to a workspace and scheme; as well a new "sdk" parameter that you will probably understand what it is here for, if you need a list of the available sdk on your computer, simply run the following command:

```
$ xcodebuild -showsdks
OS X SDKs:
        OS X 10.8                       -sdk macosx10.8
        OS X 10.9                       -sdk macosx10.9
iOS SDKs:
        iOS 7.1                         -sdk iphoneos7.1
iOS Simulator SDKs:
        Simulator - iOS 7.1             -sdk iphonesimulator7.1
```

This means that you can easily run the xcodebuild multiple times with different SDK to compare the results and make sure your application runs properly on all the versions of iOS you're targeting. That's even more convenient when Apple releases new versions of iOS. If you make sure to download the beta version as soon as they are available, you can easily fix the regressions due to the version change.

Our build script already uses xcpretty, a simple tool that takes the output of the xcodebuild command and displays it in a more human-readable way. We didn't paste it earlier but running the tests from the command line actually starts with building the application, which means getting the full output from Xcode, an output we don't really care about.

Let's see how we can use XCPretty to format the results so we can use them later in our continuous integration installation.

Analyzing the results

So far, we've used XCPretty in the simplest manner, but if you look at the description of the command, there are actually a few parameters we will be able to use to format the results and use them later. For now, let's just use the --test one.

```
$ xcpretty
[!] Usage: xcodebuild [options] | xcpretty
    -t, --test                Use RSpec style output
    -s, --simple              Use simple output (default)
    -k, --knock               Use knock output
        --tap                 Use TAP output
    -f, --formatter PATH      Use formatter returned from evaluating the specified Ruby file
    -c, --color               Use colorized output
        --no-utf              Disable unicode characters in output
    -r, --report FORMAT       Run FORMAT reporter
                                Choices: junit, html, json-compilation-database
    -o, --output PATH         Write report output to PATH
    -h, --help                Show this message
    -v, --version             Show version
```

The default output once transformed by XCpretty is the rspec, a testing tool for the Ruby programming language. It doesn't show any of the build log, as you probably don't care about it and only displays a list of dots and other symbols as a result:

```
$ xcodebuild -workspace Github\ Jobs.xcworkspace -scheme "Github Jobs" -sdk iphonesimulator7.1
clean test | xcpretty -ct
.

Executed 1 test, with 0 failures (0 unexpected) in 0.001 (0.001) seconds
```

This makes everything a lot clearer, especially if you are running the tests multiple times a day manually, the list of build logs can really get in the way of a "let's make these tests pass" session. On the other end, that's not really what we are here for. We want to find a way to integrate our test into the continuous platform of our choice.

Xcodebuild is not different from all the command line tools around. Like any of them, this command line tool will exit with a status code and any non-zero code should be considered as an error. Let's have a look at the error code returned by a typical xcodebuild test, using the "$?" variable available in bash after any command execution:

```
$ xcodebuild -workspace Github\ Jobs.xcworkspace -scheme "Github Jobs" -sdk iphonesimulator7.1
clean ...
** TEST SUCCEEDED **
$ echo "Exit code was $?"
Exit code was 0
```

When a test succeeded, xcodebuild exits with 0, as it should. Now let's fail the test. Open the PCSJobOffer.m file, and replace the line that assigns the title to the object's property of the same name with this (don't forget to restore your file back to the way it was after):

```
self.title = @"No job title for you!";
```

Then, re-run the test using the exact same command, and take a look at the exit code:

```
$ xcodebuild -workspace Github\ Jobs.xcworkspace -scheme "Github Jobs" -sdk iphonesimulator7.1
clean test
Test Suite 'All tests' started at 2014-06-07 22:56:54 +0000
Test Suite 'Github JobsTests.xctest' started at 2014-06-07 22:56:54 +0000
Test Suite 'PCSJobOfferTests' started at 2014-06-07 22:56:54 +0000
Test Case '-[PCSJobOfferTests testThatDictionaryIsProperlyMappedToProperties]' started.
/Users/Palleas/Projects/Apress/Github Jobs/Github JobsTests/PCSJobOfferTests.m:44: error:
-[PCSJobOfferTests testThatDictionaryIsProperlyMappedToProperties] : ((@"iOS developer") equal to
(offer.title)) failed: ("iOS developer") is not equal to ("pouet") - Title of the job offer should
be "iOS developer"
Test Case '-[PCSJobOfferTests testThatDictionaryIsProperlyMappedToProperties]' failed (0.017 seconds).
Test Suite 'PCSJobOfferTests' finished at 2014-06-07 22:56:54 +0000.
Executed 1 test, with 1 failure (0 unexpected) in 0.017 (0.017) seconds
Test Suite 'Github JobsTests.xctest' finished at 2014-06-07 22:56:54 +0000.
Executed 1 test, with 1 failure (0 unexpected) in 0.017 (0.017) seconds
Test Suite 'All tests' finished at 2014-06-07 22:56:54 +0000.
Executed 1 test, with 1 failure (0 unexpected) in 0.017 (0.094) seconds
** TEST FAILED **
$ echo $?
65
```

When you've been doing iOS programing and using the command line for a while, 65 is a really well-known exit code that is not limited to the execution of tests. In fact, this is the official documentation says about "sysexits", a file that lists the "preferable exit codes for programs":

EX_DATAERR (65)The input data was incorrect in some way. This should only be used for user's data and not system files.

If Chapter 4 about the power of the command line convinced you to use it more, be prepared to meet this guy a lot: this is pretty much the error code that always comes when xcodebuild is unable to build your application.

Now that we know that xcodebuild returns a non-zero status code at the end of a failed build, let's throw some xcpretty in to the mix and see what happens:

```
$ xcodebuild -workspace Github\ Jobs.xcworkspace -scheme "Github Jobs" -sdk iphonesimulator7.1
clean test | xcpretty -t
...
** TEST FAILED **
$ echo "Exit code was $?"
Exit code was 0
```

What happened here is really simple: when you use pipes in a command line execution, the final exit code is actually the one from the piped command, as it's the last command that was executed. Not being able to retrieve the exit code from xcodebuild would have prevented us from using xcpretty at all, but fortunately bash comes with yet another super useful internal variable named "PIPESTATUS". According to the documentation, this variable is an "Array variable holding exit status(es) of last executed foreground pipe." This means that in our case, the exit status of the xcodebuild command is the first element of this array and can be retrieved like this.

```
$ xcodebuild -workspace Github\ Jobs.xcworkspace -scheme "Github Jobs" -sdk iphonesimulator7.1
clean test | xcpretty -t
...
** TEST FAILED **
$ echo "xcodebuild exit code was ${PIPESTATUS[0]}"
xcodebuild exit code was 65
```

Finally, all we need to do is make sure that the exit value is always the one returned by the execution of xcodebuild and this can be done using "exit", a command that, well, exits the current shell with the status code provided as the first argument, like this:

```
$ xcodebuild -workspace Github\ Jobs.xcworkspace -scheme "Github Jobs" -sdk iphonesimulator7.1
clean test | xcpretty -t && exit ${PIPESTATUS[0]}
```

We finally have the perfect command to execute during the test from our continuous integration test installation but that is not enough. Indeed, when a test run fails, we want to know which test case failed specifically, or this feedback will be meaningless. Of course, you could simply look at the log from the build once in Jenkins or Bamboo, but your time would be better used looking for the piece of code causing the test to fail. What you actually need is to be able to look at the build and have a direct look at the test result. To do that, you need to export the result of your test suite into a format understandable by your continuous integration platform. Fortunately for us, the Java community solved this problem a while ago, when JUnit – a unit testing framework for the java programming language – was first integrated into a continuous integration platform. Even better, xcpretty is capable of generating this report for us.

```
$ xcodebuild -workspace Github\ Jobs.xcworkspace -scheme "Github Jobs" -sdk iphonesimulator7.1
clean test | xcpretty -t -r junit && exit ${PIPESTATUS[0]}
```

At the end of this command, an XML file will be generated in the build/reports/ folder which is convenient because this is the folder in which we are already putting everything that happens during the build: application, dSYM... Open this folder and have a look at the "junit.xml" file.

```
<?xml version='1.0' encoding='UTF-8'?>
<testsuites tests='1' failures='1'>
  <testsuite name='PCSJobOfferTests' tests='1' failures='1'>
    <testcase classname='PCSJobOfferTests' name='testThatDictionaryIsProperlyMappedToProperties'>
      <failure message='(((@&quot;iOS developer&quot;) equal to (offer.title)) failed: (&quot;iOS
developer&quot;) is not equal to (&quot; No job title for you!&quot;) - Title of the job offer
should be &quot;iOS developer&quot;'>Github JobsTests/PCSJobOfferTests.m:44</failure>
    </testcase>
  </testsuite>
</testsuites>
```

This file is not actually human readable but that's not the point, the point is that this is the format expected by most of the continuous integration platforms. Let's run our test suite from Jenkins then! Note that we will also add the test suite as part of our Bamboo build plan, so feel free to jump directly to that part if you don't really care about Jenkins.

Running tests from Jenkins

Open Jenkins, authenticate with the user you created earlier and navigate to the "Github Jobs for iOS" configure section. If you remember what we've implemented so far, our job calls the build script we wrote earlier that takes care of everything. It also retrieves the generated IPA at the end of the build, and uploads them to Testflight. That's already a pretty decent installation but we want more feedback. Now, we also want our tests to be run.

Our build script already takes care of installing the dependencies and because Jenkins doesn't have multiple jobs for one plan like Bamboo, we will simply run our test suite after the step that builds and package the application. To do that, add an "Execute shell" build action and in the command field, enter the command we've been perfecting earlier:

```
$ xcodebuild -workspace Github\ Jobs.xcworkspace -scheme "Github Jobs" -sdk iphonesimulator7.1
clean test | xcpretty -t -r junit && exit ${PIPESTATUS[0]}
```

Then, scroll down to the post-build actions, click on "Add post-build action" and select "Publish JUnit test result report". We already know that the default path to the exported JUnit result report is "build/reports/junit.xml" so fill in the "Test report XML" field with "**/build/reports/junit.xml" and press "Save".

Before you start the build, update the PCSJobOffer class to make sure the test won't pass. You can use the small change we made earlier to fail the test when we hardcoded the content of the title property to "No job title for you!" Commit that change, push this commit to your remote repository and start the build on Jenkins. If everything worked as expected, the build should have failed.

This means that when your test won't pass, the whole build will be marked as failed. In our case we are bundling everything into one simple build, because the project we are working on is super simple. If you want to split the part that runs the tests from the part that builds the application and sends it to the testers, feel free to do so. All you need to do is create a new Jenkins job!

Open the detail of the job that just ran, as shown in Figure 9-6. A new item has been added to the list of details showing the information about the git revision and everything: Test Result. As you can see, it gives you a glimpse into which test failed. Note that this item will also be visible on the "Github Jobs for iOS" main build page.

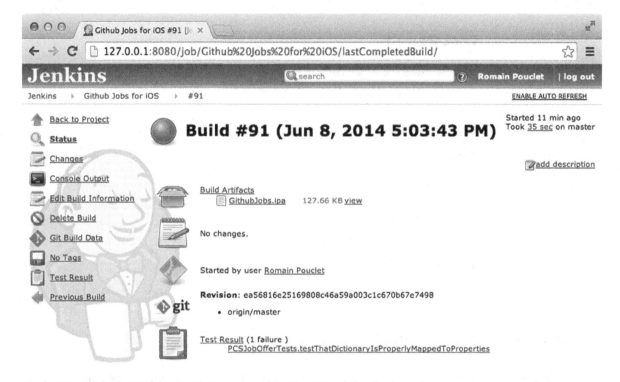

Figure 9-6. *The detail of the build that just ran shows the list of failing tests*

Of course, you probably want more details about why the test failed. After all, there can be many assertions that fail in this test case. To do that, simply click on the "Test Result" link and expand the test section by clicking on the plus sign near "PCSJobOfferTests. testThatDictionaryIsProperlyMappedToProperties" and the one near the "Stack trace". As shown in Figure 9-7, you see directly why the test failed.

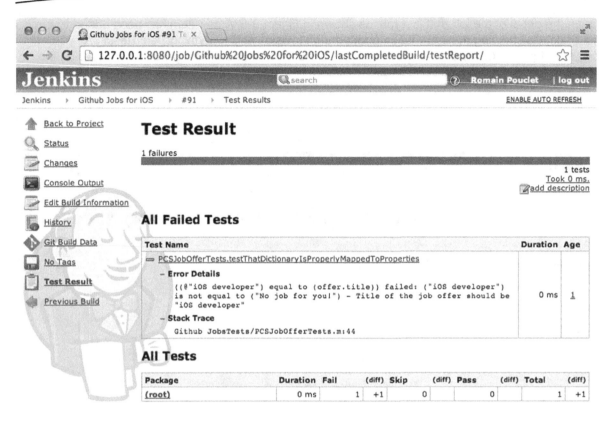

Figure 9-7. The test report shows in detail which test failed and why

That's pretty much all there is to know about running your unit tests from a continuous integration platform like Jenkins, mostly because we already have a job that was configured earlier and that we are using great tools such as xcpretty to handle the hard job for us. In the following sections, we will see how to run our tests from Bamboo and using an Xcode bot.

Running tests from Bamboo

Once again, the people who made Bamboo went for a slightly more complex approach when it comes to running testing operations. In fact, this is what it says in the configure plan "Stages" section:

> *Each stage within a plan represents a step within your build process. A stage may contain one or more jobs which Bamboo can execute in parallel. For example, you might have a stage for compilation jobs, followed by one or more stages for various testing jobs, followed by a stage for deployment jobs.*

Since we've already configured a build job and a deploying job, let's add a testing job! This is exactly what we mentioned previously about splitting the whole continuous integration process into multiple jobs.

Click on the "Add Job" button and select "Clone an existing job" so you don't have to re-enter all the information about the repository to clone. Fill in "Job Name" with "Automated testing" and press "Create job". Click on the "Automated Testing" job in the list and remove the two script build phases that, well, build the application and zip the dSYM folder as we won't need it.

Add a first script task that will install the dependencies for us. In the "Task description" field, enter "Installing the dependencies" and in the "Script body" one, fill "pod install". Press Save. Add a second script task that will actually execute the test. In the "Task description" field enter "Running the test suite" and in the "Script body" one, fill the command we used earlier, just like we did on Jenkins, and press "Save".

```
xcodebuild -workspace "Github Jobs.xcworkspace" -scheme "Github Jobs" -sdk iphonesimulator7.1
clean test | xcpretty -t -r junit && exit ${PIPESTATUS[0]}
```

Finally, add one last "JUnit Parser" task that will look for the junit xml report. In the "Task description" field enter "Parsing the JUnit test reports" and in the "custom results directories" fill "**/build/reports/junit.xml". Then, press "Save". We mentioned in the chapter about Bamboo that, as with Jenkins, the tasks run sequentially. Right now the JUnit task is happening right after the script one that ran the test suite. This means that when the test fails (as it is right now), the task arching the Junit reports will not be executed. To fix that, drag the "Junit Parser" task into the "Final Tasks" section, as shown in Figure 9-8.

Figure 9-8. *The JUnit Parser task has to be moved to the Final Tasks section or it won't be run when the tests fail*

When you are ready, run the whole "Github Jobs for iOS" plan: it will run the job that builds and packages the application and the one that runs the test suite and publishes the reports. Click on the "Automated Testing" job once it has finished running and select the "Tests" tab. As you can see in Figure 9-9, it shows the details of the failing tests. What's even better – and that's one of the perks of using a product from the Atlassian company – is that you can create a Jira issue directly from that failing test case in particular.

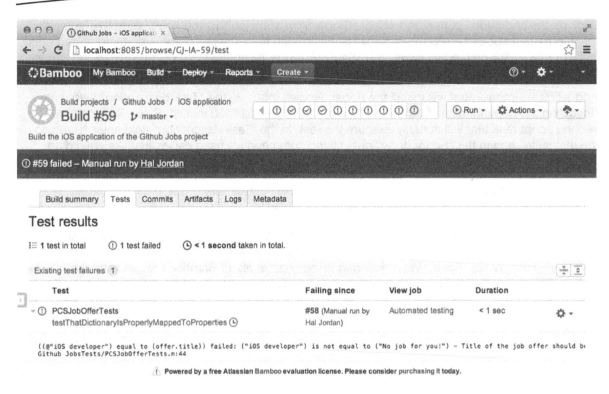

Figure 9-9. *The tests reports are available from a tab in the build details page*

That's two continuous integration platforms we've covered so let's run our tests one more time using Apple's continuous integration solution: XCode bots.

Running tests using an Xcode bot

We've already created a bot whose sole purpose was to build the application and archive it later so users can download it. This bot is named "Github Jobs (nightly build)" and is run every day at 1:00 AM. We could simply add the execution of tests to its list of tasks but instead we are going to create a new bot that will run the unit tests every time we push new commits to the remote repository.

Open the "Github Jobs" project in Xcode and in Product and using what you already know, create a bot that runs every time new commits are pushed to the remote repository (which is polled every 5 minutes) and select only the "Perform test action" task. Last time we created a bot that would only build and archive the application, now we only want testing. Because of this, as you can see on Figure 9-10, the Xcode Service will be able to run the tests on multiple devices and simulators, which is super convenient to make sure that bugs related to 32- versus 64-bit architecture are not here any more.

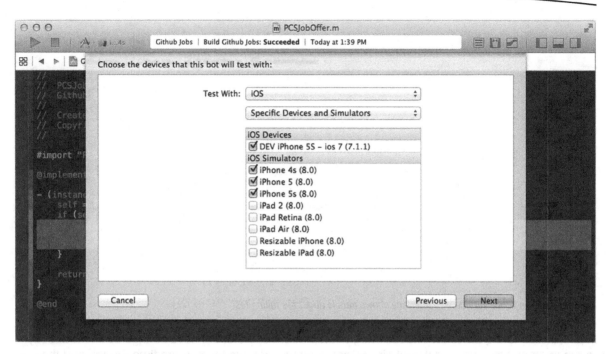

Figure 9-10. *The Xcode service allows you to run test on multiple devices*

Note that this capture not only shows simulators but also works on devices. As a matter of fact, there are multiple options in the Devices combo box that will allow you to run your test suite against all iOS devices or all iOS simulators. Of course, you don't necessarily have multiple spare devices you can leave plugged into the computer in charge of running all the tests. You may, for example, use a couple of testing devices during the day. That's when the nightly build would come in handy: create a bot that will run the tests against all the simulators during the day and another one that would run the tests on devices during the night. Creating a bot is super easy and only takes a few minutes, so why not take advantage of it?

Once the bot has finished running the test suite, open the details of the integration either from Xcode or your browser and look at the results. As expected, the test failed on all the simulators, as shown in Figure 9-11. Remember that Xcode 6 is still in beta at the time we are writing this book so please ignore the two errors displayed in this figure.

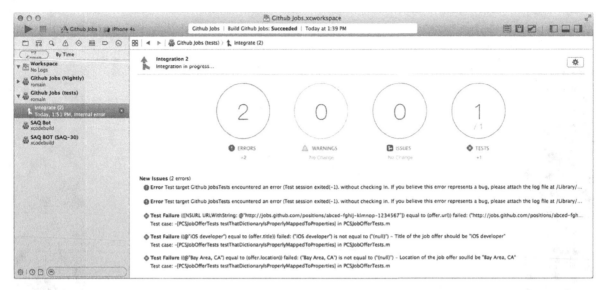

Figure 9-11. *The Xcode service web interface shows details about the failing test*

In all fairness to the other continuous integration platforms, we could have configured them directly to run multiple times using different simulators. That would have taken more time though and the result would have been a lot less clear. Yet again, that's one of the advantages of using a continuous integration tool dedicated to one platform.

Summary

In this chapter, we introduced the not-so-new concept of unit testing. If you've been able to write and run unit tests from Xcode since version 2, it's only three major releases later that Apple made them first-class citizens of your development process. It's no longer possible to create a project without unit tests, you can easily run very specific test cases and running your test automatically from your continuous integration platform is only a few clicks away.

First, we talked about what unit testing is and how it will help you go home with a little more peace of mind than if you were only relying on your skills to ensure that your product was stable. Then, we updated our continuous integration process on Bamboo, Jenkins, and created a dedicated Xcode Bot.

The next chapter will cover the final piece to the feedback provided by our continuous integration installation: quality assurance.

Chapter 10

Quality assurance

Let's have a look at what we've done in the previous chapters. We built a very simple application that retrieves a short list of iOS jobs in New York and displays the details of the openings in Safari mobile. Then, we learned how to release the application manually to your team using only Xcode and iTunes, even if we admitted it was a bad idea. Finally, we covered how to build the application from the command line, so we could build the application on a regular schedule using a few of the main continuous integration platforms: Jenkins and Bamboo, the open-source solution versus the enterprise-friendly one. We also introduced you to the tools released by Apple with Xcode 5: XCode service for OS X Server and XCode Bots. Finally, we took our continuous integration to the next level by automatically running the test suite that came with our project. This chapter will introduce you to one final notion: quality assurance, another feedback your continuous integration platform can provide.

First, I'll explain what quality assurance means and how it may be helpful to you and your project. Then, we'll talk about the action of running analyzing tools against your code without running it, a.k.a. static analysis. There are, in fact, multiple tools out there that will help you track complex pieces of code and other unused variables.

What is quality assurance?

Your continuous integration installation allows you to know if your application successfully builds and if your test runs, but it does not indicate whether the code you wrote for a feature or a bug fix didn't harm your product. It does not mean you haven't made mistakes like leaping over a vital security check because of a misplaced goto instruction. It does not means that you declared a variable and forgot to use it, nor does it mean that you haven't forgotten to put some code in an "if" statement.

"Harm" may seem like a harsh term but think about the developer that will have to go back to this particular piece of code six months from now, pulling his hair because of your method with 17 levels of if statements. There is no such thing as perfect code and even an experienced developer with 20 years of doing Objective-C can make mistakes. That's where quality assurance tools come in handy. Because they are automated, there is no arguing about being right or wrong. They are simply following a set of rules, running specific analysis, and giving you a report. For this reason, you won't fail an automated build because it is too complicated, you won't fail a build because you have a few 200+ long lines of code, and you sure won't fail your build because you are not unit testing 100% of your code. They will simply provide you with another kind of feedback that will help you write better code.

Static analysis

If you've been doing iOS development long enough, you've probably heard of things like LLVM (formerly called "Low Level Virtual Machine") and Clang. To put things in order, Clang is a tool that relies on LLVM. It comes with a lot of handy features like compiling, refactoring, and, of course, static analyzing your code. Let's see how it works.

First, you need to understand that there isn't only one way to do static analysis because this term simply means that the code will be analyzed without actually running it. It's the opposite of what is logically called "dynamic analysis". Warnings generated by a static analysis are similar to the ones you get in Xcode when you are trying to store a NSArray in a property that was declared as a NSString. Those are compiler warnings and they share the same spirit. Of course, they can detect simple issues like that, but as they evolved, static analysis tools took things a step further by starting to reason about the semantics of the code.

They are now capable of detecting potential bugs, which can reduce the amount of redundant unit tests you may have to write, and let you focus on the ones that actually test your code, not your platform.

There are few downsides to static analysis that need to be taken into account. First, these tools usually run slower than simple compilation and for good reason: they are not simply transforming the code, they are actually trying to locate potential bugs in it. That requires running complex algorithms against the parsed code and that will cost you time.

Also these tools are not magic, they will only be able to detect bugs it has been programed to find. They are also not perfect and can sometimes detect bugs that are actually perfectly normal lines of code. Those are called "false-positives" and must be reported to make the tool better and even more trustworthy.

For all these reasons, static analysis tools must not fail your build but that does not mean they are not helpful: once again there is no silver bullet, but none of the tools we've shown so far actually are.

Let's perform a simple static analysis on the code we wrote for the Github Jobs for iOS application. For now, you will only need the command line.

Performing a simple static analysis using clang

Clang comes as one of the developer tools provided by Xcode command line utilities that you've already installed, either because you needed things like the make command to be able to install homebrew or simply because we nicely asked you to in the chapter about command line. However, it does not come with the static-analysis tool, you'll have to download it manually.

There is a dedicated section about the Clang-based static analyzing tool available at `http://clang-analyzer.llvm.org/`. Navigate to this website to download the latest binary available. At the time we are writing this book, the latest release is the #276, which was released on February 19, 2014.

Download and decompress this archive to the folder of your choice (we are putting it into the "Tools" folder). This is where you will find the "scan-build" binary that runs the actual analysis.

```
$ cd ~/Tools
$ curl -O http://clang-analyzer.llvm.org/downloads/checker-276.tar.bz2
$ tar -zxvf checker-276.tar.bz2
$ cd checker-276
$ ./scan-buid -h
USAGE: scan-build [options] <build command> [build options]

ANALYZER BUILD: checker-276 (2014-02-18 22:53:01)
...
```

You must think of the scan-build command as some kind of proxy because of the way it works. The simplest use of this command would be "scan-build xcodebuild". It would build the application and use the output of the xcodebuild command to know which files to analyze. You probably know the command to build the application from the command line by heart by now. Simply call scan-build at the beginning of that command. Before you do, you should add the "~/Tools/checker-276" folder in your PATH environment variable to make things easier for you. We are keeping the full path in the command for now for the sake of the exercise. This command will run as expected, you will only see scan-build-related instructions before and after the xcodebuild one.

```
$ ~/Tools/checker-276/scan-build xcodebuild -workspace Github\ Jobs.xcworkspace -scheme Github\
Jobs clean build
scan-build: Using '/Users/Palleas/Tools/checker-276/bin/clang' for static analysis
Build settings from command line:
    CLANG_ANALYZER_EXEC = /Users/Palleas/Tools/checker-276/bin/clang
    CLANG_ANALYZER_OTHER_FLAGS =
    CLANG_ANALYZER_OUTPUT = plist-html
    CLANG_ANALYZER_OUTPUT_DIR = /var/folders/1v/d8vqkw8x23ndw49f5vs3fzw00000gn/T/scan-
build-2014-06-13-225334-95796-1
    RUN_CLANG_STATIC_ANALYZER = YES

Xcodebuild classic output...

** BUILD SUCCEEDED **

The following commands produced analyzer issues:
        AnalyzeShallow Github\ Jobs/PCSViewController.m
(1 command with analyzer issues)
scan-build: 1 bugs found.
scan-build: Run 'scan-view /var/folders/1v/d8vqkw8x23ndw49f5vs3fzw00000gn/T/scan-
build-2014-06-13-225403-95826-1' to examine bug reports.
```

The first block is important. It contains a few build settings that can be used or overridden, like we've done before with the "xcodebuild" command and the CONFIGURATION_BUILD_DIR one. The first one shows the path to the Clang executable being used. Clang's static organizer tool comes with its own version of Clang, as you can see in the "bin" subdirectory in the folder you decompressed.

You can easily override this setting using the "--use-analyzer" option, for example, to use the exact same compiler you're using on a day-to-day basis when you work with Xcode:

```
$ ~/Tools/checker-276/scan-build --use-analyzer=Xcode xcodebuild -workspace Github\
Jobs.xcworkspace -scheme Github\ Jobs clean build
scan-build: Using '/Applications/Xcode.app/Contents/Developer/Toolchains/XcodeDefault.xctoolchain/
usr/bin/clang' for static analysis
Build settings from command line:
    CLANG_ANALYZER_EXEC = /Applications/Xcode.app/Contents/Developer/Toolchains/XcodeDefault.
xctoolchain/usr/bin/clang
```

By using "Xcode" instead of an actual path to the Clang executable, scan-build will use xcrun to locate the full path to the version of the Clang executable used by Xcode.

The other important parameters are the two ones about the output of the command: CLANG_ANALYZER_OUTPUT and CLANG_ANALYZER_OUTPUT_DIR. They respectively contain the kind of report that needs to be generated and the path where it will be stored. In fact, the output displayed after the execution of the command shows where to find this report. As it turns out the code we wrote for the Github Jobs application contains a bug. Let's have a look at the report that was generated. As displayed, all you need to do is call the "scan-view" command. The default behavior of this command is to start a web server on your computer and to open the report properly formatted, as shown in Figure 10-1.

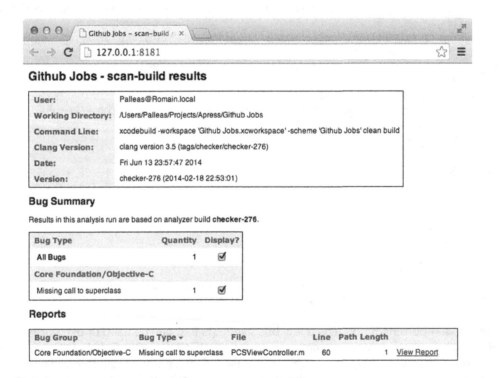

Figure 10-1. The formatted report generated by clang static analyzer shows one bug

To be honest, this mistake was not expected at the time we were writing this book but that was a good opportunity to see the benefits of using a static analyzer. We indeed forgot to call the [super viewWillAppear]. It's not very important because we're not subclassing a "container view-controller" like UINavigationController. In fact, the comment near the "viewWillAppear" declaration says:

```
// Called when the view is about to made visible. Default does nothing
```

What is even more interesting is that this bug isn't detected when you use the Clang executable provided by the latest stable version of Xcode: 5.1.1 (5B1008). That's the issue we talked about in Chapter 2 when we mentioned the Git integration in Xcode. Because of Apple's slow release process, you can easily end up a little behind with the developer tools. In fact, if you look at Clang's changes log about the latest release we are using right now (available at `http://clang-analyzer.llvm.org/release_notes.html`), you can see the following:

> *Includes a new "missing call to super" warning, which looks for common pattern in iOS/OS X APIs that require chaining a call to a super class's implementation of a method.*

In all fairness to Apple Xcode 6, which was only released as a beta at the time we are writing this book, comes with the latest version of Clang and supports these new features. We've already talked about the xcrun tool and the DEVELOPER_DIR environment variable, so you should be able to check the versions of both Clang executables.

This report was generated in a human-readable way. Of course a computer could parse it easily so you can integrate it in your continuous integration platform, after all this is very simple HTML code. There is another way though. The results of the analysis can be exported as... that's right: plist files. You can use the –plist option so the generation of the html report file is skipped, as the default export format will generate both properly-list files and html. The –o option can also be used to decide where to store the reports, instead of using the temporary folder:

```
$ scan-build -plist -o build xcodebuild -workspace Github\ Jobs.xcworkspace -scheme Github\ Jobs clean build
```

Once the command has run, you can easily find the reports related to the PCSViewController class by navigating to the report directory and then all the way to a "PCSViewController.plist" file that will contain a list of anomalies described in the following format:

```
<dict>
    <key>kind</key>
    <string>event</string>

    <key>location</key>
    <dict>
     <key>line</key><integer>60</integer>
     <key>col</key><integer>1</integer>
     <key>file</key><integer>0</integer>
    </dict>
```

```
<key>depth</key>
<integer>0</integer>
<key>extended_message</key>

<string>The &apos;viewWillAppear:&apos; instance method in UIViewController subclass
&apos;PCSViewController&apos; is missing a [super viewWillAppear:] call</string>

<key>message</key>
<string>The &apos;viewWillAppear:&apos; instance method in UIViewController subclass
&apos;PCSViewController&apos; is missing a [super viewWillAppear:] call</string>
</dict>
```

As you might expect, this is far easier to be parsed and analyzed from other software, for example Xcode. The thing is, there is no point in running a static code analysis on a continuous integration platform if the one you run on your own computer returns different results. Fortunately, there is a command made just for that purpose that comes with the checker archive called "set-xcode-analyzer". Just like the "xcode-select" command that changes the path to the developer directory at a global level, this command must be run as a super user. Close Xcode and run the following command:

```
$ sudo set-xcode-analyzer --use-checker-build=/Users/Palleas/Tools/checker-276
(+) Using Clang bundled with checker build: /Users/Palleas/Tools/checker-276
(+) Searching for xcspec file in:  /Applications/Xcode.app/Contents
(+) processing: /Applications/Xcode.app/Contents/PlugIns/Xcode3Core.ideplugin/Contents/
SharedSupport/Developer/Library/Xcode/Plug-ins/Clang LLVM 1.0.xcplugin/Contents/Resources/Clang
LLVM 1.0.xcspec
```

This command will locate the path to a Xcode specification file (xcspec) and change the path to the directory that contains the static analyzer you want to use. This has several purposes. The first one is, of course, to be able to use the latest versions of the analyzer in your own version of XCode so you get the same results. The second, more important one, is that due to the fact that the Xcode service for OS X Server requires a path to a valid Xcode developer directory, you will be able to run static analysis via an Xcode bot always using an up-to-date version of the static analyzer! Now that we know how it works, let's update the bot we created in the previous chapter, the one that runs the unit tests, to also run static code analysis.

Performing a Static analysis from an Xcode bot

Open the settings of the Github Jobs (nightly) Bot that we created earlier and change its name to simply "Github Jobs". Navigate to the "Schedule" step, check the "Perform analyze action" and press "Save". Press "integrate" to manually start the Xcode bot and wait until it's over. As you can see in Figure 10-2, a bug has been found, but the analysis did not fail the build because of it.

Figure 10-2. The integration is over. The build succeeded but a bug was found by the static analyzer

This way, every 5 minutes if you've pushed changes to your remote repository, your test suite will be run just like before, but you'll also get feedback about your code thanks to the Clang static analysis. You are now capable of using your Xcode bot at full potential: running tests, static analysis, and archiving the builds. Knowing how easy it was to create an Xcode bot from Xcode (apart from the cocoapods part, indeed) there really is no reason not to use them.

Integrating the static analysis using Clang in other continuous integration platform like Jenkins and Bamboo would be just as easy. There is a Jenkins plugin for that, even if it has not been updated since March 2013, so you'd have to pray the report format hasn't changed much in the latest releases of the Clang static analyzer. At this time there does not seem to be a Bamboo plugin for that, but if you think about it, it would not be very hard to integrate it anyway. It needs to call a specific command line instruction and archive the result, that would be simple HTML "artifacts". You could then create a deployment process that would publish those results to a dedicated web server.

Because there is nothing new in showing how to execute a command line instruction from a Bamboo build, we will instead introduce you to an alternative static analyzer: oclint.

Using OCLint to Get Additional Feedback

We mentioned earlier that there are different kinds of static analysis tools, as the term static only mean that the analysis is performed without actually running the code. There are already a lot of checks that Clang static analyzer will run for you but OCLint is a tool that can perform other tests related to code smells, unused variables and other general bad practices. Just like Clang's, OCLint comes as a standard executable and can be downloaded from the website or compiled manually. Note that choosing the later solution will cost you a few hours of your time, so you might consider the downloading solution.

Navigate to OCLint download page available at http://oclint.org/downloads.html and select the archive of the latest stable build. Download it, decompress the archive, and add the "bin" folder to your PATH.

```
$ curl -O http://archives.oclint.org/nightly/oclint-0.9.dev.43e26f7-x86_64-darwin-12.4.0.tar.gz
$ tar -zxvf oclint-0.9.dev.43e26f7-x86_64-darwin-12.4.0.tar.gz
$ PATH=$PATH:/Users/Palleas/Tools/oclint-0.9.dev.43e26f7/bin
$ oclint -version
LLVM (http://llvm.org/):
  LLVM version 3.3svn
  Optimized build.
  Built Jun 16 2013 (17:54:11).
  Default target: x86_64-apple-darwin13.2.0
  Host CPU: corei7-avx
```

The main site explains how to run OCLint on a single file, but if you try to do the same on one of the files of your project, you will probably get an error saying that the "UIKIt.h" file cannot be found. There is a reason why iOS projects are built using xcodebuild. Yes, it calls Clang under the hood but with very specific parameters about the build settings, the warnings to detect, the framework to link, and the flags to add. Remember DEBUG=1?

OCLint can be run on one single file, but only if it knows exactly how to build that file. If you take a look at xcodebuild output, you will be able to see what command is used for each file. It looks something like this:

```
/Applications/Xcode.app/Contents/Developer/Toolchains/XcodeDefault.xctoolchain/usr/bin/clang -x
objective-c-header -arch armv7s -fmessage-length=145 -fdiagnostics-show-note-include-stack -fmacro-
backtrace-limit=0 -fcolor-diagnostics -std=gnu99 -fmodules -fmodules-cache-path=/Users/Palleas/
Library/Developer/Xcode/DerivedData/ModuleCache -Wno-trigraphs -fpascal-strings -O0 -Wno-missing-
field-initializers -Wno-missing-prototypes -Wno-implicit-atomic-properties -Wno-receiver-is-weak
-Wno-arc-repeated-use-of-weak -Wno-missing-braces -Wparentheses -Wswitch -Wunused-function -Wno-
unused-label -Wno-unused-parameter -Wunused-variable -Wunused-value -Wempty-body -Wuninitialized
-Wno-unknown-pragmas -Wno-shadow -Wno-four-char-constants -Wno-conversion -Wconstant-conversion
-Wint-conversion -Wbool-conversion -Wenum-conversion -Wshorten-64-to-32 -Wpointer-sign -Wno-newline-
eof -Wno-selector -Wno-strict-selector-match -Wundeclared-selector -Wno-deprecated-implementations
-DDEBUG=1 -DCOCOAPODS=1 -isysroot /Applications/Xcode.app/Contents/Developer/Platforms/iPhoneOS.
platform/Developer/SDKs/iPhoneOS7.1.sdk... (it's actually three times longer than that)
```

Don't worry, you won't have to copy this command and run it for each file you want to analyze using OCLint. It has an approach similar to the one used by Clang static analyzer that acts as a proxy to the build command that compiles the application. There is a file format called the "JSON compilation database" which specification is available at the following URL: http://clang.llvm.org/docs/JSONCompilationDatabase.html. Basically this file contains a list of items with a file, a path to the directory containing this file, and a command to build this file:

```
{
  "directory": "Github Jobs",
  "file": "PCSAppDelegate.m",
  "command": "/Applications/Xcode.app/Contents/Developer/Toolchains/XcodeDefault.xctoolchain/usr/
bin/clang -x objective-c -arch armv7..."
}
```

This file can be easily generated thanks to a python tool provided by OCLint that will look for the output of the xcodebuild command and turn it into a "compile_commands.json". This tool is located in the bin folder of the OCLint package you've downloaded. If, as we told you earlier, you put this directory into your PATH, then it should be available as well. First run the xcodebuild command with the proper arguments and store the output into a dedicated file, then run the "oclint-xcodebuild" tool:

```
$ xcodebuild -workspace Github\ Jobs.xcworkspace -scheme Github\ Jobs -configuration Debug clean
build | tee xcodebuild.log
$ oclint-xcodebuild
```

> **Note**   that we are using *tee*, a very convenient tool that copies the standard input to standard output, while copying it in one or many files. This way you can copy the output into a log file but still have a look at the output in your terminal.

Now that we have the result of the xcodebuild command transformed into a proper JSON compilation database file, we are ready to use OCLint and actually analyze our files, using a tool that will take the content of the JSON compilation database file and transform it into an actual oclint command.

```
$ oclint-json-compilation-database
1 error generated.
1 error generated.
1 error generated.
...
[OCLint (http://oclint.org) v0.8rc1]

oclint: error: violations exceed threshold
P1=0[0] P2=30[10] P3=221[20]
```

The error message we get is due to the amount of errors OCLint has detected. Each error has a priority and there are a maximum number of errors OCLint will accept before exiting. By default, less than 20 priority 3 violations are allowed, 10 violations for priority 2, and no priority 1 violation can be tolerated. When one of these limits is reached, OCLint will exit with a non-zero status code that will fail the build.

We are getting so many errors because it's not only our code that was analyzed, but also the one from SVProgressHUD, for example, and you're not necessarily responsible for the quality of code coming from third party libraries. Of course, feel free to contribute to open-source code when you notice obvious mistakes, but that's not really the point here. What is important is that results about the code from third party libraries are less relevant to you. That's why there is an OCLint option to ignore folders you don't really care about. In our case that's the Pods folder:

```
$ oclint-json-compilation-database -e Pods
```

There are multiple outputs available: HTML, plain text, JSON and XML are a few of them. You can specify the kind of report you want to use and where to save it using the "-report-type" and the "-o. Those parameters are available for OCLint, not for oclint-json-compilation database. That's why we have to separate the first one from the second one using "--". Any character positioned after these "--" will be passed as an argument to the generated oclint command.

To generate an HTML-based report similar to the one shown in Figure 10-3, use the following command:

```
$ oclint-json-compilation-database -v -e Pods/SVProgressHUD -- -report-type html -o
oclint_result.html
```

OCLint Report

Summary

Total Files	Files with Violations	Priority 1	Priority 2	Priority 3	Compiler Errors	Compiler Warnings	Clang Static Analyzer
14	4	0	0	36	210	0	0

File	Location	Rule Name	Priority	Message
/Users/Palleas/Projects/Apress/Github Jobs/Github Jobs/PCSViewController.m	25:1	long line	3	Line with 110 characters exceeds limit of 100
/Users/Palleas/Projects/Apress/Github Jobs/Github Jobs/PCSViewController.m	28:1	long line	3	Line with 140 characters exceeds limit of 100
/Users/Palleas/Projects/Apress/Github Jobs/Github Jobs/PCSViewController.m	30:1	long line	3	Line with 116 characters exceeds limit of 100
/Users/Palleas/Projects/Apress/Github Jobs/Github Jobs/PCSViewController.m	32:1	long line	3	Line with 152 characters exceeds limit of 100
/Users/Palleas/Projects/Apress/Github Jobs/Github Jobs/PCSViewController.m	33:1	long line	3	Line with 173 characters exceeds limit of 100

Figure 10-3. The HTML reports shows the list of errors that were detected by OCLint

The report shows a list of violations with, as mentioned earlier, a priority. It also shows the position in the file and more importantly, the rule that wasn't followed (here we are getting a lot of errors because of the long line rule) with an error message.

This long line rule is subjective, especially when it comes to Cocoa APIs. There is in fact, a 148 characters long method name for the "NSBitmapImageRep". What's great with OCLint is that you can tweak the constants of some of the rules, like the long line one. To do so, simply use the "-rc" option that takes a property name and its value. Because it seems a bit ridiculous to be working on a huge iMac screen and get a warning because a line is 110 characters long when only 100 is allowed, let's bump the limit to 120. That way, a lot of warnings should go away. 120 is a pretty big number though, if you still have long line warnings after that (Figure 10-3 shows that we do) maybe a small refactoring could be the solution.

```
$ oclint-json-compilation-database -v -e Pods/SVProgressHUD -e Xcode/DerivedData -e
/Applications/Xcode.app/ -- -report-type html -o oclint_result.html -rc=LONG_LINE=120
```

This long line rule is typically the kind of rule that should be customized to suit the needs of your team because once it's settled, there is no arguing needed, the 140 characters long line in PCSVIewController is indeed too long and we should consider fixing that.

You may have noticed that there is a "Clang Static Analyzer" column. This may answer the question you might be asking to yourself: "Do I really need OCLint when I have Clang?" OCLint doesn't aim at replacing Clang; it only provides additional feedback about the quality of your code. To make things easier though, OCLint can automatically invoke the Clang static analyzer. This way, only one, unified report will be generated. Using the "-enable-clang-static-analyzer" argument to enable this feature or not is really up to you.

Now that we know how it works, let's integrate the report in our Jenkins' job.

Integrating OCLint into Jenkins

Once again, relying on the developer to run this kind of tool is not the smartest idea. Voluntarily or not, he or she will forget to run it. For that reason, we will integrate OCLint into Jenkins so the static analysis is performed regularly

Because Jenkins does not have a clean way of grouping jobs by project, we will simply add a new build phase to the existing job that will run OCLint. Before we do, remember that we need the output of the xcodebuild command so we can transform it into a JSON compilation database file. It would be a waste of resources to re-build the application. Let's update the script we are using to build the app to have the log copied into a "xcodebuild.log" file.

Open the bin/cibuild file and at the end of the xcodebuild command (but before the call to xcpretty!) add a call to tee. The command should look like this:

```
xcodebuild -workspace "$WORKSPACE" -scheme "$SCHEME" -configuration "$CONFIGURATION"
CONFIGURATION_BUILD_DIR="$BUILD_DIR" clean build | tee "$BUILD_DIR/xcodebuild.log" | xcpretty -c
```

Commit this change and push it to the remote repository. We will be able to use it in our new build phase, but before we do, let's talk about a new kind of report we haven't mentioned yet: PMD. Originally, PMD is also a static rule-set based source code analyzer, but for the Java platform. By now, you shouldn't be surprised to have yet another tool used in a continuous integration platform that comes from Java. Because Jenkins understands the format PMD static analysis reports are written in, pretty much all languages that come with a static analysis tool provides a way to generate reports in this format.

In our case an error, here called "violation" of the long line rule, would be represented as follow:

```
<file name="/Users/Palleas/Projects/Apress/Github Jobs/Github Jobs/PCSViewController.m">
        <violation begincolumn="1" endcolumn="195" beginline="56" endline="56" priority="5"
rule="long line">
        Line with 195 characters exceeds limit of 100
        </violation>
</file>
```

You already know how to set the format of the report generated by the oclint command. Simply replace html with "pmd" and change the name of the report from "oclint_result.html" to "oclint_result.xml". To keep things clean, we will put the report in the build folder.

From the Github Jobs for iOS job configuration, click on the "Add build phase" button and select "Execute shell". Fill in the text area that appears with the few commands we mentioned earlier to convert the log from xcodebuild to a compilation database and call OCLint:

```
$ oclint-xcodebuild "$WORKSPACE/build/xcodebuild.log"
$ oclint-json-compilation-database -v -e Pods/SVProgressHUD -- -report-type pmd -o
"$WORKSPACE/build/oclint_result.xml" -rc=LONG_LINE=130
```

This will generate a report in the build directory in a format understandable by Jenkins. The final step is simply to collect this report so Jenkins can present it in a more user-friendly way, using a plugin. Even if the PMD format is a really well known format, it's not natively supported by Jenkins.

Navigate to the Jenkins configuration section and select the "manage plugin" section. Go to the "available" section and look for the "PMD plugin". There are a few plugins capable of parsing and presenting PMD files but this one will do just fine. Install this plugin without restarting Jenkins and go back to the Github Jobs for iOS configuration panel.

As you may expect, collecting the report will happen in a post-build action. Click on the "Add post-build action" and select "Publish PMD analysis results". The rest of the process is nothing we haven't seen before. The post-build action simply adds a pattern to the files to collect, a bit like the one we used to collect artifacts. Fill in the "PMD results" field with "**/build/oclint_result.xml" and press the "Advanced" button to display some of the power-user features that come with this plugin.

Select the "run always" option. We know that OCLint may fail the build if too many errors are detected in your code. When this happens, the reports are generated anyway and not collecting those reports would not make a lot of sense. Press the "Save" button and start a new build.

Once the build has run, a new item is available is the project's sidebar: "PMD Warnings". As shown in Figure 10-4, the report is pretty similar to the HTML one generated by OCLint. The obvious advantage is having this report formatted and integrated into Jenkins.

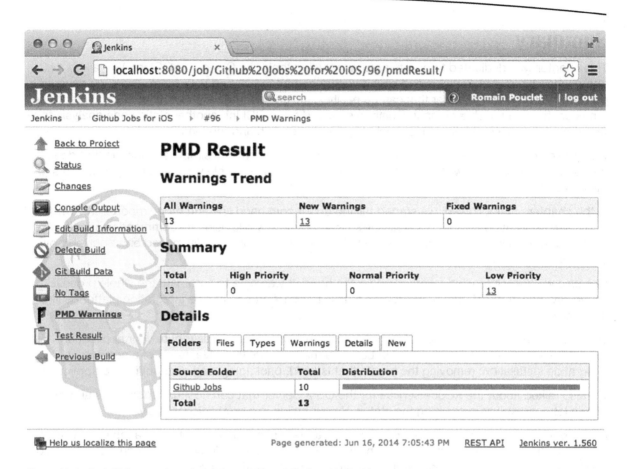

Figure 10-4. Each XML report is retrieved, formatted, and displayed in Jenkins

> **Note**   The build has failed because too many lines of code are over the 120 characters limit and it's really up to you to decide how to fix this issue. There are three options you can play with: -max-priority-1, -max-priority-2 and -max-priority-3. These options will increase the number of errors OCLint will accept before failing the build. The other solution would be to increase, once more, the number of characters allowed on a line of code.

Integrating quality checks in Bamboo would be pretty similar to what we've done in Jenkins. The main difference, once again, is that it would be done in a separate job. This way the build, the test, and the static analysis could be performed in parallel. The only trouble is that at this point, there is no decent plugin for Bamboo that can handle PMD files, so we won't be able to cover it.

Summary

This chapter was dedicated to quality assurance using tools like Clang and OCLint. We talked a bit about what quality assurance is and how it can be helpful to you and your team. Then, we covered in detail the Clang static analyzer that can be easily installed and integrated with the OS X server to be run every time you push a commit. Finally, we moved on to OCLint, another static code analysis tool that provides a different kind of feedback, like lines of code being too long.

We have now reached the end of this journey. We started with a very simple application that does a very simple job: calling a web-service, displaying the results in a table view, and using Safari to show the details of a job offer.

In the chapters that followed, we started talking about command line and more importantly how to build your application without using Xcode's User Interface, while using its command line tools. We started with a small tool that handled the whole process for us and finally moved on to our very own build script written in bash.

Because we knew everything worked under the hood, it was time to automate the whole process, so we saw how to build our application on a daily basis using continuous integration platforms like Jenkins and Bamboo.

Then, we needed a small break, so we covered the required steps to distribute your application to your beta testers at the end of a build because that's one of the advantages of a continuous integration installation: removing the hassle that is build, packaging, and distributing the application.

We also talked about the XCode service for the OS X Server that can host git repositories and run Xcode jobs, as well as presenting the status of your builds in a pretty elegant way.

At this point, we had a really decent continuous integration installation that was capable of building the application when new commits were pushed. All we had left to do was to configure our tools so they could provide us with more feedback: unit testing and static analysis.

Our installation is not perfect, but we've pretty much showed you how everything works. What is important here is that you saw (I hope!) that continuous integration is nothing to be afraid of, but something that can provide very helpful feedback and help you write better code and better applications.

Index

▌D, E, F

▌G

▌H, I

▌J, K

■ X, Y, Z

Get the eBook for only $10!

Now you can take the weightless companion with you anywhere, anytime. Your purchase of this book entitles you to 3 electronic versions for only $10.

This Apress title will prove so indispensible that you'll want to carry it with you everywhere, which is why we are offering the eBook in 3 formats for only $10 if you have already purchased the print book.

Convenient and fully searchable, the PDF version enables you to easily find and copy code—or perform examples by quickly toggling between instructions and applications. The MOBI format is ideal for your Kindle, while the ePUB can be utilized on a variety of mobile devices.

Go to www.apress.com/promo/tendollars to purchase your companion eBook.